Nikon® D5500™

FOR DUMMIES®

A Wiley Brand

by Julie Adair King

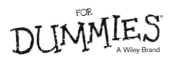

Nikon® D5500™ For Dummies®

Published by: **John Wiley & Sons, Inc.,** 111 River Street, Hoboken, NJ 07030-5774, www.wiley.com

Copyright © 2015 by John Wiley & Sons, Inc., Hoboken, New Jersey

Published simultaneously in Canada

For general information on our other products and services, please contact our Customer Care Department within the U.S. at 877-762-2974, outside the U.S. at 317-572-3993, or fax 317-572-4002. For technical support, please visit www.wiley.com/techsupport.

Wiley publishes in a variety of print and electronic formats and by print-on-demand. Some material included with standard print versions of this book may not be included in e-books or in print-on-demand. If this book refers to media such as a CD or DVD that is not included in the version you purchased, you may download this material at http://booksupport.wiley.com. For more information about Wiley products, visit www.wiley.com.

Library of Congress Control Number: 2015937168

ISBN: 978-1-119-10211-3 (pbk); ISBN 978-1-119-10200-7 (ebk); ISBN 978-1-119-10192-5 (ebk)

Manufactured in the United States of America

10 9 8 7 6 5 4 3 2 1

Contents at a Glance

Table of Contents

Introduction

*N*ikon. The name has been associated with top-flight photography equipment for generations. And the introduction of the D5500 has only enriched Nikon's well-deserved reputation, offering all the control that a diehard photography enthusiast could want while providing easy-to-use, point-and-shoot features for the beginner.

In fact, the D5500 offers so *many* features that sorting them all out can be more than a little confusing, especially if you're new to digital photography, SLR photography, or both. For starters, you may not even be sure what SLR means or how it affects your picture-taking, let alone have a clue about all the other techie terms you encounter in your camera manual — *resolution, aperture, white balance,* and so on. And if you're like many people, you may be so overwhelmed by all the controls on your camera that you haven't yet ventured beyond fully automatic picture-taking mode.

Therein lies the point of *Nikon D5500 For Dummies.* Throughout this book, you can discover not just what each bell and whistle on your camera does but also when, where, why, and how to put it to best use. Unlike many photography books, this one doesn't require any previous knowledge of photography or digital imaging to make sense of things, either. In classic *For Dummies* style, everything is explained in easy-to-understand language, with lots of illustrations to help clear up any confusion.

In short, what you have in your hands is the paperback version of an in-depth photography workshop tailored specifically to your Nikon picture-taking powerhouse.

A Quick Look at What's Ahead

This book is organized into four parts, each devoted to a different aspect of using your camera. Although chapters flow in a sequence that's designed to take you from absolute beginner to experienced user, I've also tried to make each chapter as self-standing as possible so that you can explore the topics that interest you in any order you please.

Here's a brief preview of what you can find in each part of the book:

- **Part I: Fast Track to Super Snaps:** Part I contains two chapters to help you get up and running. Chapter 1 guides you through initial camera setup, shows you how to view and adjust camera settings, and walks you through the steps of taking your first pictures using the Auto exposure mode. Chapter 2 introduces you to other exposure modes and also explains basic picture options such as Flash mode, Shutter Release mode, Image Size (resolution), and Image Quality (JPEG or Raw).

✔ **Part II: Taking Creative Control:** Chapters in this part help you unleash the full creative power of your camera by detailing the advanced shooting modes (P, S, A, and M). Chapter 3 covers the critical topic of exposure; Chapter 4 explains how to manipulate focus; and Chapter 5 discusses color controls. Chapter 6 summarizes techniques explained in earlier chapters, providing a quick-reference guide to the camera settings and shooting strategies that produce the best results for portraits, action shots, landscape scenes, and close-ups. Chapter 7 shifts gears, moving from still photography to HD movie recording with your D5500.

✔ **Part III: After the Shot:** This part offers two chapters, both dedicated to tasks you do after you press the shutter button. Chapter 8 explains how to review your pictures on the camera monitor and connect your camera to a TV for large-screen playback. Chapter 9 topics include rating, deleting, and protecting photos, downloading images to your computer or to a tablet or smartphone, processing Raw files, and preparing pictures for online sharing.

✔ **Part IV: The Part of Tens:** In famous *For Dummies* tradition, the book concludes with two top-ten lists containing additional bits of information and advice. Chapter 10 details options for customizing your camera, including changing the function of some buttons and entering a copyright notice that your camera can add to your picture files. Chapter 11 covers the photo-editing and effects tools found on the camera's Retouch menu and also shows you how to use the Effects exposure mode to add special effects to movies and photos as you record them. At the end of the chapter, I show you how to create a slide show featuring your best work.

Icons and Other Stuff to Note

If this isn't your first *For Dummies* book, you may be familiar with the large, round icons that decorate its margins. If not, here's your very own icon-decoder ring:

The Tip icon flags information that will save you time, effort, money, or some other valuable resource, including your sanity. Tips also point out techniques that help you get the best results from specific camera features.

When you see this icon, look alive. It indicates a potential danger zone that can result in much wailing and teeth-gnashing if ignored. In other words, this is stuff that you really don't want to learn the hard way.

Lots of information in this book is of a technical nature — digital photography is a technical animal, after all. But if I present a detail that is useful mainly for impressing your technology-geek friends, I mark it with this icon.

I apply this icon either to introduce information that is especially worth storing in your brain's long-term memory or to remind you of a fact that may have been displaced from that memory by another pressing fact.

Additionally, I need to point out these extra details that will help you use this book effectively:

- ✔ **Other margin art:** Replicas of some of your camera's buttons and onscreen symbols also appear in the margins of some paragraphs. I include these to provide a quick reminder of the appearance of the button or feature being discussed.

- ✔ **Software menu commands:** In sections that cover software, a series of words connected by an arrow indicates commands that you choose from the program menus. For example, if a step tells you to "Choose File ➪ Convert Files," click the File menu to unfurl it and then click the Convert Files command on the menu.

Beyond the Book

If you have Internet access, you can find a bit of extra content online, including this book's Cheat Sheet.

- ✔ The Cheat Sheet found at www.dummies.com/cheatsheet/nikond5500 contains a quick-reference guide to all the buttons, dials, switches, and exposure modes on your camera. Log on, print it out, and tuck it in your camera bag for times when you don't want to carry this book with you.

- ✔ In addition, find a few articles at www.dummies.com/extras/nikon offering additional advice about your camera and photography in general. For example, you can find an article about the seven Picture Control settings that come with your camera.

Practice, Be Patient, and Have Fun!

To wrap up this preamble, I want to stress that if you initially think that digital photography is too confusing or too technical for you, you're in very good company. *Everyone* finds this stuff mind-boggling at first. So take it slowly, experimenting with just one or two new camera settings or techniques at first. Then, every time you go on a photo outing, make it a point to add one or two more shooting skills to your repertoire.

I know that it's hard to believe when you're just starting out, but it really won't be long before everything starts to come together. With some time, patience, and practice, you'll soon wield your camera like a pro, dialing in the necessary settings to capture your creative vision almost instinctively.

So without further ado, I invite you to grab your camera, a cup of whatever it is you prefer to sip while you read, and start exploring the rest of this book. Your D5500 is the perfect partner for your photographic journey, and I thank you for allowing me, through this book, to serve as your tour guide.

Part I
Fast Track to Super Snaps

getting started
with your
Nikon
D5500

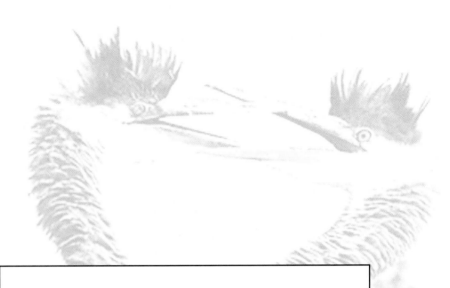

In this part . . .

- ✔ Familiarize yourself with the basics of using your camera, from attaching lenses to navigating menus.

- ✔ Find step-by-step instructions for point-and-shoot photography in Auto mode.

- ✔ Try out Live View shooting and customize the Live View display.

- ✔ Find out how to select the shutter-release mode, exposure mode, Image Size (picture resolution), and Image Quality (file type, JPEG or Raw).

- ✔ Discover options available for flash photography in different exposure modes.

First Steps, First Shots

Shooting for the first time with a camera as sophisticated as the Nikon D5500 can produce a blend of excitement and anxiety. On one hand, you can't wait to start using your new equipment, but on the other, you're a little intimidated by all its buttons, dials, and menu options.

Well, fear not: This chapter provides the information you need to start getting comfortable with your D5500. The first section walks you through initial camera setup; following that, you can discover how to view and adjust picture settings and get my take on some basic setup options. At the end of the chapter, I walk you step-by-step through taking your first pictures using Auto mode, which offers point-and-shoot simplicity until you're ready to step up to more advanced options.

Preparing the Camera for Initial Use

After unpacking your camera, you have to assemble a few parts. In addition to the camera body and the supplied battery (be sure to charge it before the first use), you need a lens and a memory card. Later sections in this chapter provide details about working with lenses and memory cards, but here's what you need to know up front:

- **Lens:** You can mount a wide range of lenses on your D5500, but some aren't compatible with all camera features. For example, to enjoy auto-focusing, you need an AF-S or AF-I lens. (The 18–55mm and 18–140mm lenses available as a kit with the D5500 body are both AF-S lenses.) Your camera manual offers details about lens compatibility.

The *AF* in AF-S stands for *autofocus,* and the *S* stands for *silent wave,* a Nikon autofocus technology. AF-I lenses are older, professional-grade (expensive) lenses that are no longer made but may be available on the secondhand market.

- **SD (Secure Digital) memory card:** Your camera accepts only this type of card. Most SD cards carry the designation SDHC (for *High Capacity*) or SDXC (for *eXtended Capacity*), depending on how many gigabytes (GB) of data they hold. SDHC cards hold from 4GB to 32GB of data; the SDXC moniker is assigned to cards with capacities greater than 32GB.

With camera, lens, battery, and card within reach, take these steps:

1. **Turn the camera off.**

2. **Install the battery into the compartment on the bottom of the camera.**

3. **Attach a lens.**

   First, remove the caps that cover the front of the camera and the back of the lens. Then align the *mounting index* (white dot) on the lens with the one on the camera body, as shown in Figure 1-1. After placing the lens on the camera mount, rotate the lens toward the shutter-button side of the camera. You should feel a solid click as the lens locks into place.

4. **Insert a memory card.**

   Open the card-slot cover on the right side of the camera and orient the card as shown in Figure 1-2 (the label faces the back of the camera). Push the card gently into the slot and

Mounting index dots

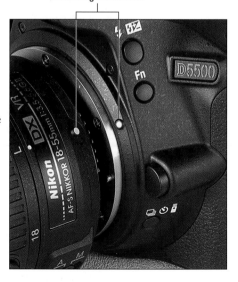

Figure 1-1: Align the white dot on the lens with the one on the camera body.

close the cover. The memory-card access light, labeled in the figure, illuminates briefly to let you know that the camera recognizes the card.

5. **Rotate the monitor to the desired viewing position.**

When you first take the camera out of its box, the monitor is positioned with the screen facing inward, protecting it from scratches and smudges. Gently lift the right side of the monitor up and away from the camera back. You can then rotate the monitor to move it into the traditional position on the camera back, as shown on the left in Figure 1-3, or swing the monitor out to get a different viewing angle, as shown on the right.

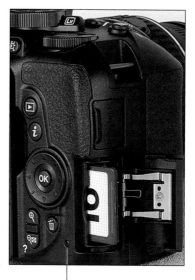

Memory-card access light

Figure 1-2: Insert the memory card with the label facing the back of the camera.

6. **Turn the camera on.**

7. **Set the language, time zone, and date.**

When you power up the camera for the first time, you can't do anything until you respond to onscreen prompts asking you to select your language, time zone, date, and time. The date/time information is included as *metadata* (hidden data) in the picture file. You can view metadata in some playback display modes (see Chapter 8) and in certain photo programs, including Nikon ViewNX 2. (Refer to Chapter 9.)

Multi Selector/OK button

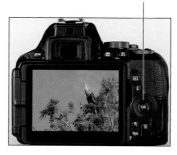 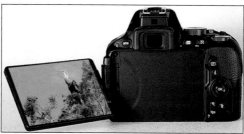

Figure 1-3: Here are just two possible monitor positions.

The easiest way to adjust the settings is to use the touchscreen: Just tap an option to select it. On the final screen (date/time), tap OK to finalize your choices. You also can do things the old-fashioned way, using the Multi Selector and OK button, both labeled in Figure 1-3. Press the edge of the Multi Selector up and down to scroll the highlight cursor vertically; press right/left to travel horizontally. Again, press OK after making your selections on a screen.

(You can find more details about using the touchscreen and adjusting camera settings later in this chapter.)

8. **Adjust the viewfinder to your eyesight.**

This step is critical; if you don't set the viewfinder to your eyesight, subjects that appear out of focus in the viewfinder might actually be in focus, and vice versa. If you wear glasses while shooting, adjust the viewfinder with your glasses on — and don't forget to reset the viewfinder focus if you take off your glasses or your prescription changes.

You control viewfinder focus through the adjustment dial labeled in Figure 1-4. (In official lingo, it's called the *diopter adjustment dial.*) After taking off the lens cap and making sure that the camera is turned on, look through the viewfinder and press the shutter button halfway. In dim lighting, the flash may pop up. Ignore it for now and concentrate on the row of data that appears at the bottom of the viewfinder screen. Rotate the dial until that data appears sharpest. The markings in the center of the viewfinder, which relate to autofocusing, also become more or less sharp. Ignore the scene you see through the lens; that won't change because you're not actually focusing the camera. When you finish, press down on the flash unit to close it if necessary.

9. **If using a retractable lens, unlock and extend the lens.**

The 18–55mm kit lens sold with the D5500 (and featured in this book) is a retractable lens, sometimes called a *pancake* lens. The beauty of this type of lens is that when you're not shooting, you can retract the lens barrel so that the camera takes up less space in your camera bag. However, before you can take a picture, you must unlock and extend the lens. Figure 1-5 shows the lens in its retracted (left image) and extended (right image) positions.

To extend the lens, press the lens lock button, highlighted in Figure 1-5, while rotating the lens barrel toward the shutter button side of the camera. To retract the lens, press the button while rotating the lens in the other direction.

That's all there is to it — the camera is now ready to go. From here, my recommendation is that you keep reading this chapter to familiarize yourself with the main camera features and basic operation. But if you're anxious to

Viewfinder adjustment dial

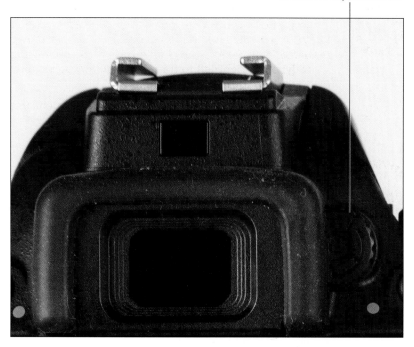

Figure 1-4: Rotate this dial to set the viewfinder focus for your eyesight.

Lens lock button

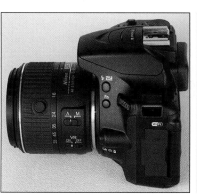 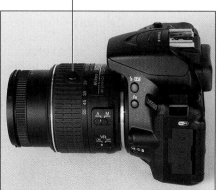

Figure 1-5: If using a retractable lens, press the lens lock button while rotating the lens barrel to extend and retract the lens.

take a picture right away, I won't think any less of you if you skip to the very last section of the chapter, which guides you through the process. Just promise that at some point, you'll read the pages in between, because they actually do contain important information.

Checking Out External Controls

Scattered across your camera's exterior are numerous features that you use to change picture-taking settings, review your photos, and perform various other operations. In later chapters, I discuss all your camera's functions in detail and provide the exact steps to follow to access them. This section provides just a basic "what's this thing do?" guide to each control. (Don't worry about memorizing the button names; throughout the book, I show pictures of buttons in the page margins to help you know exactly which one to press.)

Keep in mind, too, that you can adjust many settings by simply tapping the touchscreen, which is sometimes faster and easier than fiddling with the camera buttons. I provide an introduction to using the touchscreen later in this chapter.

Topside controls

Your virtual tour begins with the bird's-eye view shown in Figure 1-6. There are a number of features of note here:

- **Shutter button/Power switch:** Okay, I'm pretty sure you already figured out this combo button. But you may not be aware that you need to press the shutter button in two stages: Press and hold the button halfway and wait for the camera to initiate exposure metering and, if you're using autofocusing, to set the focusing distance. Then press the button the rest of the way to take the picture.

- **Mode dial:** With this dial, you set the camera to fully automatic, semi-automatic, or manual exposure mode. Setting the dial to Effects enables you to apply special effects as the image or movie is captured; the Scene setting accesses automatic modes designed for specific types of shots (portraits, landscapes, and so on). Chapter 2 introduces you to each exposure mode.

- **Command dial:** After you activate certain camera features, you rotate this dial, labeled in the figure, to select a setting. For example, to choose a shutter speed when shooting in shutter-priority (S) mode, you rotate the Command dial.

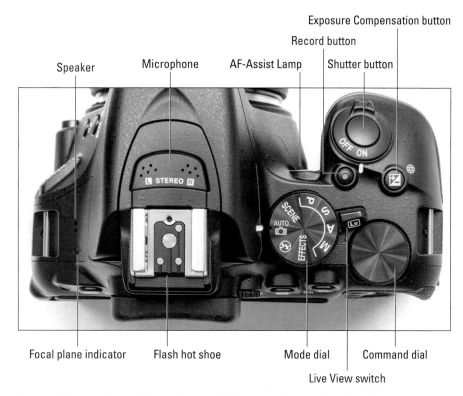

Figure 1-6: Rotate the Live View switch to shift from viewfinder to Live View photography.

✔ **Exposure Compensation button:** This button relates to Exposure Compensation, a feature that enables you to tweak exposure when using some autoexposure modes, including P, S, and A as well as many Scene modes. (I cover this feature in Chapter 3.) Press the button while rotating the Command dial to set the amount of Exposure Compensation.

In M (manual exposure) mode, pressing the button while rotating the Command dial adjusts the aperture setting.

✔ **Live View switch:** Rotate this switch to turn *Live View* on and off. In Live View mode, the scene in front of the lens appears on the monitor, and you can't see anything through the viewfinder. You then can compose a still photo using the monitor or begin recording a movie. The last section of this chapter introduces you to Live View photography; see Chapter 7 for help with movie making.

✔ **Record button:** After shifting to Live View mode, press this button to start recording a movie. Press again to stop recording.

- ✓ **AF-assist lamp:** When you use autofocusing in a dark setting, the camera may emit a beam of light from this lamp; the light helps the camera find its focus target. The lamp also lights when you use red-eye reduction flash and the Self-Timer shutter-release mode, both covered in Chapter 2. In situations where the light could be distracting, you can disable it through the Custom Setting menu. Open the Autofocus section of the menu and then set the Built-in AF-assist Illuminator option to Off.

- ✓ **Flash hot shoe:** *Hot shoe* is a photography term for a terminal that enables you to connect an external flash head. On the D5500, the hot shoe also serves as a mounting platform for the optional Nikon ME-1 stereo microphone.

- ✓ **Microphone:** If you don't attach an external microphone, movie audio is recorded using the camera's internal microphone, labeled in Figure 1-6.

- ✓ **Speaker:** When you play a movie, the sound comes wafting out of these holes.

- ✓ **Focal plane indicator:** When you need to know the exact distance between your subject and the camera, the focal plane indicator is the key. The mark indicates the plane at which light coming through the lens is focused onto the camera's image sensor. Basing your measurement on this mark produces a more accurate camera-to-subject distance than using the end of the lens or another external point on the camera body as your reference point.

Back-of-the-body controls

On the back of the camera, you find the following features, all labeled in Figure 1-7.

- ✓ **Wireless remote sensor:** This sensor is one of two receivers that picks up the infrared signal from the optional ML-L3 wireless remote control. The other receiver is on the front-right side of the camera, near the bottom of the hand grip.

- ✓ **Menu button:** Press this button to access menus of camera options. See "Navigating Menus," later in this chapter, for details.

- ✓ **Viewfinder adjustment dial:** Rotate this dial to adjust the viewfinder focus to your eyesight; see the first section of this chapter for details.

- ✓ **Eye sensor:** This little window senses when you put your eye to the viewfinder and, in response, turns off the monitor to save battery power.

- ✓ **Info button:** When using the viewfinder to compose photos, press this button to display the Information screen, which shows key camera settings and various bits of information, such as the battery status. To turn off the screen, press Info again.

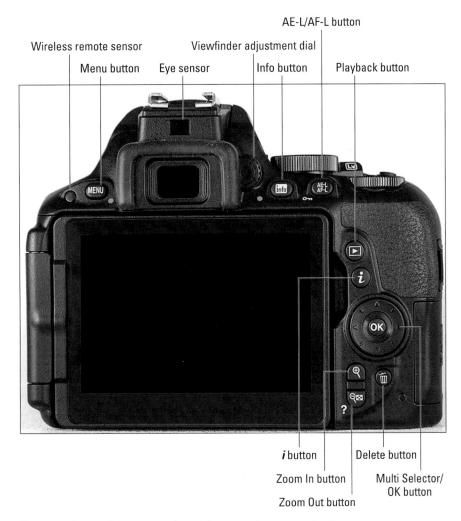

Figure 1-7: For quick access to primary picture settings, press the *i* button.

You also can display the screen by pressing the shutter button halfway and releasing it.

In Live View mode, pressing the button changes the type and amount of data that appears on the preview.

✔ **AE-L/AF-L button:** During shooting, pressing this button initiates autoexposure lock (AE-L) and autofocus lock (AF-L). Chapter 3 explains autoexposure lock; Chapter 4 talks about autofocus lock.

In playback mode, pressing the button activates the Protect feature, which locks the picture file — hence the little key symbol that appears near the button — so that it isn't erased if you use the picture-delete functions. See Chapter 9 for details. (The picture *is* erased if you format the memory card, however.)

 ✔ **Playback button:** Press this button to switch the camera to picture-review mode. Chapter 8 details playback features.

 ✔ ***i* button:** During shooting, pressing this button activates a control strip that enables quick access to certain picture settings. I provide details in the later section "Adjusting Settings via the Control Strip." Press ***i*** again to exit the control strip. In Playback mode, pressing the button brings up a menu that enables you to rate your photos, edit them using the Retouch menu features, and tag them for later wireless transmission to a smart phone or tablet.

✔ **Multi Selector/OK button:** This dual-natured control plays a role in many camera functions. You press the outer edges of the Multi Selector left, right, up, or down to navigate camera menus and access certain other options. At the center of the control is the OK button, which you press to finalize a menu selection or another camera adjustment.

 In this book, the instruction "Press the Multi Selector left" means to press the left edge of the control. "Press the Multi Selector right" means to press the right edge, and so on.

 ✔ **Delete button:** Sporting a trash can icon, the universal symbol for delete, this button enables you to erase pictures from your memory card. Chapter 9 explains the steps.

 ✔ **Zoom In button:** In still-photo playback mode, pressing this button magnifies the currently displayed image and also reduces the number of thumbnails displayed at a time. Note the plus sign in the middle of the magnifying glass — plus means enlarge. During movie playback, press the button to increase audio volume.

 ✔ **Zoom Out button:** This button has three primary purposes:

- *Display help screens:* If you see a question-mark symbol on the screen, press the button to display helpful information about the function you're currently using.

- *Display thumbnails during playback:* In playback mode, pressing the button enables you to display multiple image thumbnails on the screen; thus the little thumbnail grid on the button face.

- *Reduce magnification of displayed photo:* If you magnify an image during playback, pressing the button reduces the magnification amount. The magnifying glass with the minus sign tips you off to this function.

The Zoom Out button also comes into play when you use certain other camera features, such as applying changes from the Retouch menu. During movie playback, pressing the button lowers the sound volume.

Front-left features

The front-left side of the camera, shown in Figure 1-8, sports these features:

 ✔ **Flash button:** In the advanced exposure modes (P, S, A, and M), as well as in Food Scene mode, pressing this button raises the built-in flash. (In other modes, the camera decides whether the flash is needed.) By holding down the button and rotating the Command dial, you can adjust the Flash mode (fill flash, red-eye reduction, and so on). In some exposure modes, you can adjust flash power by pressing the button while simultaneously pressing the Exposure Compensation button and rotating the Command dial. Check out Chapter 2 for details on flash options.

 ✔ **Function (Fn) button:** By default, this button gives you quick access to the ISO setting, which controls the camera's sensitivity to light. (Chapter 3 explains.) If you don't adjust that setting often, you can use the button to perform a variety of other operations. Chapter 10 shows you how to change the button's purpose. (*Note:* All instructions in this book assume that you haven't changed the function.)

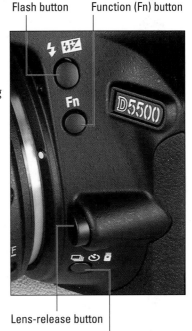

Flash button   Function (Fn) button

Lens-release button

Release mode button

Figure 1-8: Press the Flash button to use the built-in flash in P, S, A, or M mode.

✔ **Lens-release button:** Press this button to disengage the lens from the camera's lens mount so that you can remove the lens. (If you're using the retractable 18–55mm kit lens, be sure to collapse the lens first.)

 ✔ **Release Mode button:** Press this button to display a screen where you can select the shutter-release mode. By default, the option is set to Single Frame, which results in one picture each time you press the shutter button. You can explore other options in Chapter 2.

Hidden connections

Hidden under covers on the left and right sides of the camera are ports for attaching various accessories and cables, as shown in Figure 1-9:

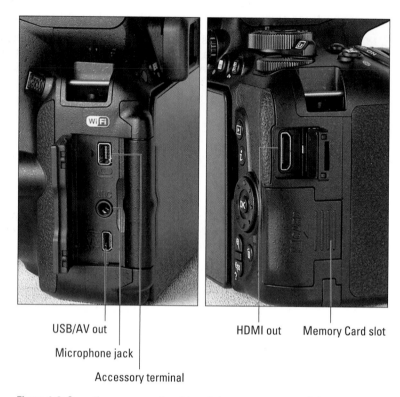

USB/AV out   HDMI out   Memory Card slot

Microphone jack

Accessory terminal

Figure 1-9: Open the covers on the sides of the camera to reveal these connections.

- ✔ **Accessory terminal:** This terminal accepts the following accessories: Nikon MC-DC2 remote shutter-release cable; WR-1 and WR-R10 wireless remote controllers; and GP-1/GP-1A GPS units. I don't cover these optional accessories, but the manual that comes with each device can get you up and running.

- ✔ **Microphone jack:** If you're not happy with the audio quality provided by the internal microphone, you can plug in an external microphone, such as the Nikon ME-1 mic. The jack accepts a 3.5mm plug.

- ✔ **USB and A/V port:** Through this port, you can connect your camera to your computer via USB connection for picture downloading. The same port enables you to connect the camera to a television via an A/V cable for picture playback. Nikon supplies the cables you need for both connections in the camera box; see Chapter 8 for information on television connections and Chapter 9 for help with downloading pictures.

- ✔ **HDMI port:** You can use this port, found on the right side of the camera, to connect your camera to a high-definition TV, but you need to buy an HDMI cable to do so. Look for a cable that has a Type C connector on one end (this end goes into the camera) and a regular, Type A connector on the other end. Chapter 8 offers details on television playback.

Just below the HMDI port is the memory-card slot, shown covered in the figure. (See the first section of this chapter for help installing a memory card.) If you turn the camera over, you find a tripod socket, which enables you to mount the camera on a tripod that uses a ¼ -inch screw, plus the battery chamber.

What about that Wi-Fi label on the top-left side of the camera? It's just there to remind you that you can transfer images to a tablet or smartphone via Wi-Fi, which I show you how to do in Chapter 9.

Enabling and Using the Touchscreen

When manufacturers first started putting touchscreens on dSLRs, I thought, "Meh, just a gimmick." But after discovering how much easier it is to adjust camera settings by using the touchscreen instead of pressing buttons and rotating dials — well, let's just say that I was wrong in my initial assessment. Yes, I said it: "I was wrong."

If you've used a smartphone, tablet, or other touchscreen device, working with the camera's touchscreen will feel familiar. Just as with those devices, you communicate with the camera via these *gestures,* which are specific ways to touch the screen:

- ✔ **Tap:** Tap a finger lightly on the screen. When navigating menus like the ones shown in Figure 1-10, for example, tap a menu icon (labeled on the left in the figure) to display that menu and then tap a menu item to select it and display available options for that item.

- ✔ **Drag (or swipe):** Drag your finger up, down, right, or left across the screen. For example, in a menu like the one shown on the left in Figure 1-10, dragging your finger up and down the screen scrolls the display through the pages of the menu.

✔ **Flick:** Drag a finger quickly across the screen. You use this gesture during playback, flicking left or right to quickly scroll from one photo to the next.

✔ **Pinch in/pinch out:** *Pinching* enables you to quickly adjust the magnification of an image during picture playback. To magnify the image, pinch out. That is, place your thumb and your pointer finger in the center of the screen and then drag both fingers outward to the edges of the screen. To zoom out, pinch in, dragging your thumb and finger from the outer edge of the screen toward the center.

By default, the touchscreen is enabled for both shooting and playback. But you can disable it entirely or use it just for playback if you wish. The following steps walk you through the process of adjusting this option and give you some practice in using the touchscreen:

1. **Press the Menu button to display the menus.**

   Sadly, there's no touchscreen control that takes you to the menus.

2. **Tap the Setup menu icon (wrench symbol) to select that menu, as shown on the left in Figure 1-10.**

3. **Tap the Touch Controls option, highlighted in the figure.**

   You see the screen shown on the right in Figure 1-10.

4. **To turn the touchscreen off for shooting functions but leave it enabled for playback, tap Playback Only. To disable the touchscreen altogether, tap Disable.**

   On many screens, a return arrow icon appears in the top-right corner of the screen (refer to Figure 1-10). Tap this icon to exit the screen without making any changes to the current setting.

Setup menu icon   Exit without making change

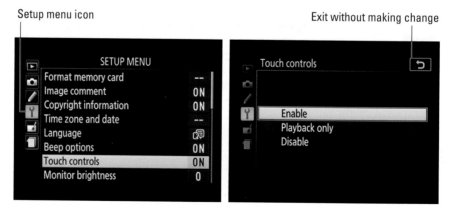

Figure 1-10: Enable or disable the touchscreen via this Setup menu option.

Keep in mind that if you choose Playback Only or Disable, you can't use the touchscreen to revert to the original, Enable, setting. Instead, you must use the Multi Selector and OK button to do the job. (See the next section for help navigating menus using these controls.)

A couple final tips about the touchscreen:

✔ **The Information screen tells you the touchscreen status.** To display this screen, available during regular, viewfinder photography, press the Info button or press the shutter button halfway and release it. At the top of the screen, the icon labeled in Figure 1-11 indicates that touchscreen is turned on for both playback and shooting. The symbol disappears if you change the Touch Controls setting to Playback Only or Disable.

Touchscreen enabled symbol

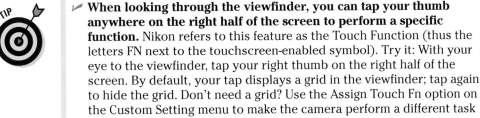

Figure 1-11: This symbol tells you that the touchscreen is active for both shooting and playback.

✔ **On the Information and Live View displays, a white border around a symbol indicates that you can tap that symbol to access the setting.** For example, the border around the *i* symbol in the lower-right corner of the Information display (refer to Figure 1-11) tells you that you can tap that area to perform the same action as pressing the *i* button.

✔ **When looking through the viewfinder, you can tap your thumb anywhere on the right half of the screen to perform a specific function.** Nikon refers to this feature as the Touch Function (thus the letters FN next to the touchscreen-enabled symbol). Try it: With your eye to the viewfinder, tap your right thumb on the right half of the screen. By default, your tap displays a grid in the viewfinder; tap again to hide the grid. Don't need a grid? Use the Assign Touch Fn option on the Custom Setting menu to make the camera perform a different task when you tap. Chapter 10 has details.

If you swing the monitor out to the left side of the camera, you can tap anywhere on the monitor to take advantage of the Touch Function. You still must have your eye to the viewfinder to make this feature work, however. It's not available for Live View photography or movie shooting.

    ✏ **During Live View shooting, you can tap the screen to set focus and take a picture.** You also can tell the camera to set focus only when you tap. The last section of this chapter tells you more about this feature, known as the Touch Shutter.

    ✏ **Don't apply a screen protector.** Applying a screen protector can actually damage the monitor and make it less responsive to your touch.

Navigating Menus

Although you can change some settings by using the camera's external buttons or by tapping touchscreen symbols, other options are accessible only via the menus. To access the menus, press the Menu button. You see a screen similar to the one shown in Figure 1-12. The icons along the left side of the screen represent the available menus. To the right of the icon strip are options associated with the current menu. Table 1-1 offers a quick guide to the menus.

Here's what you need to know to work your way though menu screens:

    ✏ **To select a different menu:** Tap the menu's icon or press the Multi Selector up or down to highlight an icon. (If a menu option is currently highlighted on the right side of the screen, as in Figure 1-12, first press the Multi Selector left to activate the icon strip.)

    ✏ **To select and adjust a menu option:** Again, you can take advantage of the touchscreen or use the Multi Selector:

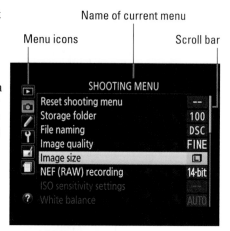

Figure 1-12: The scroll bar indicates that the menu is a multi-page affair.

        • *Touchscreen:* If you see a scroll bar on the right side of the window as in Figure 1-12, swipe up or down to scroll to the next page of menu options. Tap the option you want to adjust. Settings available for the selected item then appear. Tap the setting you want to use. Or, to exit without making any changes, tap the return arrow in the upper-right corner of the screen.

        • *Multi Selector/OK button:* First, press the Multi Selector right to jump from the menu-icon column to the list of menu items. Then press up or down to scroll the menu until the option you want to change is highlighted. Press OK to display the available settings. Repeat the old up-and-down scroll routine until the choice you prefer is highlighted. Then press OK.

Table 1-1	D5500 Menus	
Symbol	**Open This Menu . . .**	**To Access These Functions**
▶	Playback	Viewing, deleting, and protecting pictures
📷	Shooting	Basic photography settings
✏	Custom Setting	Advanced photography options and some basic camera operations
🔧	Setup	Additional basic camera operations
🖌	Retouch	Photo and movie editing options
📑 📄	My Menu/Recent Settings	Your custom menu or 20 most recently used menu options

In some cases, a right-pointing triangle appears next to a menu item. That's your cue to tap that item or to press the Multi Selector right to display a submenu.

Items that are dimmed in a menu aren't available in the current exposure mode. For access to all settings, set the Mode dial to P, S, A, or M.

✔ **To select items from the Custom Setting menu:** Displaying the Custom Setting menu, represented by the Pencil icon, takes you to a screen that contains six submenus that carry the labels A through F, as shown in Figure 1-13. Each submenu holds clusters of options related to a specific aspect of the camera's operation. To get to those options, tap the submenu name or highlight it with the Multi Selector and press OK.

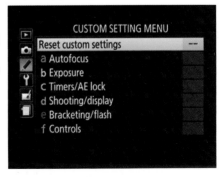

Figure 1-13: The Custom Setting menu contains six submenus of advanced options.

In the Nikon manual, instructions reference the Custom Setting menu items by a menu letter and number. For example, "Custom Setting a1" refers to the first option on the a (Autofocus) submenu. I try to be more specific, however, so I use the actual setting names. (Really, we all have enough numbers to remember, don't you think?)

After you jump to the first submenu, you can simply scroll up and down the list to view options from other submenus. You don't have to keep going back to the initial menu screen and selecting a submenu.

✔ **Create a custom menu or view your 20 most recently adjusted menu items:** The sixth menu is actually two menus that share an apartment: Recent Settings and My Menu, both shown in Figure 1-14. Each menu contains a Choose Tab option as the last item on the menu; select this option to shift between the two menus.

Here's what the two menus offer:

- *Recent Settings:* This screen lists the 20 menu items you ordered most recently. To adjust those settings, you don't have to wade through all the other menus to look for them — head to the Recent Settings menu instead.

   To remove an item from the Recent Settings menu, use the Multi Selector to highlight the item and press Delete. Press Delete again to confirm your decision. (If you tap the item in the menu, you pull up that item's options screen and you must tap the return arrow at the top of the screen to exit back to the menu. You can then press Delete.)

- *My Menu:* From this screen, you can create a custom menu that contains your favorite options. Chapter 10 details the steps.

Recent Settings/My Menu icon

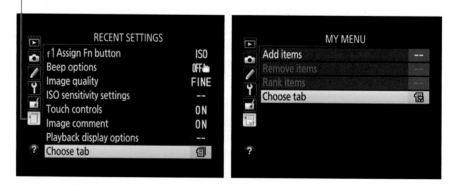

Figure 1-14: The Recent Settings menu offers quick access to the last 20 menu options you selected; the My Menu menu enables you to design a custom menu.

Viewing Critical Picture Settings

Your D5500 gives you the following ways to monitor important picture-taking settings:

- **Information display:** The left screen in Figure 1-15 gives you a look at this display, which appears when you first turn on the camera and then disappears after a few seconds. To redisplay it, take either of these steps:

  - *Press the Info button.* Press once to display the screen; press again to turn off the monitor.

  - *Press the shutter button halfway and release it.* Pressing and holding the button halfway down turns off the screen and fires up the autofocusing and exposure metering systems. Because those two systems use battery power, you may want to avoid this technique when the battery is running low.

  If your Information screen appears different than the ones shown in this book, don't freak out: The camera actually offers six Information screen display styles. You choose your favorite via the Info Display Format option on the Setup menu; Chapter 10 has details.

- **Live View display:** In Live View mode, where you compose pictures using the monitor, the shooting data appears atop the live preview (refer to the right side of Figure 1-15). To switch to Live View mode, rotate the Live View switch (top of the camera, next to the Mode dial).

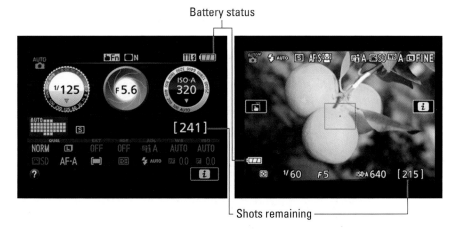

Figure 1-15: Press the Info button to view picture-taking settings on the monitor.

You can vary the type of data displayed on the Live View screen by pressing the Info button. See the last section of this chapter for information about this issue and about Live View shooting in general.

✔ **Viewfinder:** You also can view some settings at the bottom of the viewfinder, as shown in Figure 1-16. The information that appears depends on the exposure mode.

You can display gridlines in the viewfinder, as shown on the right in the figure. The gridlines help you ensure the alignment of objects in your photo — for example, to make sure that the horizon is level in a landscape. When your eye is up to the viewfinder and the touchscreen is enabled, tap the right half of the monitor to toggle the grid on and off. (If the monitor is swung to the side of the camera, you can tap anywhere on the screen.) This trick works only if you stick with the default Touch Function setting on the Setup menu, however. You also can hide and display the grid via the Viewfinder Grid Display option, found on the Shooting/Display section of the Custom Setting menu.

If what you see in Figures 1-15 and 1-16 looks like a confusing mess, don't worry. Many settings relate to options that won't mean anything to you until you explore the advanced exposure modes (P, S, A, and M). But make note of the following bits of data that are helpful in any exposure mode:

✔ **Battery status indicator:** A full-battery icon (refer to Figure 1-15) shows that the battery is fully charged; if the icon appears empty, look for your battery charger.

Just for good measure, the camera also displays a low-battery symbol in the viewfinder (refer to the left image in Figure 1-16). If the symbol blinks, the camera won't take more pictures until you charge the battery.

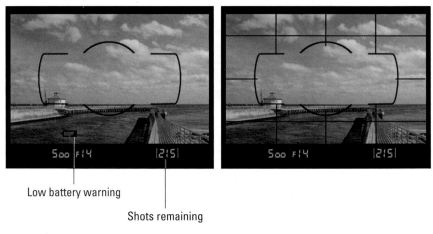

Low battery warning

Shots remaining

Figure 1-16: Picture settings also appear at the bottom of the viewfinder (left); enable the grid for help with aligning objects in the frame (right).

✔ **Shots remaining:** Labeled in Figures 1-15 and 1-16, this value indicates how many more pictures you can store on the memory card. If the number exceeds 999, the initial *K* appears, to indicate that the value is in the thousands. For example, 1.0K means that you can store 1,000 more pictures (*K* is a universally accepted symbol indicating 1,000 units). The number is rounded down to the nearest hundred. So if the card has room for, say, 1,230 more pictures, the value reads 1.2K.

Also, remember that the viewfinder display, Live View screen, and Information screen automatically shut off after a specific period of inactivity to preserve battery power. See Chapter 10 for details about altering these auto-shutdown times, which you accomplish through the Auto Off Timers option, found in the Timers/AE Lock section of the Custom Setting menu. Normal is the default setting.

Adjusting Settings via the Control Strip

The Information display isn't just for checking current picture-taking settings; it also provides a control strip that gives you quick access to some of the most critical of those settings. Here's how it works for viewfinder photography (that is, when you're not shooting in Live View mode):

1. **Display the Information screen by pressing the Info button or pressing the shutter button halfway and releasing it.**

2. **Press the *i* button or tap the *i* symbol on the screen, labeled on the left in Figure 1-17.**

   The top part of the display dims, and the two rows of settings at the bottom of the screen become accessible, as shown on the right in Figure 1-17. The currently selected setting appears highlighted, and its name is displayed above the control strip. For example, in Figure 1-17, the Image Quality option is selected.

3. **Select the setting you want to change.**

   Either tap the setting or use the Multi Selector to highlight it and then press OK. Either way, the next screen displays the available settings for the option.

4. **Adjust the setting as desired.**

   Again, you can tap the setting or highlight it and then press OK. Either way, the camera returns you to the control strip screen. You can then adjust another setting, if needed.

5. **To exit the control strip, press the *i* button or tap the exit symbol, labeled on the right in Figure 1-17.**

   You also can just give the shutter button a quick half-press and release it to exit the control strip.

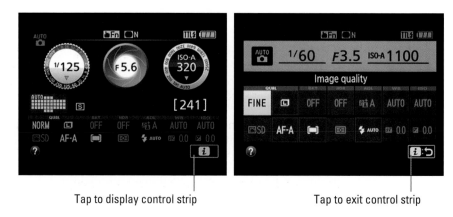

Tap to display control strip   Tap to exit control strip

Figure 1-17: Press the *i* button or tap the *i* icon (left) to activate the control strip (right).

Displaying Help screens

If you see a question mark in the lower-left corner of a screen, as shown on the left in the figure here, tap that question mark or press the Zoom Out button to display information about the active setting. For example, the right screen here shows the Help screen associated with the White Balance option. Tap the return arrow or press Zoom Out again to exit the Help screen. (For some screens, the question mark appears in a different position.)

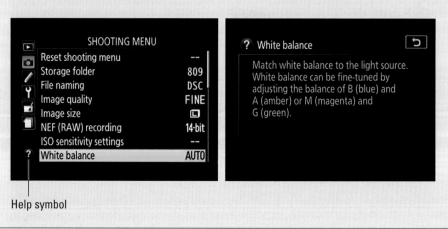

Help symbol

Familiarizing Yourself with the Lens

Because I don't know which lens you're using, I can't give you full instructions on its operation. But the following basics apply to most Nikon AF-S lenses as well as to certain other lenses that support autofocusing — you should explore the lens manual for specifics, of course:

- **Focusing:** First, set the lens to automatic or manual focusing by moving the focus-method switch on the lens. For example, Figure 1-18 shows the switch as it appears on the 18–55mm kit lens sold with the D5500. (The 18–140mm kit lens has the same switch.) Move the switch to the A position for autofocusing and to M for manual focusing.

  - *Autofocusing:* Press and hold the shutter button halfway. See the last section of this chapter for details on autofocusing in the Auto exposure mode; visit Chapter 4 for details on controlling the autofocusing system.

  - *Manual focusing:* After setting the lens switch to M, rotate the focusing ring on the lens barrel. The position of the focusing ring varies depending on the lens; I labeled the one found on the 18–55mm lens in Figure 1-18. Chapter 4 has additional tips on manual focusing, too.

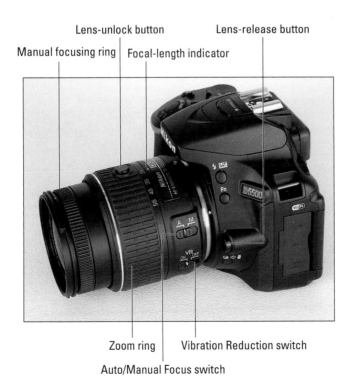

Lens-unlock button Lens-release button

Manual focusing ring | Focal-length indicator

Zoom ring | Vibration Reduction switch

Auto/Manual Focus switch

Figure 1-18: Here are a few features that may be found on your lens.

✔ **Zooming:** If you bought a zoom lens, it has a movable *zoom ring.* Figure 1-18 shows the location of the zoom ring on the 18–55mm lens. To zoom in or out, rotate the ring.

You can determine the current focal length of the lens by looking at the number that's aligned with the white dot labeled *focal-length indicator* in Figure 1-18. (If you're new to the term *focal length,* the sidebar "Focal length and the crop factor," elsewhere in this chapter, explains the subject.)

✔ **Enabling Vibration Reduction:** Many Nikon lenses offer *Vibration Reduction,* which compensates for small amounts of camera shake that can occur when you handhold the camera. Camera movement during the exposure can produce blurry images, so turning on Vibration Reduction can help you get sharper handheld shots. When you use a tripod, however, turn the feature off so that the camera doesn't try to compensate for movement that isn't occurring. Turn Vibration Reduction on or off by using the VR switch (refer to Figure 1-18). The available settings vary depending on the lens, so again, see the lens manual for details.

Vibration Reduction is initiated when you depress the shutter button halfway. If you pay close attention, the image in the viewfinder may appear to be a little blurry immediately after you take the picture. That's a normal result of the Vibration Reduction operation and doesn't indicate a problem with your camera or focus. Also understand that a blurry image can be the result of using a too-slow shutter speed when photographing a moving subject; Vibration Reduction isn't intended to handle that focus issue.

✔ **Removing a lens:** If you use a retractable lens such as the 18–55mm kit lens, collapse the lens before you remove it. (Press the lock button on the lens and then rotate the lens barrel; refer to Figure 1-5.)

With any type of lens, turn the camera off before removing the lens. Then press the lens-release button (refer to Figure 1-18), and turn the lens toward that button until it detaches from the lens mount. Put the rear protective cap onto the back of the lens and, if you aren't putting another lens on the camera, cover the lens mount with its cap, too.

Always switch lenses in a clean environment to reduce the risk of getting dust, dirt, and other contaminants inside the camera or lens. Changing lenses on a sandy beach, for example, isn't a good idea. For added safety, point the camera body slightly down when performing this maneuver; doing so helps prevent any flotsam in the air from being drawn into the camera by gravity.

TIP

Focal length and the crop factor

The angle of view that a lens can capture is determined by its _focal length,_ or in the case of a zoom lens, the range of focal lengths it offers. Focal length is measured in millimeters.

According to photography tradition, a focal length of 50mm is described as a "normal" lens. Most point-and-shoot cameras feature this focal length, which is a medium-range lens that works well for the type of snapshots that users of those kinds of cameras are likely to shoot.

A lens with a focal length under 35mm is characterized as a _wide-angle_ lens because at that focal length, the camera has a wide angle of view, making it good for landscape photography. A short focal length also has the effect of making objects seem smaller and farther away. At the other end of the spectrum, a lens with a focal length longer than 80mm is considered a _telephoto_ lens and is often referred to as a _long lens._ With a long lens, the angle of view narrows and faraway subjects appear closer and larger, which is ideal for wildlife and sports photographers.

Note, however, that the focal lengths stated here and elsewhere in the book are _35mm equivalent_ focal lengths. Here's the deal: For

reasons that aren't really important, when you put a standard lens on most digital cameras, including the D5500, the available frame area is reduced, as if you took a picture on a camera that uses 35mm film negatives and cropped it. (Nikon refers to the image sensors used in this type of camera as a DX sensor.)

This _crop factor_ varies depending on the camera, which is why the photo industry adopted the 35mm-equivalent measuring stick as a standard. With the D5500, the crop factor is roughly 1.5. In the figure here, the red line indicates the image area that results from the 1.5 crop factor.

When shopping for a lens, it's important to remember this crop factor to make sure that you get the focal length designed for the type of pictures you want to take. Just multiply the lens focal length by 1.5 to determine the actual angle of view. Not sure which focal length to choose? Point your web browser to http://imaging.nikon.com, click the link for Nikkor lenses, click the Related Links item, and then click the link for the Nikkor Lens Simulator. Using this interactive tool, you can see exactly how different focal-length lenses capture the same scene.

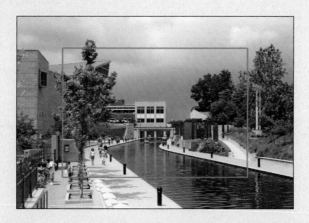

Working with Memory Cards

As the medium that stores your picture files, the memory card is a critical component of your camera. See the steps at the start of this chapter for help installing a card; follow these tips for buying and maintaining cards:

✓ **Buying SD cards:** Again, you can use regular SD cards, which offer less than 4GB of storage space; SDHC cards (4GB–32GB); and SDXC cards (more than 32GB). Aside from card capacity, the other specification to note is *SD speed class,* which indicates how quickly data can be moved to and from the card (the *read/write speed*). For best performance, especially for movie recording, I recommend a speed class rating of 6 or 10 (currently the fastest SD speed class rating).

Some cards may also carry another designation, UHS-1, 2, or 3. These UHS labels refer to a new technology designed to boost data transmission speeds above the normal Speed Class 10 rate. Your camera can use UHS-1 cards, but Nikon doesn't promise compatibility with UHS-2 or -3 cards.

✓ **Formatting a card:** The first time you use a new memory card or insert a card that's been used in other devices, you need to *format* it to prepare it to record your pictures. You also need to format the card if you see the blinking letters *FOR* in the viewfinder or if the monitor displays a message requesting formatting.

Formatting erases everything on your memory card. So before you format a card, be sure that you've copied any data on it to your computer. After doing so, get the formatting job done by selecting Format Memory Card from the Setup menu.

✓ **Removing a card:** After making sure that the memory card access light is off, indicating that the camera has finished recording your most recent photo, turn off the camera. Open the memory card door, depress the memory card slightly, and then let go. The card rises a little way out of the slot, enabling you to grab it by the tail and remove it.

If you turn on the camera when no card is installed, the symbol [-E-] appears in the lower-right corner of the viewfinder, and the image area of the viewfinder displays a blinking memory card symbol. A message on the monitor also nudges you to insert a memory card. If you have a card in the camera and you get these messages, try taking out the card and reinserting it. (Turn off the camera first.)

✓ **Handling cards:** Don't touch the gold contacts on the back of the card. (See the right card in Figure 1-19.) When cards aren't in use, store them in the protective cases they came in or in a memory card wallet. Keep cards away from extreme heat and cold as well.

✔ **Locking cards:** The tiny switch on the side of the card, labeled *Lock switch* in Figure 1-19, enables you to lock your card, which prevents any data from being erased or recorded to the card. If you insert a locked card into the camera, a message on the monitor alerts you, and the symbol [d blinks in the view-finder.

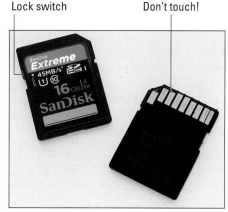

Lock switch   Don't touch!

Figure 1-19: Avoid touching the gold contacts on the card.

You can protect individual images from accidental erasure by using the camera's Protect feature, which I cover in Chapter 9. Note, though, that formatting the card *does* erase even protected pictures; the safety feature prevents erasure only when you use the camera's Delete function.

✔ **Using Eye-Fi memory cards:** Your camera works with *Eye-Fi memory cards,* which are special cards that enable you to transmit your files wirelessly to your computer and other devices. That's a cool feature, but, unfortunately, the cards themselves are more expensive than regular cards and require some configuring that I don't have room to cover in this book. For more details, visit `www.eye.fi`.

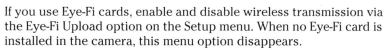

If you use Eye-Fi cards, enable and disable wireless transmission via the Eye-Fi Upload option on the Setup menu. When no Eye-Fi card is installed in the camera, this menu option disappears.

Of course, for transferring files to a smartphone or tablet, you can instead use the camera's built-in Wi-Fi feature. Chapter 9 shows you how. This feature doesn't permit transferring files to a computer, however.

Taking a Few Final Setup Steps

Your camera offers scads of options for customizing its performance, some of which I discuss earlier in this chapter. Later chapters explain settings related to actual picture-taking, such as those that affect flash behavior and autofocusing, and Chapter 10 talks about some options that are better left at their default settings until you're fully familiar with your camera. That leaves just the handful of options covered in the next two sections that I recommend you consider at the get-go.

Cruising the Setup menu

The following options live on the Setup menu, which is the one marked with the little wrench icon. The menu, which appears in Figure 1-20, is a three-page affair (only Page 1 is visible in the figure); drag up and down the touchscreen or use the Multi Selector to scroll through the menu and access these settings:

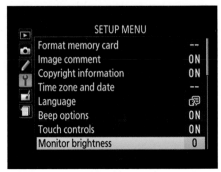

Figure 1-20: Visit the Setup menu to customize the camera's basic operation.

- ✓ **Beep Options:** By default, your camera beeps after certain operations, such as after it sets focus when you shoot in autofocus mode. When the touchscreen is enabled, it also sounds a beep every time you tap a screen item. Select this menu item if you need the camera to hush up.

  You get two sound controls: For the Beep On/Off option, select Off (Touch Controls Only) to silence just touchscreen sounds; choose Off to disable the beep for all operations. The Pitch option lets you set the volume to High or Low.

- ✓ **Monitor Brightness:** This option enables you to make the display brighter or darker. But if you take this step, what you see on the monitor may not be an accurate rendition of the picture exposure. I recommend that you keep the brightness at the default setting (0).

- ✓ **Slot Empty Release Lock:** This cryptically named feature determines whether the camera lets you take a picture when no memory card is installed in the camera. If you set it to Enable Release, you can take a temporary picture, which appears in the monitor with the word *Demo* but isn't recorded anywhere. The feature is provided mainly for use in camera stores, enabling salespeople to demonstrate the camera without having to keep a memory card installed. I can think of no good reason why anyone else would change the setting from the default, Release Locked.

- ✓ **Wi-Fi:** This option controls the built-in Wi-Fi transmitter, which enables you to link your camera to a smartphone or tablet. (See Chapter 9 for details.)

  To save battery power, keep the Wi-Fi feature turned off, as it is by default, until you're ready to connect the camera to your smart device.

- ✓ **Conformity Marking:** I bring this one up just so that you know you can ignore it: When you select the option, you see logos indicating that the camera conforms with certain camera-industry standards. I know you'll sleep better at night with that information.

- ✓ **Firmware Version:** Select this option to view which version of the camera *firmware,* or internal software, your camera runs. You see the firmware items C and L. At the time this book was written, C was version 1.00; L was 2.008.

Keeping your camera firmware up to date is important, so visit the Nikon website (www.nikon.com) regularly to find out whether your camera sports the latest version. You can find detailed instructions at the site on how to download and install any firmware updates.

Custom Setting options

Check the status of these Custom Setting menu options before you shoot your first pictures, too:

- ✔ **File Number Sequence:** This option, found on the Shooting/Display sub-menu and highlighted in Figure 1-21, controls how the camera names your picture files. When the option is set to Off, as it is by default, the camera restarts file numbering at 0001 every time you format the memory card or insert a new memory card. Numbering is also restarted if a new image-storage folder is created. (Chapter 10 explains folders.)

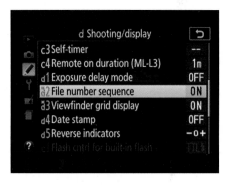

  This setup can cause problems over time, creating a scenario where you wind up with multiple images that have the same filename — not on the current memory card, but when you download images to your computer. So set the option to On (refer to Figure 1-21). Note that when you get to picture number 9999, file numbering is still reset to 0001, however. The camera automatically creates a new folder to hold your next 9,999 images.

  Figure 1-21: Danger, Will Robinson! Change the File Number Sequence option to On to avoid winding up with multiple pictures that have the same filename.

  As for the Reset option, it enables you to assign the first file number (which ends in 0001) to the next picture you shoot. Then the camera behaves as if you selected the On setting.

  Should you be a really, _really_ prolific shooter and snap enough pictures to reach image 9999 in folder 999, the camera will refuse to take another photo until you choose that Reset option and either format the memory card or insert a brand-new one.

- ✔ **Date Stamp:** Using this option, you can imprint on the photo the shooting date, the date and time, or the number of days between the day you took the picture and another date that you specify. This feature works only with pictures that you shoot in the JPEG file format; see the Chapter 2 section related to the Image Quality setting for details about file formats.

The default Date Stamp setting, Off, is the way to go; you don't need to permanently mar your photos to find out when you took them. Every picture file includes a hidden vat of text data, or *metadata,* that records the shooting date and time as well as all the camera settings you used — f-stop, shutter speed, and lots more. You can view this data during playback and, after downloading, in the free software provided with your camera as well as in many photo programs.

Restoring default settings

Should you ever want to return your camera to its original, out-of-the-box state, the camera manual contains a complete list of most of the default settings. Look on the pages that introduce each of the menus.

You can also partially restore default settings by taking these steps:

- ✔ **Reset all Shooting Menu options:** Open the Shooting menu and select Reset Shooting Menu. Note that resetting the menu does not affect the Storage Folder option, which is a concern only if you create custom folders, as outlined in Chapter 10.

- ✔ **Reset all Custom Setting Menu options:** Choose Reset Custom Settings at the top of the Custom Setting menu.

  Resetting the Custom Setting menu restores the File Number Sequence option to its default, Off, which is most definitely Not a Good Thing. If you restore the menu defaults, be *sure* that you revisit that option and return it to the On setting. See the preceding section for details.

- ✔ **Restore critical picture-taking settings *without* affecting all options on the Custom Setting menu:** Use the two-button reset method: Press and hold the Menu button and the Info button simultaneously for longer than 2 seconds. (The little green dots near these two buttons are a reminder of this function.) See the camera manual for a list of exactly which settings are restored.

Shooting Your First Pictures in Auto Mode

Your camera is loaded with features for the advanced photographer, enabling you to exert precise control over options such as f-stop, shutter speed, ISO, flash power, and much more. But you don't have to wait until you master those topics to take great pictures, because your camera also offers point-and-shoot simplicity through its Auto exposure mode.

The next two sections walk you through the process of taking a picture in Auto mode using autofocusing and the default picture settings. (Before taking these steps, you may want to visit the preceding section and follow the instructions there for returning the camera to its default state.) The first section explains normal, through-the-viewfinder shooting; the second section shows you how to take a picture in Live View mode.

Viewfinder photography in Auto mode

When you use the viewfinder to compose photos, follow these steps to take a picture:

1. **Set the Mode dial to Auto, as shown in Figure 1-22.**

2. **Set the lens focusing method to auto.**

   You make this shift using a switch on the side of the lens. On the lens featured in this book, as well as with the 18–140 mm kit lens, set the switch to A.

3. **Looking through the viewfinder, frame your subject so that it appears within the autofocus brackets, labeled in Figure 1-23.**

4. **Press and hold the shutter button halfway down.**

   At this point, the following occurs:

   - *Exposure metering begins.* The autoexposure meter analyzes the light and selects the initial exposure settings. The camera continues monitoring the light up to the time you take the picture, however, and may adjust the exposure settings if lighting conditions change.

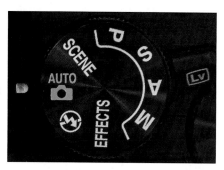

Figure 1-22: Set the Mode dial to Auto for point-and-shoot simplicity.

Autofocus brackets

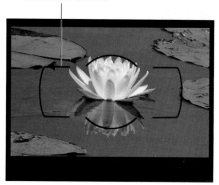

Figure 1-23: Frame your subject so that it's within the area surrounded by the autofocus brackets.

- *The built-in flash pops up if the camera thinks additional light is needed.* If you're in a situation where flash is prohibited, return to Step 1 and change the Mode dial setting from Auto to Auto Flash Off, which is the setting between Auto and Effects (refer to Figure 1-22). This shooting mode does the same thing as Auto but disables flash.

- *The autofocus system begins to do its thing.* In dim light, the AF-assist lamp may shoot out a beam of light to help the camera measure the distance between your subject and the lens so that it can better establish focus. (This assumes that you have not turned the feature off via the Custom Setting menu.)

- *The shots remaining value changes to display the buffer capacity, as shown in Figure 1-24.* The buffer is a temporary storage tank where the camera stores picture data until it has time to record that data to the memory card. This system exists so that you can take a continuous series of pictures without waiting between shots until each image is written to the card. When the buffer is full, you can't take another picture until the camera catches up with its recording work.

5. **Check the focus indicators in the viewfinder.**

When the camera has established focus, one or more of the focus points turns red for a split second. The red focus points represent the areas of the frame used to set the focusing distance. (Typically, the camera focuses on the object closest to the camera.) Then a single black focus point appears, as shown in Figure 1-24. At the bottom of the viewfinder, the focus indicator, labeled in the figure, lights to give you further notice that focus has been achieved.

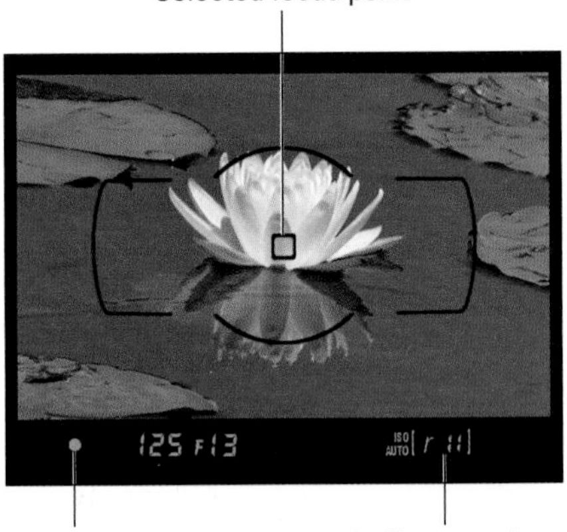

Selected focus point

Focus indicator light　　　Buffer capacity

Figure 1-24: The green light indicates that the camera locked focus on the object under the focus point.

If the subject isn't moving, autofocus remains locked as long as you hold the shutter button halfway down. But if the camera detects subject motion, it adjusts focus up to the time you press the button fully to record the picture. As your subject moves, keep it within the autofocus brackets to ensure correct focusing.

6. Press the shutter button the rest of the way to record the image.

If the camera refuses to take the picture, don't panic: This error is likely related to autofocusing. By default, the camera insists on achieving focus before it releases the shutter to take a picture. You can press the shutter button all day, and the camera just ignores you if it can't set focus.

Try backing away from your subject a little — you may be exceeding the minimum focusing distance of the lens. If that doesn't work, the subject just may not be conducive to autofocusing. Highly reflective objects, scenes with very little contrast, and subjects behind fences are some of the troublemakers. The easiest solution? Switch to manual focusing and set focus yourself.

While the camera sends the image data to the memory card, the memory card access lamp lights. Don't turn off the camera or remove the memory card while the lamp is lit or else you may damage both camera and card.

When the recording process is finished, the picture appears briefly on the camera monitor. If the picture doesn't appear or you want to take a longer look at the image, see Chapter 8, which covers picture playback.

Live View photography in Auto mode

Most aspects of shooting in Live View are the same as for viewfinder photography. Autofocusing, however, works quite differently. Here are the steps to take a picture in Auto mode using the default settings:

1. Set the Mode dial to Auto, as shown in Figure 1-25.

Or, if you need to ensure that the camera's flash doesn't fire, choose the Auto Flash Off mode (the setting between Auto and Effects on the Mode dial).

2. Rotate the Live View switch (refer to Figure 1-25).

The viewfinder goes dark, and the scene in front of the lens appears on the monitor, along with some shooting data, as shown in Figure 1-26. The figures show the default Live View display; see the tips at the end of this step list for other display options.

Live View switch

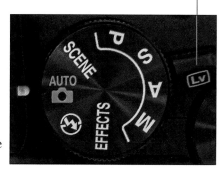

Figure 1-25: Rotate the Live View switch once to enter Live View mode; rotate a second time to return to viewfinder shooting.

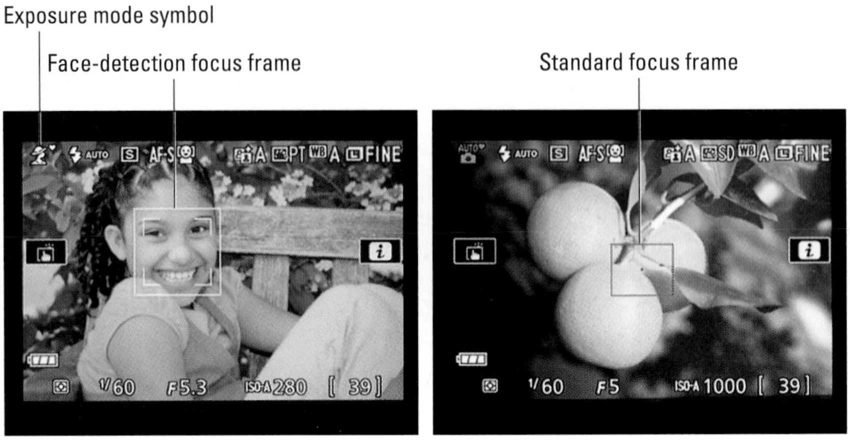

Exposure mode symbol

Face-detection focus frame

Standard focus frame

Figure 1-26: For portraits, a focus box appears automatically over the subject's face (left); otherwise, you see a focus box in the center of the screen (right).

3. **Compose your shot.**

4. **Check the position of the focusing frame; if necessary, adjust the frame so that it's over your subject.**

The autofocus frame that appears depends on your subject:

- *Portraits:* By default, the camera uses an autofocusing option called Face Priority AF-area mode. If it detects a face, it displays a yellow focus box over it (refer to the left side of Figure 1-26). In a group portrait, you may see several boxes: The one that includes the interior corner marks (refer to the figure) indicates the face that will be used to set the focusing distance. To use a different face as the focus point, use the Multi Selector to move the focus box over it.

- *Other subjects:* Anytime the camera can't detect a face, it switches to Wide Area AF-area mode, with the focus point indicated by a red box in the center of the screen (refer to the right side of Figure 1-26). Again, use the Multi Selector to move the focus box over your subject. Press the OK button to move the focus box quickly back to the center of the frame.

You also can set focus by tapping your subject on the screen, but if the Touch Shutter feature is enabled, the camera immediately takes the picture after you tap. See the list at the end of this section for details. For now, stick with using the Multi Selector to position the focus box.

5. Press the shutter button halfway to set focus and initiate exposure metering.

When focus is set, the focus box turns green and you hear a beep (assuming that you didn't disable it via the Setup menu). In dim lighting, the built-in flash pops up (unless you selected the Auto Flash Off setting in Step 1).

In Live View mode, the camera always locks focus when you press the shutter button halfway, even if the subject is moving. If you want the camera to track focus on a moving subject, you must shift from the default Focus mode option, AF-S (for single-servo autofocus), to AF-F (full-time servo) mode. Chapter 4 explains the details.

6. Press the shutter button all the way down to record the picture.

The photo appears briefly on the monitor, and then the live preview reappears.

After you press the shutter button halfway in Step 5, the camera may shift automatically to one of four Scene modes that are designed to capture specific types of subjects. The exposure mode symbol labeled in Figure 1-26 is your cue that this switch was made. For example, in the left screen in the figure, the camera shifted to Portrait mode, represented by the lady with a hat. The other three Scene modes that the camera may select are Landscape (mountain symbol); Close Up (flower symbol); and Night Portrait (head-and-shoulders with a star). If you see the word *Auto* with a heart, as on the right screen of the figure, the camera is sticking with ordinary Auto mode. If you prefer to select a Scene type directly, see the first section of Chapter 2.

To close out this chapter, here are a few important pointers to remember when you use Live View mode:

✔ **Press the Info button to change the type of data that's displayed on the monitor.** You can choose from five displays:

- *Detailed Photo Indicators:* Reveals extensive shooting data for still photography (refer to Figure 1-26). The display uses this mode by default. (I detail each value or symbol as I explain the relevant features later in the book.)

- *Movie Indicators:* Displays data related to movie recording, as shown on the upper-left screen in Figure 1-27. The transparent gray bar that appears along the top and bottom of the screen shows how much of the vertical image area is excluded from the frame if you set the movie resolution to a setting that produces a 16:9 frame aspect ratio. (The only setting that doesn't produce this ratio is 640 x 424, which captures a 3:2 frame, the same as a still photo.) I discuss this option, along with other movie-recording topics, in Chapter 7.

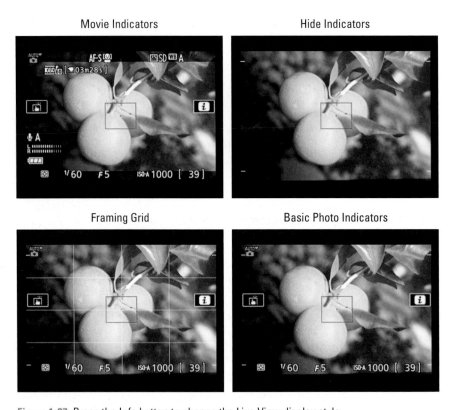

Figure 1-27: Press the Info button to change the Live View display style.

- *Hide Indicators:* Displays only the markings shown in the upper-right corner in Figure 1-27.

- In this display mode, as well as in the two described next, you may see four tiny, horizontal markers near the corners of the display. They take the place of the shaded bars indicating the 16:9 frame area that appears in Movie Indicators mode.

- *Framing Grid:* Adds a grid and the 16:9 framing marks (refer to the lower-left corner of Figure 1-27).

- *Basic Photo Indicators:* Presents only the basic exposure settings plus the aforementioned movie frame-area markers, as shown in the lower-right corner in the figure.

✔ **If you enable the Touch Shutter feature, you can tap anywhere on the screen to set focus and snap the picture.** To turn this feature on and off, tap the symbol labeled in Figure 1-28.

Even when the Touch Shutter feature is disabled, you can still tap the screen to set focus when using autofocus. You then use the shutter button to take the picture.

✏ **To access the Live View control strip, press the *i* button or tap the icon labeled in Figure 1-28.** See the earlier section "Adjusting Settings via the Control Strip" for help with using this time-saving feature.

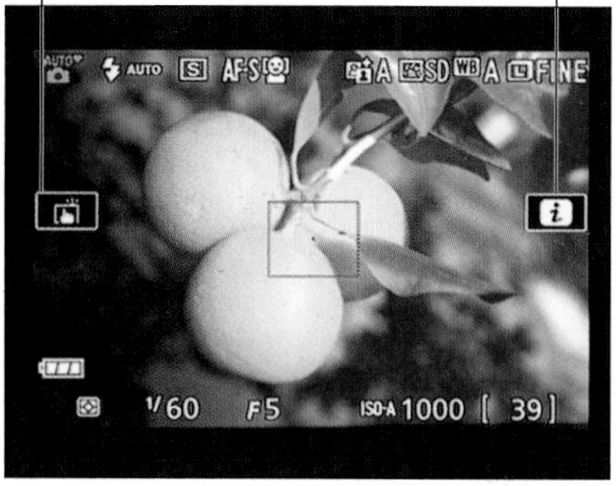

✏ **Cover the viewfinder to prevent light from seeping into the camera and affecting exposure.** Nikon sells a cover designed for this purpose: the DK-5 Eyepiece cap, about $4. Slide the rubber eyecup that surrounds the viewfinder up and out of the groove that holds it in place; then slide the cover down into the groove. (Orient the cover so that the Nikon label faces the viewfinder.)

Tap to display control strip

Touch Shutter symbol

Figure 1-28: These symbols relate to the Touch Shutter and Information display control strip.

✏ **The monitor turns off by default after ten minutes of inactivity.** When monitor shutdown is 30 seconds away, a countdown timer appears in the upper-left corner of the screen. You can adjust the shutdown timing via the Auto Off Timers option, found on the Timers/AE Lock submenu of the Custom Setting menu; Chapter 10 has details.

✏ **Using Live View for an extended period can harm your pictures and the camera.** In Live View mode, the camera's innards heat up more than usual, and that extra heat can create the proper electronic conditions for *noise,* a defect that gives your pictures a speckled look. Perhaps more importantly, the increased temperatures can damage the camera. For that reason, Live View is automatically disabled if the camera detects a critical heat level. In extremely warm environments, you may not be able to use Live View mode for long before the system shuts down.

When the camera is 30 seconds or fewer from shutting down, the countdown timer appears in order to let you know how many seconds remain for shooting. The warning doesn't appear during picture playback or when menus are active, however.

✏ **Aiming the lens at the sun or another bright light also can damage the camera.** Of course, you can cause problems by doing this even during viewfinder shooting, but the possibilities increase when you use Live View. You can harm not only the camera's internal components but also the monitor (not to mention your eyes).

✔ **Some lights may interfere with the Live View display.** The operating frequency of some types of lights, including fluorescent and mercury-vapor lamps, can create electronic interference that causes the monitor display to flicker or exhibit odd color banding. Changing the Flicker Reduction option on the Setup menu may resolve this issue. At the default setting, Auto, the camera gauges the light and chooses the right setting for you. But you also can choose from two specific frequencies: 50 Hz and 60 Hz. (In the United States and Canada, the standard frequency is 60 Hz; in Europe, it's 50 Hz.)

Reviewing Five Essential Picture-Taking Options

In This Chapter

▶ Selecting an exposure mode

▶ Changing the shutter-release mode

▶ Choosing the right Image Size (resolution) setting

▶ Understanding the Image Quality setting: JPEG or Raw?

▶ Adding flash

*E*very camera manufacturer strives to ensure that your initial encounter with the camera is a happy one. To that end, the D5500's default settings are designed to make it easy to take a good picture the first time you press the shutter button. The camera is set to the Auto exposure mode, which means that all you need to do is frame, focus, and shoot, as outlined at the end of Chapter 1.

Although the default settings deliver acceptable pictures in many cases, they don't produce optimal results in every situation. You may be able to take a decent portrait in Auto mode, for example, but by tweaking a few settings, you can turn that decent portrait into a stunning one.

This chapter helps you start fine-tuning the camera settings by explaining five basic picture-taking options: exposure mode, shutter-release mode, image size, image quality, and flash. They're not the most exciting features (don't think I didn't notice you stifling a yawn), but they make a big difference in how easily you can capture the photo you have in mind. You should review these settings before each photo outing.

Choosing an Exposure Mode

The first setting to consider is the exposure mode, which you select via the Mode dial, shown in Figure 2-1. Your choice determines how much control you have over two critical exposure settings — aperture and shutter speed — as well as many other options, including those related to color settings and flash photography.

Your choices fall into three categories: fully automatic, semiautomatic, and manual. The next three sections provide the background you need to choose the option.

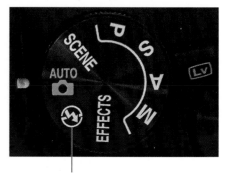

Auto Flash Off

Figure 2-1: The Mode dial determines how much input you have over exposure, color, and other picture options.

Fully automatic exposure modes

My guess is that you bought this book for help with using the camera's advanced exposure modes, so that's what the rest of this book covers. But until you have time to digest that information — or if you just need a break from thinking about the advanced options — you can take advantage of the following point-and-shoot modes:

- **Auto and Auto Flash Off:** The camera analyzes the scene and selects what it considers the most appropriate settings to capture the image. The only difference between the two modes is that the Auto Flash Off setting, labeled in Figure 2-1, disables flash. In Auto mode, you can choose from several Flash modes, which I detail later in this chapter. Chapter 1 shows you how to use the Auto Flash Off setting as well as plain ol' Auto.

- **Scene modes:** You also get a batch of automatic modes designed to capture specific subjects in ways deemed best according to photography tradition. For example, in Portrait mode, skin tones are manipulated to appear warmer and softer, and the background appears blurry to bring attention to your subject, as shown on the left in Figure 2-2; in Landscape mode, greens and blues are intensified, and the camera tries to maintain sharpness in both near and distant objects, as shown on the right in the figure.

To experiment with Scene modes, set the Mode dial to Scene. An icon representing the current Scene mode appears in the upper-left corner of the screen, as shown on the left in Figure 2-3. Rotate the Command dial to shift to the scene selection screen, as shown on the right; keep spinning the dial or tap the left/right scroll arrows to cycle through the Scene types. (The figures show how things look when you're using the viewfinder to frame shots; the display looks slightly different in Live

View mode, but you adjust the setting using the same te
lock in your setting and return to shooting mode, press
button halfway and release it.

Portrait mode   Landscape mode

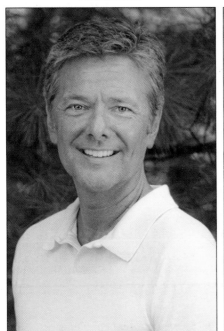   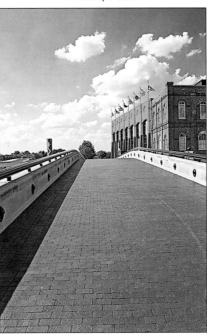

Figure 2-2: Portrait mode produces pleasant skin tones and a soft background; Landscape mode delivers vivid colors and keeps both foreground and background objects sharp.

Current Scene mode

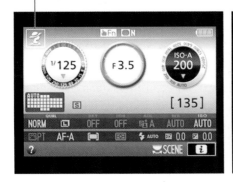   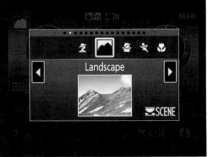

Figure 2-3: After setting the Mode dial to Scene, rotate the Command dial to scroll through additional Scene types.

After you exit the selection screen, you can tap the question mark icon in the lower left corner of the monitor (or press the Zoom Out button) to display a Help screen with more information about the chosen mode.

For the most part, the process of taking pictures in the Scene modes is the same as for shooting in Auto mode. For a few Scene modes, however, some variations come into play:

- *Close Up, Candlelight, and Food:* In Auto mode (and in most Scene modes), the camera selects the focus point, typically focusing on the object closest to the lens. But in these three modes, the center focus point is used by default, so frame the picture with your subject under that point. To choose a different focus point, look through the viewfinder and then press the Multi Selector left/right/up/down until the point you prefer is highlighted. (You may need to give the shutter button a quick half-press to wake up the camera before you can do so.)

  In Food mode, you also control whether the flash fires. If you want to use flash, press the flash button on the left side of the camera to raise the built-in flash. Close the flash unit to go flash free.

- *Sports and Pet Portrait:* Again, the center focus point is selected by default, and you can choose a different point by using the Multi Selector. Start by framing your subject under the focus point, and then press and hold the shutter button halfway. If the subject leaves the selected focus point, the camera looks to the other focus points for focusing information, adjusting focus as necessary up to the time you press the button the rest of the way to take the shot.

  Sports mode and Pet Portrait mode also use the Continuous High shutter-release setting, which means that the camera records a burst of images as long as you hold down the shutter button. See the later section "Setting the Release Mode" for more about this setting.

- ✓ **Effects:** This mode works like Auto except that the camera applies one of ten special effects to the picture. Chapter 11 provides details on Effects mode and also explains how you can apply effects to existing pictures by using options on the Retouch menu.

Because all these modes are designed to make picture-taking simple, they prevent you from accessing many camera features. You can control the rest of the settings covered in this chapter and also adjust certain aspects of the camera's autofocusing behavior (Chapter 4 tells you how), but that's about it. Options that are off-limits appear dimmed on the menus and Information and Live View displays. If you press a button that leads to an advanced setting, the monitor displays a message telling you that the option is unavailable.

Scene modes in focus (or not)

When you focus the camera, you determine the point of sharpest focus. The distance to which the focus zone extends from that point — photographers call it *depth of field* — depends in part on the *aperture setting,* or *f-stop,* which is an exposure control. Some Scene modes are designed to choose aperture settings that deliver a certain depth of field. The Portrait, Child, and Close Up modes, for example, try to use a wide aperture (low f-stop number) because doing so shortens the depth of field, rendering backgrounds softly focused — an artistic choice that most people prefer for those types of shots. On the flip side, Landscape mode tries to use a small aperture (high f-stop number), which produces a large depth of field, maintaining sharpness in both foreground and background objects.

However, the range of apertures that the camera can select varies, depending on the light. In dim lighting, an open aperture is needed in order to properly expose the picture, and in bright light, a small aperture may be required in order to avoid overexposing the picture. Additionally, the range of available aperture settings varies from lens to lens, and the amount of background blurring also increases as the distance between your subject and the background grows. Depth

of field is affected by the lens focal length and the subject-to-camera distance, too. Long story short: How much depth of field any Scene mode produces varies from shot to shot.

Another exposure-related control, *shutter speed,* affects how sharp moving subjects appear. At slow shutter speeds, moving objects appear blurry; at fast shutter speeds, they appear sharp.

In Sports and Pet Portrait modes, the camera tries to select a shutter speed fast enough to freeze action, but in dim lighting, that may not be possible: The less light that's available, the slower the shutter speed that's needed to expose the photo — so even in these two modes, a moving subject may appear blurry. Additionally, some Scene modes, such as Night Portrait, Night Landscape, and Candlelight, purposely choose a slow shutter speed to cope with the dark settings. For these modes, it's critical to use a tripod because any camera movement during the exposure can also blur the image.

To fully understand these issues — and to find out how to control the focus and depth of field to a greater extent than the Scene modes allow — visit Chapters 3 and 4.

Semiautomatic exposure modes (P, S, and A)

To take more creative control but still get some exposure assistance from the camera, choose one of these exposure modes, all detailed in Chapter 3:

✓ **P (programmed autoexposure):** The camera selects the aperture and shutter speed necessary to ensure a good exposure. But you can rotate the Command dial to choose from different combinations of the two to vary the creative results. For example, you might use a fast shutter speed to freeze action, or you might go in the other direction, choosing a shutter speed slow enough to blur the action, which creates a heightened sense of motion.

✔ **S (shutter-priority autoexposure):** You select the shutter speed, and the camera selects the proper aperture to properly expose the image. This mode is ideal for capturing moving subjects because it gives you direct control over the shutter speed. The fastest way to adjust the shutter speed is to rotate the Command dial.

✔ **A (aperture-priority autoexposure):** In this mode, you rotate the Command dial to choose the aperture, and the camera automatically chooses a shutter speed to properly expose the image. Because aperture affects depth of field (the distance over which objects in a scene remain acceptably sharp), this setting works well for portraits because you can select an aperture that results in a soft, blurry background, putting the emphasis on your subject. For landscape shots, on the other hand, you might choose an aperture that keeps the entire scene sharply focused so that both near and distant objects have equal visual weight.

You also can use the touchscreen to adjust the shutter speed or aperture setting: Tap the arrow box set to the right of the setting and then tap the left and right arrows that appear to change the value. See Figure 2-4, in the next section, for a look at the position of these controls. Frankly, though, using the Command dial is easier because you can keep your eye up to the viewfinder while changing the setting.

P, S, and A modes give you access to all camera features. So even if you're not ready to explore aperture and shutter speed, go ahead and set the Mode dial to P if you need to access a setting that's off-limits in the fully automated modes. The camera then operates pretty much as it does in Auto mode but doesn't limit you to the most basic picture-taking settings.

Manual exposure mode (M)

In Manual mode, you take the exposure reins completely, selecting both aperture and shutter speed as follows:

✔ **To set the shutter speed:** Rotate the Command dial.

✔ **To set the aperture:** Press the Exposure Compensation button while rotating the Command dial.

You also can adjust the two values via the touchscreen:

✔ **Viewfinder photography:** Tap the arrow box under the shutter speed or aperture setting icon (see Figure 2-4) to access the touch controls for adjusting that value. The Information screen displays a pair of arrows at either side of the selected setting, as shown on the right in the figure; tap the right arrow to raise the value, tap left to lower it. Tap the exit icon (labeled in the figure), to return to the Information screen.

✓ **Live View photography:** The shutter speed and f-stop appear in boxes at the bottom of the screen. Tap either box to display arrows that you can tap to change the current value. After adjusting the setting, tap the exit arrow to return to the normal Live View display.

Tap to adjust shutter speed

Tap to adjust f-stop

Exit screen

Tap to adjust current setting

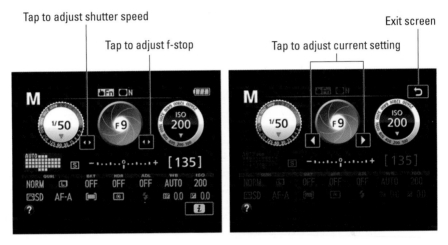

Figure 2-4: Tap the box next to the setting you want to change (left); then tap the left/right arrows to change the value.

Even in Manual exposure mode, the camera offers an assist by displaying an exposure meter to help you dial in the right settings. (See Chapter 3 for details.) You have complete control over all other picture settings, too.

One important and often misunderstood aspect of Manual exposure mode: Setting the Mode dial to M has no bearing on focusing. You can still choose manual focusing or autofocusing, assuming that your lens offers autofocusing. Just set the lens switch to the focusing method you prefer.

Setting the Release Mode

By using the Release mode setting, you tell the camera whether to capture a single image each time you press the shutter button; to record a burst of photos as long as you hold down the shutter button; or to use Self-Timer mode, which delays the image capture until a few seconds after you press the shutter button. You also get two options related to wireless remote control shooting and Quiet Shutter mode, which dampens the normal shutter-release sounds.

Why *Release mode?* It's short for *shutter-release mode.* Pressing the shutter button tells the camera to release the *shutter* — an internal light-control mechanism — so that light can strike the image sensor and expose the image. Your choice of Release mode determines when and how that action occurs.

On the Information screen and Live View display, the current Release mode is indicated by the icons labeled in Figure 2-5. In the figure, the S represents the Single Frame mode. (See the next several sections for a look at the icon representing each mode.) Note that the Live View screen in the figure shows the default data-display mode; if your screen shows a different assortment of data, press the Info button to cycle through the available display modes.

Release mode

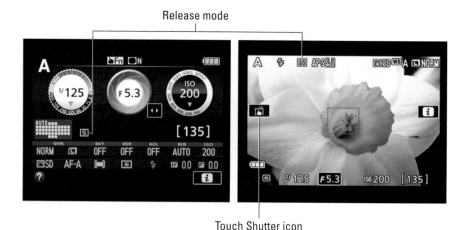

Touch Shutter icon

Figure 2-5: This S represents the Single Frame shutter-release option, which produces one picture for each press of the shutter button.

Also pay attention to the status of the Touch Shutter when you shoot in Live View mode. The Touch Shutter has two settings: On and Off. When the icon appears as shown on the right in Figure 2-5, the Touch Shutter is on. At this setting, the camera sets focus when you touch the screen and releases the shutter button when you lift your finger from the screen. Tap the icon to turn off the shutter-release portion of the feature; you can then tap your subject to set focus on that part of the screen and use the shutter button to record the picture. You can use the Touch Shutter to record only one photo at a time; the burst mode options (Continuous High and Continuous Low) aren't compatible with the Touch Shutter.

To adjust the Release mode setting, use these methods:

 ✔ **Release Mode button:** Press this button, labeled in Figure 2-6, to display the selection screen shown in Figure 2-7. Then tap the setting you want to use. Or, if the touchscreen is disabled, use the Multi Selector to highlight a setting and then press OK.

For even faster results, press and hold down the Release Mode button. When the selection screen appears, rotate the Command dial to highlight a setting. Then release the button to return to shooting mode.

 Shooting menu: Scroll to the second page of the menu to find the setting, as shown in Figure 2-8.

With those basics out of the way, the next few sections explain how each Release mode works.

Single Frame and Quiet Shutter Release modes

 Single Frame Release mode captures one picture each time you release the shutter, whether you're using the Touch Shutter in Live View mode or the plain old shutter button. Single Frame is the default setting for all exposure modes except the Sports and Pet Portrait Scene modes.

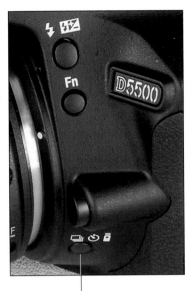

Release Mode button

Figure 2-6: The Release Mode button offers the fastest access to the setting.

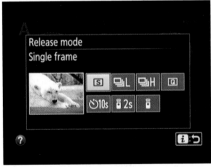

Figure 2-7: After this screen appears, tap the Release Mode option you want to use.

Quiet Shutter mode works just like Single Frame mode but makes less noise as it goes about its business. First, the camera disables the beep that it emits by default when it achieves focus. Additionally, Quiet Shutter mode affects the operation of the internal mirror that causes the scene coming through the lens to be visible in the viewfinder. Normally, the mirror flips up when you press the shutter button and then flips back down after the shutter opens and closes. This mirror movement makes some noise. In Quiet Shutter mode, you can prevent the mirror from flipping back down by keeping the shutter button fully pressed after the shot. Or, if you use the Touch Shutter, keep your finger on the monitor. This way, you can delay the sound made by the final mirror movement to a moment when the noise won't be objectionable.

Even in Quiet mode, the camera beeps when you tap the touchscreen. To turn that sound effect off, set the Beep Options setting on the Setup menu to Off (touch controls only).

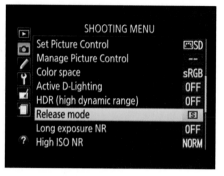

Figure 2-8: The Release Mode option is also found on the Shooting menu.

Continuous (burst mode) shooting

Continuous Low and Continuous High enable *burst mode* shooting. That is, the camera records a continuous series of images for as long as you hold down the shutter button, making it easier to capture fast-paced action. Remember that these two modes don't play nice with the Touch Shutter function available in Live View mode; you must use the shutter button to trigger the shutter release.

Here's how the two modes differ:

✔ **Continuous Low:** The camera can capture as many as 3 frames per second (fps).

✔ **Continuous High:** Records as many as 5 fps, depending on the Image Quality setting, which I cover later in this chapter. If you select the Image Quality setting that produces 14-bit Raw (NEF) files, the maximum frame rate is 4 fps.

A few critical details about these two Release modes:

✔ **You can't use flash.** Continuous mode doesn't work with flash because the time that the flash needs to recycle between shots slows down the capture rate too much. If flash is enabled, you get one shot per each press of the shutter button, as in Single Frame mode.

✔ **Images are stored temporarily in the memory buffer.** The camera has some internal memory — a *buffer* — where it stores picture data until it has time to record all the photos in a burst of shots to the memory card. The number of pictures the buffer can hold depends on certain camera settings, such as Image Quality. When you press the shutter button halfway, the shots remaining value in the lower-right corner of the viewfinder and Live View display changes to show an estimate of how many pictures will fit in the buffer.

After shooting a burst of images, wait for the memory card access light to go out before turning off the camera. (The light is in the lower-right corner of the camera back.) That's your signal that the camera has moved all data from the buffer to the memory card. Turning off the camera before that happens may corrupt the image file.

✔ **Your mileage may vary.** The number of frames per second depends on several factors, including shutter speed. To achieve the highest rate, the shutter speed must be 1/250 second or faster. Additionally, although you can capture as many as 100 frames in a single burst, the frame rate can drop if the buffer gets full.

✔ **Continuous Low is enough for all but the fastest action.** Unless you're shooting a subject that's moving at a really fast pace, not too much changes between frames when you shoot at 5 fps. So, when you use Continuous High, you typically wind up with lots of shots that show the exact same thing, wasting space on your memory card. Continuous Low usually gives you plenty of frames to capture the shot without the unnecessary file bloat.

Self-timer shooting

You're no doubt familiar with Self-Timer mode, which delays the shutter release for a few seconds after you release the shutter button or, in Touch Shutter mode, when you lift your finger from the monitor. After you take that step, the AF-assist lamp on the front of the camera starts to blink, and the camera emits a series of beeps (assuming that you didn't disable its voice via the Beep Options setting on the Setup menu). A few seconds later, the camera captures the image.

By default, the camera waits ten seconds after you press the shutter button and then records a single image. But you can tweak the delay time and capture as many as nine shots at a time. Set your preferences by using the Self-Timer option, found in the Timers/AE Lock section of the Custom Setting menu and shown in Figure 2-9. Here's what you need to know about the two settings:

✔ **Self-Timer Delay:** Choose a delay time of 2, 5, 10, or 20 seconds. The selected delay time appears with the Self-Timer symbol in the Information and Live View displays.

✔ **Number of Shots:** Specify how many frames you want to capture with each press of the shutter button; the maximum is nine. When you record multiple frames, shots are taken at 4-second intervals.

Two more points about self-timer shooting:

✔ **You must reselect the Self-Timer setting for each picture (or series of frames) you want to shoot.** After the specified number of shots are captured, the camera exits Self-Timer Release mode and then returns to the Release mode you used before your Self-Timer shot(s). Turning off the camera also resets the Release mode.

✔ **Cover the viewfinder during self-timer shooting.** Otherwise, light may seep into the camera through the viewfinder and affect exposure.

You may want to purchase the optional Nikon DK-5 eyepiece cap, made just for this purpose. The cap costs around $4.

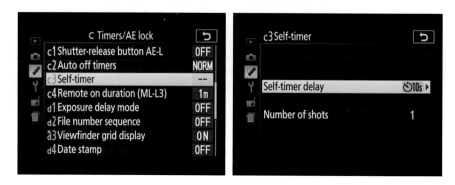

Figure 2-9: You can adjust the self-timer capture delay and the number of frames taken with each press of the shutter button.

Wireless remote control modes

Two other Release mode settings relate to the Nikon ML-L3 wireless remote control and work as follows:

- **Delayed Remote:** After you press the shutter-release button on the remote unit, the AF-assist lamp blinks for about two seconds, and then the camera takes the picture.

- **Quick Response Remote:** The image is captured immediately. In this mode, the AF-assist lamp blinks after the shot is taken.

Normally, the camera cancels out of the remote control modes if it doesn't receive a signal from the remote after about one minute. You can adjust this timing by using the Remote On Duration option, located on the Timers/ AE Lock submenu of the Custom Setting menu. The maximum delay time is 15 minutes; keep in mind that a shorter delay time saves battery life. After the delay time expires, the camera resets itself to either Single Frame, Quiet Shutter, or Continuous Low or Continuous High mode, depending on which mode you last used. The Release mode is also reset to one of those modes if you turn off the camera.

As with self-timer shooting, it's a good idea to cover the viewfinder when you're using these modes, to prevent exposure problems that can be caused by light entering the camera through the viewfinder.

These Release modes are not meant to be used with a wired remote control (which you connect to the Accessory terminal port on the left side of the camera). Select one of the other Release mode settings, and then press the shutter-release button on the remote to trigger the shutter. Wired or wireless, see your remote's operating guide for more details on using the unit.

Additionally, if you own a smartphone or tablet, you can connect it to the camera via Wi-Fi and then use the device to trigger the shutter release. Chapter 9 details this feature.

Investigating other shutter-release options

In addition to the official Release mode setting, your camera offers two other features related to triggering the shutter release: Exposure Delay Mode and Interval Timer Shooting. Check them out in the next two sections.

Exposure Delay Mode

One component of a dSLR camera is a mirror that moves every time you press the shutter button. The vibration caused by the mirror action can cause a small amount of blur when you use a very slow shutter speed, shoot with a long telephoto lens, or take extreme close-ups.

To cope with that issue, some cameras offer *mirror-lockup* shooting, which delays opening the shutter until after the mirror movement is complete. Although the D5500 doesn't offer mirror-lockup shooting — its mirror-lockup function is provided solely for the purpose of accessing the sensor for cleaning — it does offer another solution: Exposure Delay Mode. When you enable this feature, the camera waits about 1 second after the mirror is raised to release the shutter, ensuring that the mirror movement is complete before the image is recorded.

Look for the Exposure Delay Mode option in the Shooting/Display section of the Custom Setting menu, as shown in Figure 2-10. You can use Exposure Delay Mode with any Release mode. Just don't forget that you enabled the feature or else you'll drive yourself batty trying to figure out why the camera isn't responding to your shutter-button finger. I say this from experience. . . .

d Shooting/display	↰
c1 Shutter-release button AE-L	OFF
c2 Auto off timers	NORM
c3 Self-timer	--
c4 Remote on duration (ML-L3)	1m
d1 Exposure delay mode	ON
d2 File number sequence	OFF
d3 Viewfinder grid display	ON
d4 Date stamp	OFF

Figure 2-10: Exposure Delay Mode helps ensure that the movement of the camera's internal mirror doesn't create image blur.

Interval Timer Shooting

With Interval Timer Shooting, you can set the camera to automatically release the shutter at intervals ranging from seconds to hours apart. This feature enables you to capture a subject as it changes over time — a technique commonly known as *time-lapse photography* — without having to stand around pressing the shutter button the whole time.

Be aware that you can't take advantage of this feature during Live View photography or when the Autobracketing or HDR options are enabled. (Chapter 3 explains autobracketing and HDR photography.)

Assuming those restraints aren't in place, here's how to set up the camera for time-lapse photography:

1. Set the Release mode to Single Frame or Quiet Shutter.

 The fastest way to access the setting is to press the Release Mode button on the front-left side of the camera.

2. Display the Shooting menu and select Interval Timer Shooting (as shown on the left in Figure 2-11).

The screen on the right in Figure 2-11 appears.

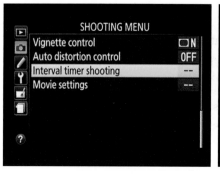
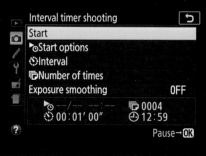

Figure 2-11: The Interval Timer Shooting feature enables you to do time-lapse photography.

3. To begin setting up your capture session, select Start Options as shown on the right in Figure 2-12.

You get two choices:

- *Now:* Select this option to begin capturing frames after you complete the shooting setup.

- *Choose start day and start time:* Select this setting, as shown on the right in Figure 2-12, to delay the start of the interval shooting session. On the next screen, use the touchscreen or Multi Selector to set the date, hour, and minute that you want the interval captures to begin. Tap OK or press the OK button to lock in your choices.

The Start Time option is based on a 24-hour clock, as is the Interval option (explained next). The current time appears in the lower-right corner of the screen and is based on the date/time information you entered when setting up the camera.

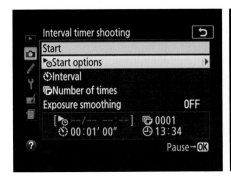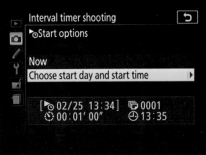

Figure 2-12: You can specify the starting time of the interval captures.

4. **Set the Interval and Number of Times options.**

   Access these options via the initial Interval Timer screen (right screen in Figure 2-11). A few points to note:

   - *Interval:* This setting determines the delay time between each capture. The left column box is for the hour setting; the middle, minutes; and the right, seconds. Make sure that the delay time between frames is longer than the shutter speed you plan to use.

   - *Number of times:* Slightly misnamed, this option determines how many frames the camera records during a single interval-timing shooting session.

   Remember to tap OK or press the OK button after adjusting each setting.

5. **Enable or disable Exposure Smoothing.**

   The final option, Exposure Smoothing, tells the camera to try to match the exposure of each shot to the one taken previously. Obviously, if your goal is a series of frames that show how the subject appears as the sun rises and falls, you should turn this option off, as it is by default. You may want to enable it, however, if you're shooting a subject that will be illuminated with a consistent light source throughout the entire shooting time or if the light may change only slightly, such as when recording a hummingbird at a feeder during an afternoon.

   The Exposure Smoothing option doesn't work in the M (manual) expo-sure mode unless you enable Auto ISO Sensitivity, which gives the camera permission to increase the ISO setting as necessary to maintain a consistent exposure. You can locate that option via the ISO Sensitivity

Settings item on the Shooting menu. (The next chapter explains this setting, which determines how much the camera reacts to light.)

6. **Verify the interval setup and then choose Start to begin the capture setting.**

Your selected timer settings appear at the bottom of the main Interval Timer Shooting screen, as shown in Figure 2-13.

If you selected Now as the Start Time option in Step 3, the first shot is recorded about 3 seconds after you select Start. If you set a delayed start time, the camera displays the message *Timer Active* for a few seconds.

A few final factoids:

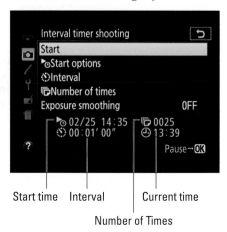

Figure 2-13: Your chosen capture settings appear at the bottom of the main Interval Timer Shooting screen.

✔ **Interval Timer Shooting isn't available for Live View photography or Effects exposure mode.** The menu option is disabled any time Live View is enabled or the Mode dial is set to Effects.

✔ **The card access light blinks while Interval Timer Shooting is in progress.** It's the little light just above the Delete button on the back of the camera.

✔ **You can't adjust camera settings while the interval sequence is in progress.** Make sure that everything is set up to your liking before you begin the interval-shooting session.

✔ **If you're autofocusing, be sure that the camera can focus on your subject.** The camera initiates focusing before each shot. See Chapter 4 for details about autofocusing.

✔ **To pause or cancel interval timing, press the OK button.**

You then see a screen similar to the one in Figure 2-14. Choose from three options:

• *Restart shooting immediately:* Select Restart.

• *Restart at a later date/time:* Select Start Options. Then choose Start Day and Start Time and enter the date and time that you want to resume interval shooting. Return to the screen shown in Figure 2-14 and choose Restart.

• *Exit interval shooting:* Select Off. Or just turn the camera off or change the Mode dial setting.

✓ **To prevent exposure miscues, cover the viewfinder.** This prevents light from entering the viewfinder and fooling the exposure meter.

✓ **When the interval sequence is complete, the Interval Timer Shooting menu option is reset to Off.** The card access light stops blinking shortly after the final image is recorded to the memory card.

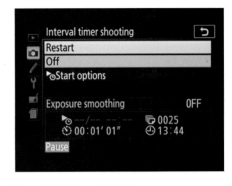

Figure 2-14: Press the OK button to pause or cancel interval photography.

One final piece of advice for this section: The camera battery may not contain enough juice for time-lapse photography sessions that span many hours. If you do a lot of this kind of shooting, you may want to invest in the AC power supply. Also be sure that your memory card has enough empty space to hold all your interval shots. If the camera runs out of card space, the interval countdown will continue but no shots will be recorded until you insert a new memory card.

Checking Image Size and Image Quality

Your preflight camera check should also include a look at the Image Size and Image Quality settings. The first option sets picture resolution; the second, file type.

The names of these settings are a little misleading, though, because the Image Size setting also contributes to picture quality, and the Image Quality setting affects the file size of the picture. Because the two work in tandem to determine quality and size, it's important to consider them together. The next few sections explain each option; following that, I offer a few final tips and show you how to select the settings you want to use.

Also check out the section related to ISO in Chapter 3; very high ISO settings can also reduce image quality. In this case, a defect known as *noise* can give the picture a speckled appearance.

Considering the Image Size setting (resolution)

The Image Size setting determines how many pixels are used to create your photo. *Pixels* are the square tiles from which digital images are made; you can see some pixels close up in the right image in Figure 2-15, which shows a greatly magnified view of the eye area in the left image.

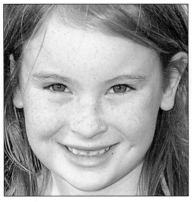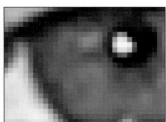

Figure 2-15: Pixels are the building blocks of digital photos.

Pixel is short for *picture element.*

The number of pixels in an image is referred to as *resolution.* You can define resolution in terms of either the *pixel dimensions* — the number of horizontal pixels and vertical pixels — or total resolution, which you get by multiplying those two values. This number is usually stated in *megapixels* (or MP, for short), with one megapixel equal to 1 million pixels.

Your camera offers three Image Size options: Large, Medium, and Small. Table 2-1 lists the resolution values for each setting. (Megapixel values are rounded off.)

Table 2-1	Image Size (Resolution) Options
Setting	**Resolution**
Large	6000 x 4000 (24.0MP)
Medium	4496 x 3000 (13.5MP)
Small	2992 x 2000 (6.0MP)

However, if you select Raw (NEF) as the Image Quality setting, images are captured at the Large setting. You can vary the resolution only for pictures taken in the JPEG format. The upcoming section "Understanding Image Quality options (JPEG or Raw)" explains file formats.

To choose the right Image Size setting, you need to understand the three ways that resolution affects your pictures:

- ✔ **Print size:** Pixel count determines the size at which you can produce a high-quality print. When an image contains too few pixels, details appear muddy, and curved and diagonal lines appear jagged. Such pictures are said to exhibit *pixelation.*

    Depending on your photo printer, you typically need anywhere from 200 to 300 pixels per linear inch, or *ppi,* for good print quality. To produce an 8 x 10 print at 200 ppi, for example, you need a pixel count of 1600 x 2000, or about 3.2 megapixels.

    Even though many photo-editing programs enable you to add pixels to an existing image — known as *upsampling* — doing so doesn't enable you to successfully enlarge your photo. In fact, upsampling typically makes matters worse.

    To give you a better idea of the impact of resolution on print quality, Figures 2-16, 2-17, and 2-18 show you the same image at 300 ppi, at 50 ppi, and then resampled from 50 ppi to 300 ppi (respectively). As you can see, there's no way around the rule: If you want quality prints, you need the right pixel count from the get-go.

300 ppi

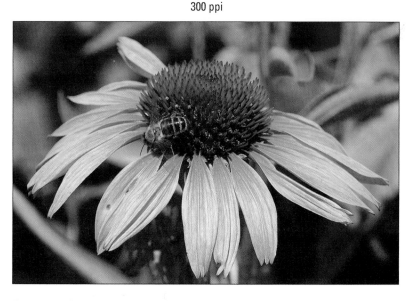

Figure 2-16: A high-quality print depends on a high-resolution original.

50 ppi

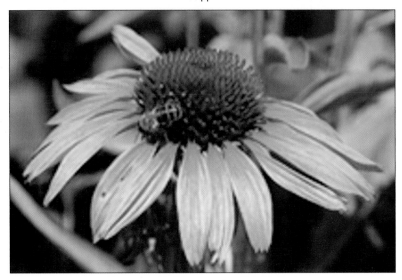

Figure 2-17: At 50 ppi, the image has a jagged, pixelated look.

50 ppi resampled to 300 ppi

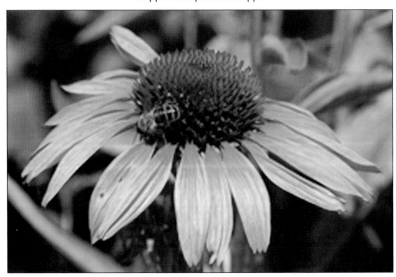

Figure 2-18: Adding pixels in a photo editor doesn't rescue a low-resolution original.

✔ **Screen display size:** Resolution doesn't affect the quality of images viewed on a monitor or television or another screen device the way it does for printed photos. Instead, resolution determines the *size* at which the image appears. This issue is one of the most misunderstood aspects of digital photography, so I explain it thoroughly in Chapter 9. For now, just know that you need *way* fewer pixels for onscreen photos than you do for prints. In fact, even the Small resolution setting creates a picture too big to be viewed in its entirety in many e-mail programs.

✔ **File size:** Every pixel increases the amount of data required to create the picture file. So a higher-resolution image has a larger file size than a low-resolution image.

Large files present several problems:

- You can store fewer images on the memory card, on your computer's hard drive, and on removable storage media such as DVDs.

- The camera needs more time to process and store the image data on the memory card after you press the shutter button. This extra time can hamper fast-action shooting.

- When you share photos online, larger files take longer to upload and download.

- When you edit photos in your photo software, your computer needs more resources and time to process large files.

As you can see, resolution is a bit of a sticky wicket. What if you aren't sure how large you want to print your images? What if you want to print your photos *and* share them online? I take the better-safe-than-sorry route, which leads to the following recommendations:

✔ **Always shoot at a resolution suitable for print.** You then can create a low-resolution copy of the image for use online. In fact, your camera offers a built-in resizing option that I cover in Chapter 9.

✔ **For everyday images, Medium is a good choice.** I find Large to be overkill for casual shooting, creating huge files for no good reason. Keep in mind that even at the Small setting, the pixel count (2992 x 2000) gives you enough resolution to produce an 8 x 10-inch print at 200 ppi.

✔ **Choose Large for an image that you plan to crop or print very large, or both.** The benefit of maxing out the resolution is that you have the flexibility to crop your photo and still generate a decently sized print of the remaining image. Figure 2-19 offers an example. When I was shooting this photograph, I couldn't get close enough to fill the frame with my main interest — the two juvenile herons at the center of the scene. But because I had the resolution cranked up to Large, I could later crop the shot to the composition you see on the right and still produce a greatlooking print. In fact, I could have printed the cropped image at a much larger size than fits here.

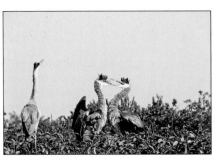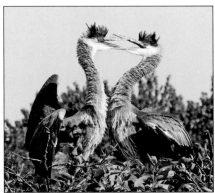

Figure 2-19: A high-resolution original (left) enabled me to crop the photo and still have enough pixels to produce a quality print (right).

✔ **Reduce resolution if shooting speed is paramount.** If the camera takes too long after you take one shot before it lets you take another, dialing down the resolution may help.

Understanding Image Quality options (JPEG or Raw)

If I had my druthers, the Image Quality option would instead be called File Type because that's what the setting controls. Here's the deal: The file type, sometimes also known as a file *format,* determines how your picture data is recorded and stored. Your choice does affect picture quality, but so does the Image Size setting, as described in the preceding section, and the ISO setting, covered in the next chapter. In addition, your choice of file type has ramifications beyond picture quality.

At any rate, your camera offers two file types: JPEG and Camera Raw — or Raw, for short, which goes by the specific moniker NEF (Nikon Electronic Format) on Nikon cameras. The next couple of sections explain the pros and cons of each format. If your mind is already made up, skip ahead to the section "Setting Image Size and Image Quality," to find out how to make your selection.

Don't confuse *file format* with the Format Memory Card option on the Setup menu. That option erases all data on your memory card; see Chapter 1 for details.

JPEG: The imaging (and web) standard

Pronounced "jay-peg," this format is the default setting on your D5500, as it is on most digital cameras. JPEG is popular for two main reasons:

- **Immediate usability:** All web browsers and e-mail programs can display JPEG files, so you can share pictures online immediately after you shoot them. You also can get a JPEG file printed at any retail photo outlet. The same can't be said for Raw (NEF) files, which must be converted to JPEG for online sharing and to JPEG or another standard format, such as TIFF, for retail printing.

- **Small files:** JPEG files are smaller than Raw files. And smaller files consume less room on your camera memory card and in your computer's storage tank.

The downside (you knew there had to be one) is that JPEG creates smaller files by applying *lossy compression*. This process actually throws away some image data. Too much compression produces a defect called *JPEG artifacting*. Figure 2-20 compares a high-quality original (left photo) with a heavily compressed version that exhibits artifacting (right photo).

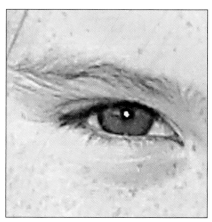 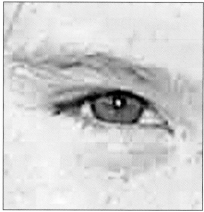

Figure 2-20: The reduced quality of the right image is caused by excessive JPEG compression.

Fortunately, your camera enables you to specify how much compression you're willing to accept. You can choose from three JPEG settings, which produce the following results:

- **JPEG Fine:** The compression ratio is 1:4 — that is, the file is four times smaller than it would otherwise be. Because very little compression is applied, you shouldn't see many compression artifacts, if any.

- ✔ **JPEG Normal:** The compression ratio rises to 1:8. The chance of seeing some artifacting increases as well. This setting is the default.

- ✔ **JPEG Basic:** The compression ratio jumps to 1:16. That's a substantial amount of compression that brings with it a lot more risk of artifacting.

Note, though, that even the Basic setting doesn't result in anywhere near the level of artifacting you see in the right image in Figure 2-20. I've exaggerated the defect in that example to help you recognize artifacting and understand how it differs from the quality loss that occurs when you have too few pixels (refer to Figures 2-16 through 2-18). In fact, if you keep the image print or display size small, you aren't likely to notice a great deal of quality difference between the Fine, Normal, and Basic compression levels. It's only when you greatly enlarge a photo that the differences become apparent.

Given that the differences between the compression settings aren't that easy to spot until you enlarge the photo, is it okay to stick with the default setting — Normal — or even drop down to Basic to capture smaller files? Well, only you can decide what level of quality your pictures demand. For me, the added file sizes produced by the Fine setting aren't a huge concern, given that the prices of memory cards fall all the time. Long-term storage is more of an issue; the larger your files, the faster you fill your computer's hard drive and the more DVDs or CDs you need for archiving purposes. But in the end, I prefer to take the storage hit in exchange for the lower compression level of the Fine setting. You never know when a casual snapshot will be so great that you want to print or display it large enough that even minor quality loss becomes a concern. And of all the defects that you can correct in a photo editor, artifacting is one of the hardest to remove.

If you don't want *any* risk of artifacting, change the file type to Raw (NEF). Or consider your other option, which is to record two versions of each file — one Raw and one JPEG. The next section offers details.

Raw (NEF): The purist's choice

The other picture file type you can create is *Camera Raw,* or just *Raw* (as in uncooked), for short.

Each manufacturer has its own flavor of Raw. Nikon's is NEF, for Nikon Electronic Format, so you see the three-letter extension NEF at the end of Raw filenames.

Raw is popular with advanced, very demanding photographers for three reasons:

- ✔ **Greater creative control:** With JPEG, internal camera software tweaks your images, adjusting color, exposure, and sharpness as needed to produce the results that Nikon believes its customers prefer. With Raw, the camera simply records the original, unprocessed image data. The photographer then copies the image file to the computer and uses special software known as a *Raw converter* to produce the actual image, making decisions about color, exposure, and so on at that point. Nikon ViewNX 2, available for free download from Nikon's website, offers a Raw converter, and the D5500 also has a built-in Raw converter. I cover both options in Chapter 9.

✔ **Higher bit depth:** *Bit depth* is a measure of how many distinct color values an image file can contain. JPEG files restrict you to 8 bits each for the red, blue, and green color components, or *channels,* that make up a digital image, for a total of 24 bits. That translates to roughly 16.7 million possible colors. On the D5500, you can set the camera to capture either 12 or 14 bits per channel when you shoot in the Raw format.

Although jumping from 8 to 12 or 14 bits sounds like a huge difference, you may never notice any difference in your photos — that 8-bit palette of 16.7 million values is more than enough for superb images. Where the extra bits can come in handy is if you adjust exposure, contrast, or color in your photo-editing program. When you apply extreme adjustments, the extra bits sometimes help avoid a problem known as *banding* or *posterization,* which creates abrupt color breaks where you should see smooth, seamless transitions. (A higher bit depth doesn't always prevent this problem, however.)

✔ **Best picture quality:** Because Raw doesn't apply the destructive compression associated with JPEG, you don't run the risk of the artifacting that can occur with JPEG.

But Raw isn't without its disadvantages:

✔ **You can't do much with your pictures until you process them in a Raw converter.** You can't share them online or put them into a text document or multimedia presentation. You can view and print them immediately if you use Nikon ViewNX 2 software, but most other photo programs require you to convert the Raw files to a standard format first, such as JPEG or TIFF. Ditto for retail photo printing.

✔ **Raw files are larger than JPEGs.** Unlike JPEG, Raw doesn't apply lossy compression to shrink files. In addition, Raw files are always captured at the maximum resolution. For both reasons, Raw files are significantly larger than JPEGs, so they take up more room on your memory card and on your computer's hard drive or other picture-storage device.

Whether the upside of Raw outweighs the down is a decision that you need to ponder based on your photographic needs and on whether you have the time to, and interest in, converting Raw files.

You do have the option to capture a picture in the Raw and JPEG formats at the same time. In this scenario, you wind up with two files: one in the Raw format and one in the JPEG format. The JPEG file can be set to either Fine, Normal, or Basic. I often take this route when I'm shooting pictures I want to share right away with people who don't have software for viewing Raw files. I upload the JPEGs to a photo-sharing site where everyone can view them, and then I process the Raw versions when I have time.

My take: Choose JPEG Fine or Raw (NEF)

At this point, you may be finding all this technical goop a bit overwhelming, so allow me to simplify things for you. Until you have the time or energy to completely digest all the ramifications of JPEG versus Raw, here's a quick summary of my thoughts on the matter:

- If you require the absolute best image quality and have the time and interest in doing the Raw conversion, shoot Raw.

- If great photo quality is good enough and you don't have time to spend processing images, stick with JPEG Fine.

- If you don't mind the added file-storage space requirement and want the flexibility of both formats, choose a Raw+JPEG option, which stores one copy of the image in each format. Set the JPEG version to Fine, Normal, or Basic depending on how you plan to use the JPEG image. Again, for top quality, choose Fine.

- If you go with JPEG only, stay away from JPEG Normal and Basic. (Remember, Normal is the default setting on your camera.) The trade-off for smaller files isn't, in my opinion, worth the risk of compression artifacts.

Setting Image Size and Image Quality

To sum up the Image Size and Image Quality information laid out in the preceding sections:

- Both options affect picture quality and file size.

- Choose a high Image Quality setting — Raw (NEF) or JPEG Fine — and the maximum Image Size setting (Large) for top-quality pictures and large file sizes.

- Combining the lowest Quality setting (JPEG Basic) with the lowest Size setting (Small) greatly shrinks files, enabling you to fit lots more pictures on your memory card, but it also increases the chances that you'll be disappointed with the quality of those pictures, especially if you make large prints.

Now for the lowdown on how to monitor and adjust the setting: First, to see which options are currently in force, check the Information screen or Live View display, in the areas labeled in Figure 2-21.

Image Quality

Image Size

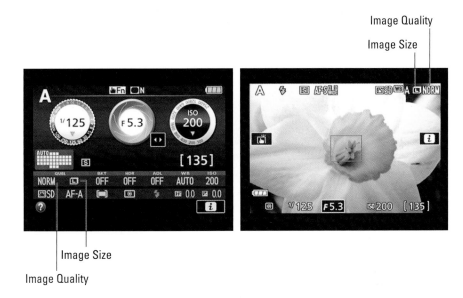

Image Size

Image Quality

Figure 2-21: The current Image Quality and Image Size settings appear here.

To adjust the settings, you have two choices:

✓ **Information display control strip:** Press the *i* button or tap the *i* icon on the Information screen to access the control strip. Choose the option you want to change — Image Size or Image Quality — to display a screen showing the available settings. For example, choosing the Image Quality option, as shown on the left in Figure 2-22, takes you to the screen shown on the right, where you can select the setting you want to use.

Notice that in the screen shown on the right in Figure 2-22, the left side of the display shows the file size that will result from your selected setting along with the number of pictures that will fit on the memory card at that size (8.6MB and 133 images, in the figure). Keep in mind that certain other factors also affect the file size, such as the level of detail and color in the subject.

✓ **Shooting menu:** As an alternative, you can adjust the settings via the Shooting menu, as shown in Figure 2-23. If you select the Image Size setting from the menu, the options screen shows the pixel counts for each setting, as shown on the right in the figure.

File Size   Shots remaining

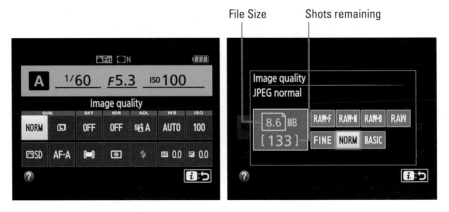

Figure 2-22: You can adjust both settings quickly via the Information display control strip.

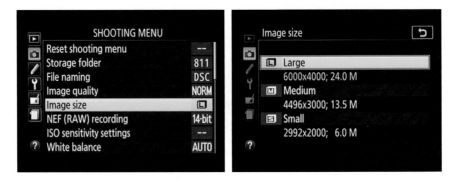

Figure 2-23: You also can set Image Size and Image Quality via the Shooting menu.

REMEMBER

When you choose the Raw (NEF) option, all pictures are automatically captured at the Large resolution setting. However, if you choose one of the Raw+JPEG settings, the JPEG version is captured at the selected Image Size setting.

In addition, you can specify the bit depth of Raw files. Make the call through the NEF (RAW) Recording option on the Shooting menu, as shown in Figure 2-24. You can choose 12 or 14 bits. If you opt for 14 bits,

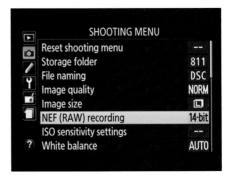

Figure 2-24: For Raw files, you can specify how many bits of color data you want to record.

which enables the file to contain more color data, understand that doing so increases the file size. A 12-bit Raw file has a size of 19.7MB; a 14-bit file, 24.4MB. See the earlier section "Raw (NEF): The purist's choice" for more information about bit depth.

Maintaining a pristine view

Often lost in discussions of digital photo defects — compression artifacts, pixelation, and noise — is the impact of plain-old dust and dirt on picture quality. But no matter what camera settings you use, you won't achieve great picture quality with a dirty lens. So clean the lens regularly, using one of the specialized cloths and cleaning solutions made for that purpose.

If you notice spots at the same position in all your images and cleaning the lens doesn't get rid of them, you have a dirty image sensor. The Setup menu offers a couple automated sensor-cleaning features:

✓ **Clean Image Sensor:** By default, an internal sensor-cleaning mechanism runs every time you turn the camera on or off. You also can perform a cleaning at any time by selecting this Setup menu option and choosing Clean Now. (Nikon recommends that you set the camera on a solid surface, base down, when you perform the cleaning.) Don't try to perform the cleaning several times in a row — if you do, the camera temporarily disables the function to protect itself. The Clean At Startup/Shutdown option enables you to specify whether you want the camera to change from the default setting to clean only at startup, only at shutdown, or never. I suggest that you stick with the default.

✓ **Image Dust-Off Ref Photo:** This feature is designed for use with Nikon Capture NX2, an optional program that I don't cover in this book. You take a reference photo that the software uses to determine the location of sensor spots. Then, when you open the photo, you can run a dust-busting operation that tries to eradicate just those dirt defects.

If you're still having issues after running the automated cleaner, a manual sensor cleaning is necessary. I don't recommend that you tackle this job yourself unless you're experienced; you can easily damage the sensor. Instead, find a camera store that offers this service. If you want to clean the sensor yourself, first make sure that the battery is fully charged. Then visit the Setup menu and select Lock Mirror Up for Cleaning, which moves the camera's mirror out of the way so that you can access the sensor. (The menu item is dimmed when the battery is low.)

Finally, to get rid of fingerprints, nose prints, and other debris from the monitor, use a blower to dislodge any loose debris and then follow up with a soft cloth or chamois made for monitor cleaning. Never use water or any other cleaning solution or try to blow away dust using compressed air, which can crack the screen.

Adding Flash

Another basic picture-taking option to consider is whether you want to use the built-in flash to illuminate your subject.

However, whether you can use the built-in flash depends on your exposure mode: The flash isn't available in Auto Flash Off mode and the following Scene modes: Landscape, Sports, Beach/Snow, Night Landscape, Sunset, Dusk/Dawn, Candlelight, Blossom, and Autumn Colors. All Effects modes except Super Vivid, Pop, Photo Illustration, and Toy Camera Effect also disable the built-in flash.

If you do a lot of flash photography, you may want to invest in an external flash head, which attaches to the hot shoe on top of your camera. When you use an external flash head, you *can* use flash in exposure modes that disable the built-in flash, with the exception of Auto Flash Off mode.

The rest of this chapter concentrates on taking advantage of the built-in flash. For help with an external flash, I need to point you to the flash manual because different flash units provide different flash settings.

Enabling and disabling flash

In certain exposure modes, flash is set by default to fire automatically if the camera thinks that the ambient light is insufficient; in other modes, you have to manually enable flash. Here's the breakdown:

✔ **Auto mode; all Scene modes that permit flash *except* Food mode; and Toy Camera Effect mode:** Flash is set to Auto by default. After you press the shutter button, the camera assesses the available light and automatically pops up the built-in flash if it finds that light lacking.

If you don't want to use flash, you may be able to disable it via the Flash mode setting. See the next section for how-tos.

✔ **Photo Illustration Effects mode:** Flash is disabled by default, but you can override that setting by changing the Flash mode setting.

✔ **P, S, A, and M modes and the Food Scene mode:** There's no such thing as automatic flash in these modes. Instead, if you want to use the built-in flash, press the Flash button on the side of the camera, labeled in Figure 2-25. Don't want flash? Just press down gently on the top of the flash to close the unit.

The camera does give you a little flash input, though: You see a blinking question mark or a flash symbol, or both, in the displays if the camera thinks you need flash. Tap the question mark symbol on the display or press the Zoom Out button, and a message appears recommending that you use flash.

Choosing a Flash mode

The *Flash mode* determines how and when the flash fires. The next section introduces the various options; following that, you can find details on how to adjust the setting.

Sorting through your Flash mode options

Your camera offers the following Flash modes, represented in the Information and Live View displays by the symbols you see in the margins here. (Skip to Figure 2-29 to see where to find the symbols in the Information and Live View displays.)

Flash button

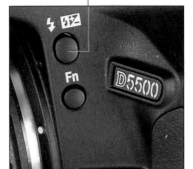

 ✓ **Auto:** The camera decides whether the flash fires. This mode isn't available in the P, S, A, M modes or the Food Scene mode.

Figure 2-25: In P, S, A, and M modes (and the Food Scene mode), raise the built-in flash by pressing the Flash button.

 ✓ **Flash Off:** In Auto exposure mode or the Scene and Effects modes that permit flash, choose this Flash mode to prevent the flash from firing. (In the P, S, A, and M modes and the Food Scene mode, simply close the flash unit if you don't want to use flash.)

✓ **Fill Flash:** You can think of this mode, available in P, S, A, M and Food Scene modes, as normal flash. You may also hear this mode called *force* flash because the flash fires no matter the amount of available light.

 Although most people think of flash as an indoor lighting option, adding flash can improve outdoor photos, too. After all, your main light source — the sun — is overhead, so although the top of the subject may be adequately lit, the front typically needs additional illumination. As an example, Figure 2-26 shows a floral image taken both with and without a flash. The small pop of light provided by the built-in flash is also beneficial when shooting subjects that happen to be slightly shaded. For outdoor portraits, a flash is even more important to properly illuminate the face; the section on shooting portraits in Chapter 6 discusses that subject and offers a look at the difference flash can make.

 Shooting with flash in bright light involves a couple of complications, however; see the sidebar "Using flash outdoors," later in this chapter, for help.

No flash   With flash

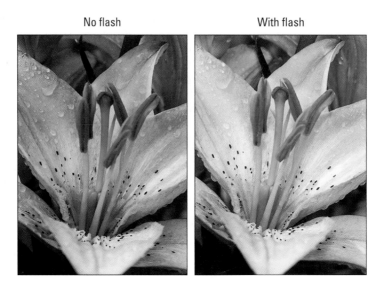

Figure 2-26: Adding flash resulted in better illumination and a slight warming effect.

↳ **Red-Eye Reduction:** *Red-eye* is caused when flash light bounces off a subject's retinas and is reflected back to the camera lens, making the subjects appear possessed by a demon. This flash mode is designed to reduce the chances of red-eye.

When you use Red-Eye Reduction mode, the AF-assist lamp on the front of the camera lights briefly before the flash fires. The subject's pupils constrict in response to the light, allowing less flash light to enter the eye and cause that glowing red reflection. Be sure to warn your subjects to wait for the flash, or else they may step out of the frame or stop posing after they see the light from the AF-assist lamp.

In Auto exposure mode as well as in certain other Scene and Effects modes that permit flash, red-eye reduction flash is just a variation of the regular Auto flash setting. That is, if the camera sees the need for flash, it fires the flash with red-eye reduction engaged. In this case, you see the word *Auto* next to the red-eye symbol. Additionally, a few Scene modes use a variation of red-eye reduction, combining that feature with a slow shutter speed. This flash mode displays the little eye icon plus the words *Auto Slow.* It's important to use a tripod and ask your subject to remain still during the exposure to avoid a blurry picture.

↳ **Slow-Sync and Rear-Sync:** In the flash modes listed so far, the flash and shutter are synchronized so that the flash fires at the exact moment the shutter opens.

Technical types call this flash arrangement *front-curtain sync,* which refers to how the flash is synchronized with the opening of the shutter. Here's the deal: The camera uses a type of shutter involving two curtains that move across the frame. When you press the shutter button, the first curtain opens, allowing light to strike the image sensor. At the end of the exposure, the second curtain draws across the frame to once again shield the sensor from light. With front-curtain sync, the flash fires when the front curtain opens.

Your camera also offers these four special sync modes:

- *Slow-Sync:* This mode, available only in the P and A exposure modes, also uses front-curtain sync but allows a shutter speed slower than the 1/60 second minimum that's in force when you use Fill Flash and Red-Eye Reduction flash. Because of the longer exposure, the camera has time to absorb more ambient light, which has two benefits: Background areas that are beyond the reach of the flash appear brighter; and less flash power is needed, resulting in softer lighting.

The downside of the slow shutter speed is, well, the slow shutter speed. Any movement of your camera or subject during the exposure can blur the picture, and the slower the shutter speed, the greater the chances of camera or subject motion. A tripod is essential to a good outcome, as are subjects that can hold very, very still. I find that the best practical use for this mode is shooting nighttime still-life subjects like the one you see in Figure 2-27. However, if you're shooting a nighttime portrait and you have a subject that *can* maintain a motionless pose, slow-sync flash can produce softer, more flattering light.

Even though the official Slow-Sync mode appears only in the P and A exposure modes, you can get the same result in the M and S modes by simply using a slow shutter speed and the normal, Fill Flash mode. You can use a shutter speed as slow as 30 seconds when using flash in those modes. In fact, I prefer using those modes when I want the slow-sync look because I can directly control the shutter speed.

- *Rear-Curtain Sync:* In this mode, available only in shutter-priority (S) and manual (M) exposure modes, the flash fires at the end of the exposure, just before the shutter closes. The classic use of this mode is to combine the flash with a slow shutter speed to create trailing-light effects like the one you see in Figure 2-28. With Rear-Curtain Sync, the light trails extend behind the moving object (my hand, and the match, in this case), which makes visual sense. If instead you use slow-sync flash, the light trails appear in front of the moving object.

You can set the shutter speed as low as 30 seconds and as high as 1/200 second in this Flash mode.

Regular flash   Slow-sync flash

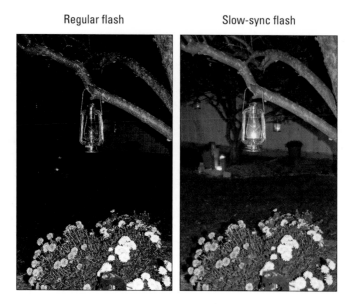

Figure 2-27: Slow-sync flash produces softer, more even lighting than normal flash in nighttime pictures.

⚡ SLOW
⚡ REAR

- *Slow-Rear:* Hey, not confusing enough for you yet? This mode enables you to produce the same motion trail effects as with Rear-Curtain Sync, but in the P and A exposure modes. The camera automatically chooses a slower shutter speed than normal after you set the f-stop, just as with regular Slow-Sync mode.

- *Slow-Sync with Red-Eye Reduction:* In P and A exposure modes, you can also combine a slow-sync flash with the red-eye reduction feature. The symbol that represents this mode is the normal red-eye eyeball combined with the word *Slow.*

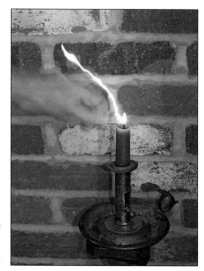

Figure 2-28: I used Rear-Curtain Sync Flash to create this candle-lighting image.

In sync: Flash timing and shutter speed

To properly expose flash pictures, the camera has to synchronize the firing of the flash with the opening and closing of the shutter. For this reason, the range of available shutter speeds is limited when you use flash. The maximum shutter speed is 1/200 second; the minimum shutter speed varies, depending on the exposure mode:

✔ **Auto, all Effects modes that permit flash, and all Scene modes except Portrait and Night Portrait:** 1/60 second

✔ **Night Portrait:** 1 second

✔ **Portrait:** 1/30 second

✔ **P, A:** 1/60 second (unless you use one of the Slow-Sync Flash modes, which permit a shutter speed as slow as 30 seconds)

✔ **S:** 30 seconds

✔ **M:** 30 seconds (for Fill Flash mode, you can exceed that limit if the shutter speed is set to Bulb or Time, which are two special shutter speeds I discuss in Chapter 3)

Setting the Flash mode

You can view the current Flash mode in the Information and Live View displays, as shown in Figure 2-29. (In Live View mode, press the Info button to cycle through the various data-display modes to get to the one shown in the figure.) The lightning bolt shown in the figures represents the Fill flash (normal flash) mode.

In the viewfinder as well as in the lower-right corner of the Live View display, you see a single lightning bolt. This symbol simply tells you that the flash is ready to fire. (You can't view the Flash mode in the viewfinder.) The symbol blinks if the camera thinks you need to add flash.

As for the TTL symbol, highlighted on the left in Figure 2-29, it represents the current setting of the Built-in Flash Cntrl (Control) option on the Custom Setting menu. TTL, which stands for *through the lens,* represents the normal flash metering operation: The camera measures the light coming through the lens and sets the flash output accordingly. Your other option is to set the flash output manually, as explained in the last section of this chapter. If you take that route, the letter *M* appears in place of *TTL.* You can choose between the two settings only when the Mode dial is set to P, S, A, or M.

To change the Flash mode, you can use these techniques:

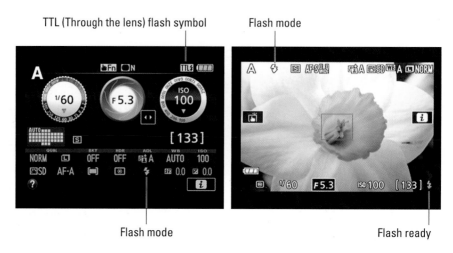

Figure 2-29: An icon representing the Flash mode appears in the displays.

 🗲 ✔ **Flash button + Command dial:** As soon as you press the button, the Flash mode option in the Information display becomes selected, as shown in Figure 2-30. The same thing happens in the Live View display, but the related symbol is at the top of the screen (refer to Figure 2-29). Either way, keep the Flash button pressed while rotating the Command dial to cycle through the available Flash modes.

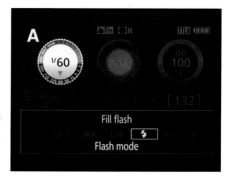

Figure 2-30: The fastest way to change the Flash mode is to hold down the Flash button and rotate the Command dial.

 ✔ **Information display control strip:** Press the *i* button or tap the *i* icon on the monitor to activate the control strip in the Information and Live View displays. Select the Flash mode option, as shown on the left in Figure 2-31, to display a screen listing the mode settings, as shown on the right in the figure. Remember that the available Flash modes depend on the exposure mode.

Adjusting the flash output

TIP

In the P, S, A, or M exposure modes, as well as in certain other modes that permit flash, you have some control over flash power, even if you stick with the default, TTL (through the lens) automatic flash metering. If you want a little more or less flash light than the camera thinks is appropriate, you can adjust the flash output by using *Flash Compensation*.

Using flash outdoors

Adding flash can often improve outdoor photos. But be aware of two "gotchas" when mixing flash and sunlight:

✔ **Colors may need tweaking.** When you combine multiple light sources, colors may appear warmer or cooler than neutral. For outdoor portraits, the warming effect is usually flattering, and I usually like the result with nature shots as well. But if you prefer a neutral color rendition, see the Chapter 5 section related to the White Balance control to find out how to address this issue. You can adjust white balance only in P, S, A, and M exposure modes.

✔ **Keep an eye on shutter speed.** Because of the way the camera needs to synchronize the firing of the flash with the opening of the shutter, the fastest shutter speed you can use with the built-in flash is 1/200 second. In bright sun, you may need to stop down the aperture significantly or lower the ISO, if possible, to avoid overexposing the image even at 1/200 second. As another option, you can place a neutral density filter over the lens; this accessory reduces the light that comes through the lens without affecting colors. Of course, if possible, you can simply move your subject into the shade.

On the flip side, the camera may select a shutter speed as slow as 1/60 second in the P and A modes, depending on the lighting conditions. If your subject is moving, it's a good idea to work in the S or M modes so that you control the shutter speed.

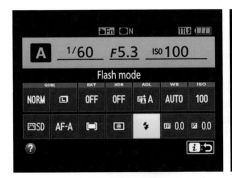 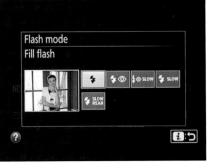

Figure 2-31: You also can adjust the Flash mode by using the normal control-strip method; press the *i* button or tap the on-screen *i* symbol to activate the control strip.

Flash Compensation settings are stated in terms of *exposure value (EV)* numbers. A setting of EV 0.0 indicates no flash adjustment; you can increase the flash power to EV +1.0 or decrease it to EV –3.0.

As an example of the benefit of this feature, look at the carousel images in Figure 2-32. The first image shows a flash-free shot. Clearly, I needed a flash to compensate for the fact that the horses were shadowed by the roof of the carousel. But at normal flash power, as shown in the middle image, the flash was too strong, creating glare in some spots and blowing out the highlights in the white mane. By dialing the flash power down to EV –1.0, I got a softer flash that straddled the line perfectly between no flash and too much flash.

No flash

Flash EV 0.0

Flash EV -1.0

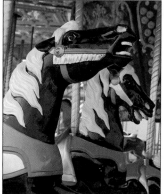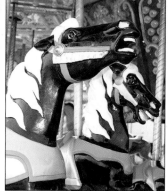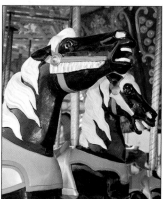

Figure 2-32: When normal flash output is too strong, dial in a lower Flash Compensation setting.

As for boosting the flash output, you may find it necessary on some occasions, but don't expect the built-in flash to work miracles even at a Flash Compensation of +1.0. The built-in flash has a maximum range of about 12 feet; it simply can't illuminate faraway objects. In other words, don't even try taking flash pictures of a darkened recital hall from your seat in the balcony — all you'll wind up doing is annoying everyone.

The current Flash Compensation setting appears in the Information display, as shown on the left in Figure 2-33. If this readout is dimmed, Flash Compensation isn't available in your current exposure mode. One quirk: Some modes that disable the built-in flash make the Flash Compensation setting available. What gives? The option is provided solely for use with an external flash head. Any adjustment you make to the camera's flash-exposure setting is added to flash-power changes you make using the controls on the flash head. The built-in flash won't fire no matter what Flash Compensation value you select.

In the Live View display, you see only a symbol indicating that Flash Compensation is enabled, as shown on the right side of the figure. Note that if the feature is turned off (set to EV 0.0), the symbol doesn't appear in the Live View display.

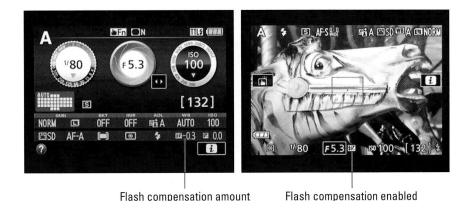

Flash compensation amount   Flash compensation enabled

Figure 2-33: These symbols represent Flash Compensation.

To adjust the amount of Flash Compensation, use either of these tricks:

▸ **Two-button-plus-Command-dial maneuver:** First, press the Flash button to pop up the built-in flash. Then press and hold the Flash button and the Exposure Compensation button simultaneously. When you press the buttons, the Flash Compensation value becomes highlighted in the Information and Live View displays, as shown in Figure 2-34. In the viewfinder, the current setting takes the place of the usual Frames Remaining value. While keeping both buttons pressed, rotate the Command dial to adjust the setting. I find that any technique that involves coordinating this many fingers a little complex, but you may find it easier than I do.

▸ **Information or Live View display control strip:** Activate the strip by tapping the *i* icon on the monitor or by pressing the *i* button. Select the Flash Compensation setting, as shown on the left in Figure 2-35, to display a screen where you can set the compensation amount, as shown on the right in the figure.

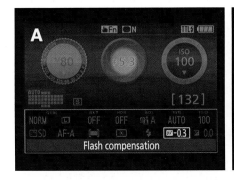
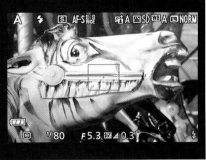

Figure 2-34: Rotate the Command dial while pressing the Flash and Exposure Compensation buttons to adjust the flash power.

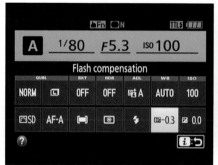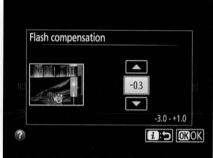

Figure 2-35: You also can adjust the setting by using the Information display control strip.

 When you use one of the Scene modes, the Flash Compensation setting is reset to 0.0 when you turn off the camera or switch to a different Scene mode. In other exposure modes, the flash-power adjustment remains in force until you reset the value, even if you turn off the camera. So be sure to check the setting before you next use the flash.

Controlling flash output manually

If you're experienced in the way of the flash, you can manually set flash output via the Flash Cntrl for Built-in Flash option, found in the Bracketing/Flash section of the Custom Setting menu. The normal setting is TTL (for automatic, through-the-lens metering), but if you select Manual, as shown on the left in Figure 2-36, you can access the power settings, which range from Full to 1/32 power.

When flash is set to manual control, the TTL icon that normally appears in the upper-right corner of the Information display (refer to Figure 2-29) is replaced by the letter *M*. In the viewfinder, an icon that looks like the Information screen's Flash Compensation icon (a lightning bolt with a plus-minus sign) blinks.

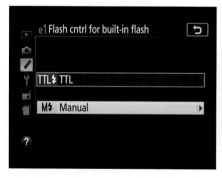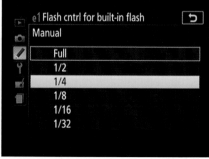

Figure 2-36: Using this option, you can control the flash output manually.

Part II
Taking Creative Control

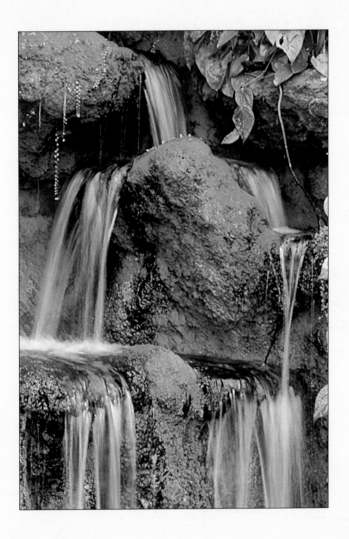

Find out how to customize your Picture Controls at www.dummies.com/extras/nikon.

In this part . . .

- ✔ Find out how to control exposure and shoot in the advanced exposure modes (P, S, A, and M).

- ✔ Master the autofocusing system and get help with manual focusing.

- ✔ Understand how to control depth of field.

- ✔ Manipulate color by using white balance and other color options.

- ✔ Get pro tips for shooting portraits, action shots, landscapes, close-ups, and more.

- ✔ Take advantage of your camera's HD movie-recording features.

3

Taking Charge of Exposure

*U*nderstanding exposure is one of the most intimidating challenges for a new photographer. Discussions of the topic are loaded with technical terms — *aperture, metering, shutter speed, ISO,* and the like. Add the fact that your camera offers many exposure controls, all sporting equally foreign names, and it's no wonder that most people throw up their hands and decide that their best option is to stick with the Auto exposure mode and let the camera take care of all exposure decisions.

You can, of course, turn out good shots in Auto mode, and I fully relate to the confusion you may be feeling — I've been there. But I can also promise that when you take things nice and slow, digesting a piece of the exposure pie at a time, the topic is *not* as complicated as it seems on the surface. I guarantee that the payoff will be worth your time, too. You'll not only gain the know-how to solve just about any exposure problem but also discover ways to use exposure to put your creative stamp on a scene.

To that end, this chapter provides everything you need to know about controlling exposure, from a primer in exposure terminology (it's not as bad as it sounds) to tips on using the P, S, A, and M exposure modes, which are the only ones that offer access to all exposure features. ***Note:*** The one exposure-related topic not covered in this chapter is flash; I discuss flash in Chapter 2 because it's among the options you can access even in Auto mode and many of the other point-and-shoot modes. Also, this chapter deals with still photography; see Chapter 7 for information on movie-recording exposure issues.

Introducing the Exposure Trio: Aperture, Shutter Speed, and ISO

Any photograph is created by focusing light through a lens onto a light-sensitive recording medium. In a film camera, the film negative serves as that medium; in a digital camera, it's the image sensor, which is an array of light-responsive computer chips.

Between a digital camera's lens and sensor are two barriers — the aperture and shutter — which work in concert to control how much light makes its way to the sensor. In the digital world, the design and arrangement of the aperture, shutter, and sensor vary depending on the camera; Figure 3-1 offers an illustration of the basic concept.

The aperture and shutter, along with a third feature — ISO — determine *exposure,* which is basically the picture's overall brightness and contrast. This three-part exposure formula works as follows:

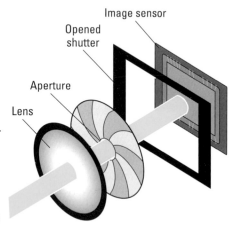

Figure 3-1: The aperture size and shutter speed determine how much light strikes the image sensor.

- ✓ **Aperture (controls amount of light):** The *aperture* is an adjustable hole in a diaphragm inside the lens. You change the aperture size to control the size of the light beam that can enter the camera.

Aperture settings are stated as *f-stop numbers,* or simply *f-stops,* and are expressed by the letter *f* followed by a number: f/2, f/5.6, f/16, and so on. The lower the f-stop number, the larger the aperture, and the more light is permitted into the camera, as illustrated by Figure 3-2. (If it seems backward to use a higher number for a smaller aperture, think

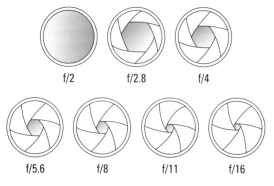

Figure 3-2: A lower f-stop number means a larger aperture, allowing more light into the camera.

of it this way: A higher value creates a bigger light barrier than a lower value.) The range of available aperture settings varies from lens to lens.

✓ **Shutter speed (controls duration of light):** The shutter works something like, er, the shutters on a window. The camera's shutter stays closed, preventing light from striking the image sensor (just as closed window shutters prevent sunlight from entering a room) until you press the shutter button. Then the shutter opens briefly to allow light that passes through the aperture to hit the sensor. The exception to this scenario is when you compose in Live View mode: When you enable Live View, the shutter opens and remains open so that the image can form on the sensor and be displayed on the monitor. When you press the shutter button, the shutter first closes and then reopens for the actual exposure.

Either way, the length of time that the shutter is open is the *shutter speed,* which is measured in seconds: 1/60 second, 1/250 second, 2 seconds, and so on.

✓ **ISO (controls light sensitivity):** *ISO,* which is a digital function rather than a mechanical structure on the camera, enables you to adjust how responsive the image sensor is to light.

The term *ISO* is a holdover from film days, when an international standards organization rated each film stock according to light sensitivity: ISO 200, ISO 400, ISO 800, and so on. On a digital camera, the sensor itself doesn't actually get more or less sensitive when you change the ISO. Instead, the light "signal" that hits the sensor is either amplified or dampened through electronics wizardry, sort of like how raising the volume on a radio boosts the audio signal. The upshot is the same as changing to a more light-reactive film stock. Using a higher ISO means that less light is needed to produce the image, enabling you to use a smaller aperture, faster shutter speed, or both.

Distilled to its essence, the image-exposure formula is this simple:

✓ Together, aperture and shutter speed determine how much light strikes the image sensor.

✓ ISO determines how much the sensor reacts to that light and thus how much light is needed to expose the picture.

The tricky part of the equation is that aperture, shutter speed, and ISO settings affect pictures in ways that go beyond exposure:

✓ Aperture affects *depth of field,* or the distance over which focus remains acceptably sharp.

✓ Shutter speed determines whether moving objects appear blurry or sharply focused.

✓ ISO affects the amount of image *noise,* which is a defect that looks like specks of colored sand.

Understanding these side effects is critical to choosing the combination of aperture, shutter speed, and ISO that will work best for your subject, so the next three sections explore each issue. If you're already familiar with this stuff and just want to know how to adjust exposure settings, skip ahead to the section "Setting Aperture, Shutter Speed, and ISO."

Aperture affects depth of field

The aperture setting, or f-stop, affects *depth of field,* which is the distance over which focus appears acceptably sharp. With a shallow depth of field, your subject appears more sharply focused than faraway objects; with a large depth of field, the sharp-focus zone spreads over a greater distance.

As you reduce the aperture size by choosing a higher f-stop number — *stop down the aperture,* in photo lingo — you increase the depth of field. As an example, see Figure 3-3. For both shots, I established focus on the fountain statue. Notice that the background in the first image, taken at f/13, is sharper than in the right example, taken at f/5.6. Aperture is just one contributor to depth of field, however; the focal length of the lens and the distance between that lens and your subject also affect how much of the scene stays in focus. See Chapter 4 for the complete story.

f/13, 1/25 second, ISO 200   f/5.6, 1/125 second, ISO 200

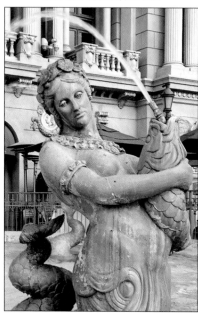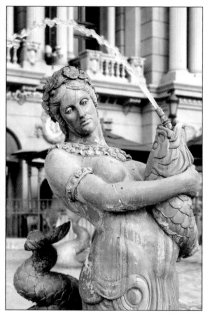

Figure 3-3: Widening the aperture (choosing a lower f-stop number) decreases depth of field.

One way to remember the relationship between f-stop and depth of field is to think of the *f* as standing for *focus*. A higher f-stop number produces a larger depth of field, so if you want to extend the zone of sharp focus to cover a greater distance from your subject, you set the aperture to a higher f-stop. Higher *f*-stop number, greater zone of sharp *focus*. (Please *don't* share this tip with photography elites, who will roll their eyes and inform you that the *f* in *f-stop* most certainly does *not* stand for focus but for the ratio between the aperture size and lens focal length — as if *that's* helpful to know if you're not an optical engineer. Chapter 1 explains focal length, which *is* helpful to know.)

Shutter speed affects motion blur

At a slow shutter speed, moving objects appear blurry; a fast shutter speed captures motion cleanly. This phenomenon has nothing to do with the actual focus point of the camera but rather on the movement occurring — and being recorded by the camera — while the shutter is open.

Compare the photos in Figure 3-3, for example. The static elements are perfectly focused in both images although the background in the left photo appears sharper because I shot that image using a higher f-stop, increasing the depth of field. But how the camera rendered the moving portion of the scene — the fountain water — was determined by shutter speed. At 1/25 second (left photo), the water blurs, giving it a misty look. At 1/125 second (right photo), the droplets appear more sharply focused, almost frozen in mid-air. How high a shutter speed you need to freeze action depends on the speed of your subject.

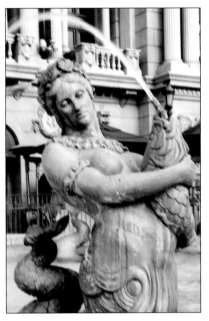

If your picture suffers from overall blur, as in Figure 3-4, the camera itself moved during the exposure, which is always a danger when you handhold a camera. The slower the shutter speed, the longer the exposure time and the longer you have to hold the camera still to avoid the blur that's caused by camera shake. Use a tripod to avoid this issue.

Figure 3-4: If both stationary and moving objects are blurry, camera shake is the usual cause.

Freezing action isn't the only way to use shutter speed to creative effect. When shooting waterfalls, for example, many photographers use a slow shutter speed to give the water even more of a blurry, romantic look than you see in my fountain example. With colorful subjects, a slow shutter can

Handholding the camera: How low can you go?

My students often ask how slow they can set the shutter speed and still handhold the camera rather than use a tripod. Unfortunately, there's no one-size-fits-all answer. The slow-shutter safety limit varies depending on a couple factors, including your physical abilities and your lens — the heavier the lens, the harder it is to hold steady. Camera shake also affects your picture more when you shoot with a lens that has a long focal length. You may be able to use a slower shutter speed with a 55mm lens than with a 200mm lens, for example.

A standard photography rule is to use the inverse of the lens focal length as the minimum handheld shutter speed. For example, with a 50mm lens, use a shutter speed no slower than 1/50 second. That rule was developed before the advent of today's modern lenses, though, which

tend to be significantly lighter and smaller than older lenses, as do cameras themselves. For example, I have a very light, superzoom lens that I can handhold at speeds as low as 1/80 second even when I zoom to focal lengths way beyond 80mm. The best idea is to do your own tests to see where your handholding limit lies. See Chapter 8 to find out how to select the picture-playback mode that enables you to see the shutter speed you used for each picture.

Remember, too, that if your lens offers Vibration Reduction, turning on that feature can compensate for small amounts of camera shake. See the lens manual to find out whether your lens offers this feature and, if so, how to enable it. (If you use a non-Nikon lens, the feature may go by another name, such as Vibration Compensation.)

produce some cool abstract effects and create a heightened sense of motion. Chapter 6 offers examples of both effects.

ISO affects image noise

As ISO increases, making the image sensor more reactive to light, you increase the risk of producing noise. *Noise* is a defect that looks like sprinkles of sand and is similar in appearance to film *grain,* a defect that often mars pictures taken with high ISO film. Figure 3-5 offers an example.

Ideally, then, you should always use the lowest ISO setting on your camera to ensure top image quality. Sometimes, though, the lighting conditions don't permit you to do so and still use the aperture and shutter speeds you need. Take my rose image as an example. When I shot these pictures, I didn't have a tripod, so I needed a shutter speed fast enough to allow a sharp handheld image. I opened the aperture to f/5.6, which was the widest setting on the lens I was using, to allow as much light as possible into the camera. At ISO 100, I needed a shutter speed of 1/40 second to expose the picture, and that shutter speed wasn't fast enough for a successful handheld shot. You see the blurred result on the left in Figure 3-6. By raising the ISO to 200, I was able to use a shutter speed of 1/80 second, which enabled me to capture the flower cleanly, as shown on the right in the figure.

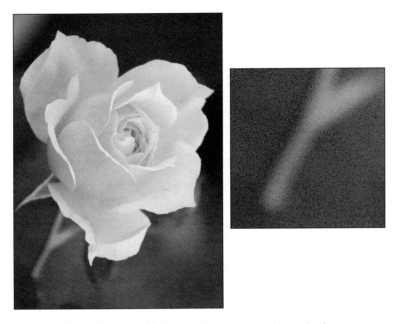

Figure 3-5: Caused by a very high ISO or long exposure time, noise becomes more visible as you enlarge the image.

ISO 100, f/5.6, 1/40 second   ISO 200, f/5.6, 1/80 second

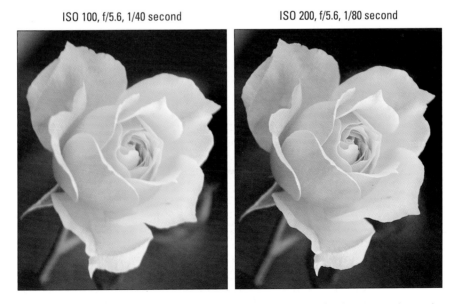

Figure 3-6: For this image, raising the ISO allowed me to bump up the shutter speed enough to capture a blur-free shot while handholding the camera.

Fortunately, you don't encounter serious noise on the D5500 until you really crank up the ISO. In fact, you may even be able to get away with a fairly high ISO if you keep the print or display size small. Some people probably wouldn't even notice the noise in the left image in Figure 3-5 unless they were looking for it, for example. But as with other image defects, noise becomes more apparent as you enlarge the photo, as shown on the right in that same figure. Noise is also easier to spot in shadow areas of the picture and in large areas of solid color.

How much noise is acceptable — and, therefore, how high of an ISO is safe — is your choice. Even a little noise isn't acceptable for pictures that require the highest quality, such as images for a product catalog or a travel shot that you want to blow up to poster size.

A high ISO isn't the only cause of noise: A long exposure time (slow shutter speed) can also produce the defect. So, how high you can raise the ISO before the image gets ugly varies, depending on shutter speed.

Your camera offers two features designed to combat both types of noise, but each has its pros and cons. See the sidebar "Dampening noise," later in this chapter, for a review of both options.

Doing the exposure balancing act

As you change any of the three exposure settings — aperture, shutter speed, and ISO — one or both of the other two must also shift to maintain the same image brightness. Say that you're shooting a soccer game and you notice that although the overall exposure looks great, the players appear slightly blurry at the current shutter speed. If you raise the shutter speed, you have to compensate with a larger aperture (to allow in more light during the shorter exposure) or a higher ISO setting (to make the camera more sensitive to the light) — or both.

Again, changing these settings impacts the image in ways beyond exposure:

- ✔ Aperture affects depth of field, with a higher f-stop number increasing the distance over which objects appear sharp.
- ✔ Shutter speed affects whether motion of the subject or camera results in a blurry photo. A faster shutter "freezes" action and also helps safeguard against all-over blur that can result from camera shake when you're handholding the camera.
- ✔ ISO affects the camera's sensitivity to light. A higher ISO makes the camera more responsive to light but also increases the chance of image noise.

When you boost that shutter speed to capture your soccer subjects, therefore, you have to decide whether you prefer the shorter depth of field that comes with a larger aperture or the increased risk of noise that accompanies a higher ISO.

Exposure stops: How many do you want to see?

In photo lingo, the word *stop* refers to an increment of exposure. To increase exposure by one stop means to adjust the aperture or shutter speed to allow twice as much light into the camera as the current settings permit. To reduce exposure a stop, you use settings that allow half as much light. Doubling or halving the ISO value also adjusts exposure by one stop.

By default, most exposure-related settings on your camera are based on one-third stop adjustments. If you prefer, you can tell the camera to present exposure adjustments in half-stop increments so that you don't have to cycle through as many settings each time

you want to make a change. Make your preferences known through the EV Steps for Exposure Cntrl setting, found in the Exposure section of the Custom Setting menu and shown here. This setting affects the shutter speed, aperture, Exposure Compensation, Flash Compensation, and exposure bracketing settings. It also determines the increment used to indicate the amount of under- or overexposure in the meter.

Obviously, the default setting, 1/3 stop, provides the greatest degree of exposure fine-tuning, so I stick with that option. In this book, instructions assume that you're using the defaults as well.

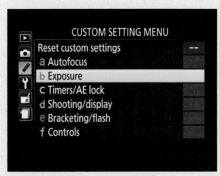

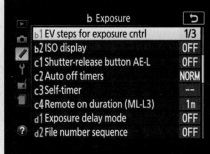

Everyone has their own approach to finding the right combination of aperture, shutter speed, and ISO, and you'll no doubt develop your own system as you become more familiar with these concepts. In the meantime, here's how I handle things:

- ✔ I use ISO 100, the lowest setting on the camera, unless the lighting conditions are so poor that I can't use the aperture and shutter speed I want without raising the ISO.

- ✔ If my subject is moving, I give shutter speed the next highest priority in my exposure decision. I might choose a fast shutter speed to ensure a blur-free photo or, on the flip side, select a slow shutter to intentionally blur that moving object, an effect that can create a heightened sense of motion.

✔ For nonmoving subjects, I make aperture a priority over shutter speed, setting the aperture according to the depth of field I have in mind. For portraits, for example, I use a large aperture — say, in the range of f/2.8 to f/5.6 — so that I get a short depth of field, creating a nice, soft background for my subject. For landscapes, I usually go the opposite direction, stopping down the aperture as much as possible to capture the subject at the greatest depth of field. (Again, remember that the range of f-stops you can choose depends on your lens.)

Keeping all this straight is a little overwhelming at first, but the more you work with your camera, the more the whole exposure equation will make sense to you. You can find tips for choosing exposure settings for specific types of pictures in Chapter 6; keep moving through this chapter for details on how to actually adjust aperture, shutter speed, and ISO.

Stepping Up to Advanced Exposure Modes (P, S, A, and M)

In the fully automatic exposure modes — Auto, Auto Flash Off, Scene modes, and Effects modes — you have little control over exposure. You may be able to choose from one or two Flash modes, and you can adjust ISO in some modes. But to gain full control over exposure, set the Mode dial to one of the advanced modes highlighted in Figure 3-7: P, S, A, or M. You also need to use these modes to take advantage of many other camera features, including some of its color and autofocus options.

Advanced exposure modes

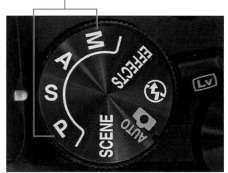

Figure 3-7: You can control exposure and certain other picture properties fully only in P, S, A, or M mode.

I introduce the P, S, A, and M modes in Chapter 2, but because they're critical to your control over exposure, I want to offer some additional information and pointers here. First, a recap of how the four modes differ:

✔ **P (programmed autoexposure):** The camera selects both aperture and shutter speed to deliver a good exposure at the current ISO setting. But you can choose from different combinations of the two for creative flexibility, which is why the official name of this mode is *flexible pro-grammed autoexposure.*

- ✓ **S (shutter-priority autoexposure):** You set the shutter speed, and the camera chooses the aperture setting that produces a good exposure at that shutter speed and the current ISO setting.

- ✓ **A (aperture-priority autoexposure):** The opposite of shutter-priority autoexposure, this mode asks you to select the aperture setting. The camera then selects the appropriate shutter speed — again, based on the selected ISO setting.

- ✓ **M (manual exposure):** In this mode, you specify both shutter speed and aperture. The brightness of your photo depends on the settings you select and the current ISO setting.

To sum up, the first three modes are semiautomatic modes that are designed to offer exposure assistance while still providing you with some creative control. Note one important point about P, S, and A modes, however: In extreme lighting conditions, the camera may not be able to select settings that will produce a good exposure, and it doesn't stop you from taking a poorly exposed photo. You may be able to solve the problem by using features designed to modify autoexposure results, such as Exposure Compensation (explained later in this chapter) or by adding flash, but you get no guarantees.

Manual mode puts all exposure control in your hands. If you're a longtime photographer who comes from the days when manual exposure was the only game in town, you may prefer to stick with this mode. If it ain't broke, don't fix it, as they say. And in some ways, manual mode is simpler than the semi-automatic modes — if you're not happy with the exposure, you just change the aperture, shutter speed, or ISO setting and shoot again. You don't have to fiddle with features that enable you to modify your autoexposure results.

My choice is to use aperture-priority autoexposure when I'm shooting stationary subjects and want to control depth of field — aperture is my *priority* — and to switch to shutter-priority autoexposure when I'm shooting a moving subject and I'm most concerned with controlling shutter speed. Frankly, my brain is taxed enough by all the other issues involved in taking pictures — what my Release mode setting is, what resolution I need, where I'm going for lunch as soon as I make this shot work — that I appreciate having the camera do some of the exposure "lifting."

However, when I know exactly what aperture and shutter speed I want to use or I'm after an out-of-the-ordinary exposure, I use manual exposure. For example, sometimes when I'm doing a still life in my studio, I want to create a certain mood by underexposing a subject or even shooting it in silhouette. The camera will always fight you on that result in the P, S, and A modes because it so dearly wants to provide a good exposure. Rather than dial in all the autoexposure tweaks that could eventually force the result I want, I simply set the mode to M, adjust the shutter speed and aperture directly, and give the autoexposure system the afternoon off.

But even when you use the M exposure mode, you're never really flying without a net: The camera assists you by displaying the exposure meter, explained next.

Checking the Exposure Meter

Before explaining how to adjust aperture, shutter speed, and ISO, I want to introduce you to your camera's most important exposure guide: the *exposure meter*. The meter tells you whether the camera thinks your picture will be properly exposed at your chosen exposure settings.

However, if and when the meter appears depends on whether you shoot in the M, P, S, or A exposure mode:

- ✔ **M mode:** The meter is always present in the Information and Live View displays, as shown in Figure 3-8, and also appears in the viewfinder data display. You can see a close-up look at how the meter looks in the view-finder in Figure 3-9.

- ✔ **P, S, and A modes:** The meter doesn't appear unless the camera antici-pates an exposure problem — for example, if you're shooting in S (shut-ter-priority autoexposure) mode, and the camera can't select an f-stop that will properly expose the image at your chosen shutter speed and ISO. You also see the meter if you enable Exposure Compensation, explained later in this chapter. In that case, the meter indicates how much Exposure Compensation is being applied.

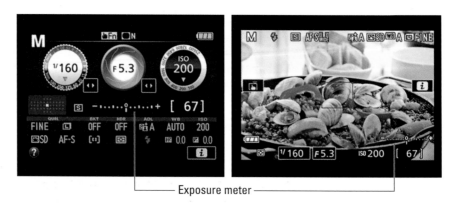

Exposure meter

Figure 3-8: In M exposure mode, the exposure meter appears in the Information and Live View displays.

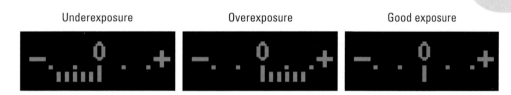

Figure 3-9: The bars under the meter indicate the amount of under- or overexposure.

Either way, here's what you need to know about using the meter:

- ✔ **Waking up the meter:** By default, the meter appears when you press the shutter button halfway and then turns off automatically after 8 seconds of inactivity to save battery power. To wake up the meter, just give the shutter button another half-press.

  You can adjust the meter's auto shutdown timing via the Auto Off Timers option, found in the Timers/AE Lock section of the Custom Setting menu. Chapter 10 has details, if you need help.

- ✔ **Reading the meter:** The minus-sign end of the meter represents underexposure; the plus sign, overexposure. If the little notches under the meter fall to the left of 0, as shown in the first example in Figure 3-9, the image will be underexposed. If the notches move to the right of 0, as shown in the second example, the image will be overexposed. When all notches except the center bar disappear, as in the third example in Figure 3-9, you're good to go.

  A couple of details to note:

  - *The markings on the meter indicate exposure stops.* The squares on either side of the 0 represent one full stop each. The small lines below, which appear only when the meter needs to indicate over- or underexposure, break each stop into thirds. So the middle readout in Figure 3-9, for example, indicates an overexposure of 1 and 2/3 stop. The left readout indicates the same amount of underexposure. (The third-stop display assumes that you haven't asked the camera to present exposure data in half-stop increments, in which case you see just one bar between each stop. Again, this feature is controlled by the EV Steps for Exposure Cntrl option, located in the Exposure section of the Custom Setting menu.)

  - *If a triangle appears at the end of the meter, the amount of over- or underexposure exceeds the two-stop range of the meter.* In other words, you have a serious exposure problem.

  - *You can reverse the meter orientation.* For photographers used to a camera that orients the meter with the positive (overexposure) side appearing on the left and the negative (underexposure) side on the right — the design that Nikon used for years — the D5500 offers the option to flip the meter to that orientation. This option also lies on the Custom Setting menu, on the Controls submenu. Look for the Reverse Indicators option, as shown in Figure 3-10. (The setting shown in the figure is the default.)

✓ **Understanding how exposure is calculated:** The information the meter reports is based on the *Metering mode,* which determines which part of the frame the camera considers when calculating exposure. At the default setting, exposure is based on the entire frame, but you can select two other Metering modes. See the next section for details.

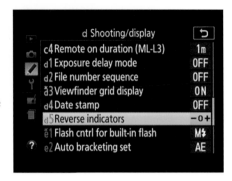

Figure 3-10: You can reverse the meter orientation.

There's one metering quirk to note with respect to Live View photography: In Live View mode, metering may be calculated differently for some scenes than when you use the viewfinder. The rationale is to produce an exposure that's close to what you see in the live preview, which gets darker or lighter as you change exposure settings in an attempt to simulate the final exposure. However, I don't recommend that you trust the preview because it can be deceiving depending on the ambient light in which you're viewing the monitor. In addition, when you apply Exposure Compensation, an option that produces a brighter or darker image in the P, S, and A modes, the monitor can't adjust itself to accommodate the full range of Exposure Compensation settings. Long story short: The meter is a more accurate indication of exposure than the live preview.

Finally, keep in mind that the meter's suggestion on exposure may not always be the one you want to follow. For example, you may want to shoot a backlit subject in silhouette, in which case you *want* that subject to be underexposed. In other words, the meter is a guide, not a dictator.

Choosing an Exposure Metering Mode

To interpret what the exposure meter tells you, you need to be aware of the current *Metering mode,* which determines which part of the frame the camera analyzes to calculate exposure. The Metering mode affects the meter reading in M mode as well as the exposure settings that the camera chooses in the fully automatic shooting modes as well as in the P, S, and A modes.

The Information display and Live View screen both contain a symbol representing the current metering mode; look in the areas labeled in Figure 3-11. You can choose from three modes, described in the following list and represented in the displays by the icons shown in the margins:

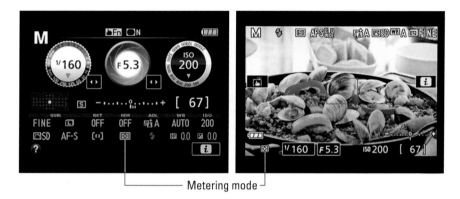

Metering mode

Figure 3-11: This symbol represents the Matrix metering mode.

 Matrix: The camera analyzes the entire frame and then selects an exposure that's designed to produce a balanced exposure.

Your camera manual refers to this mode as 3D Color Matrix II, which is the label that Nikon created to describe the specific technology used in this mode.

 Center-weighted: The camera bases exposure on the entire frame but puts extra emphasis — or *weight* — on the center of the frame. Specifically, the camera assigns 75 percent of the metering weight to an 8mm circle in the center of the frame.

 Spot: In this mode, the camera bases exposure entirely on a circular area that's about 3.5mm in diameter, or about 2.5 percent of the frame. The location used for this pinpoint metering depends on an autofocusing option called the AF-area mode. Detailed in Chapter 4, this option determines which of the camera's focus points the autofocusing system uses to establish focus. Here's how the setting affects exposure metering:

- *If you choose the Auto Area mode,* in which the camera chooses the focus point for you, metering is based on the center focus point.

- *If you use any of the other AF-area modes,* which enable you to select a specific focus point, the camera bases metering on that point.

 Because of this autofocus/autoexposure relationship, it's best to switch to one of the AF-area modes that allow focus-point selection when you want to use spot metering. In Auto Area mode, exposure may be incorrect if you compose your shot so that the subject isn't at the center of the frame.

As an example of how Metering mode affects exposure, Figure 3-12 shows the same image captured in each mode. In the matrix example, the bright background caused the camera to select an exposure that left the statue quite dark. Switching to center-weighted metering helped somewhat but didn't quite bring the statue out of the shadows. Spot metering produced the best result as far as the statue goes, although the resulting increase in exposure left the sky a little washed out.

Matrix metering   Center-weighted metering   Spot metering

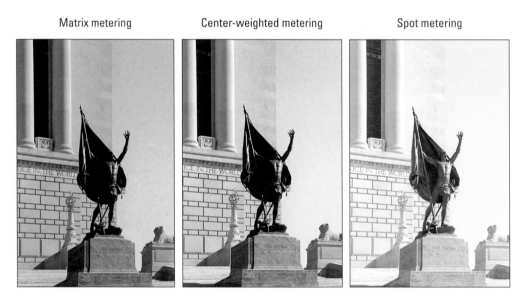

Figure 3-12: The Metering mode determines which area of the frame the camera considers when calculating exposure.

 Matrix metering is the default setting, and you can change the Metering mode only in the P, S, A, and M exposure modes. The only way to adjust the setting is via the Information display or Live View control strip, as shown in Figure 3-13. Remember: You activate the strip by pressing the *i* button or tapping the *i* symbol on the monitor.

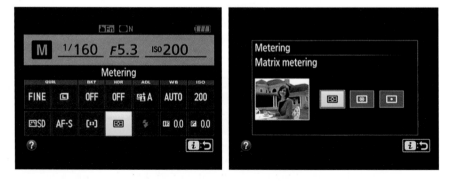

Figure 3-13: Change the Metering mode setting via the control strip.

In theory, the best practice is to check the Metering mode before you shoot and choose the one that best matches your exposure goals. But that's a bit of a pain, not just in terms of having to adjust yet one more capture setting but also in terms of having to *remember* to adjust one more capture setting. Here's my advice: Until you're really comfortable with all the other controls on your camera, just stick with the default setting, which is matrix metering. That mode produces good results in most situations, and after all, you can see in the monitor whether you disagree with how the camera metered or exposed the image and simply reshoot after adjusting the exposure settings to your liking. This option, in my mind, makes the whole Metering mode issue a lot less critical than it is when you shoot with film.

The one exception might be when you're shooting a series of images in which a significant contrast in lighting exists between subject and background. Then, switching to center-weighted metering or spot metering may save you the time spent having to adjust the exposure for each image.

Setting Aperture, Shutter Speed, and ISO

The next sections detail how to view and adjust these critical exposure settings. For a review of how each setting affects your pictures, check out the first part of this chapter.

Adjusting aperture and shutter speed

You can view the current aperture (f-stop) and shutter speed in the Information display and Live View display, as well as in the viewfinder, as shown in Figures 3-14 and 3-15. (If you don't see this data in Live View mode, press the Info button to cycle through the various display options until your screen looks similar to the one in the figure.)

In the viewfinder, shutter speeds are presented as whole numbers, even if the shutter speed is set to a fraction of a second. For example, the number 100 indicates a shutter speed of 1/100 second. When the shutter speed slows to 1 second or more, quote marks appear after the number — 1" indicates a shutter speed of one second, 4" means four seconds, and so on.

In Live View mode, the exposure system is always doing its thing while the display is active. When you're using the viewfinder to compose images, press the shutter button halfway to kick the exposure system into gear and display the current aperture and shutter speed in the viewfinder and on the Information screen. Then release the button. The next step depends on the exposure mode, as follows:

> ✔ **P (programmed autoexposure):** The camera displays its recommended f-stop and shutter speed when you press the shutter button halfway.

But you can rotate the Command dial to select a different combination of settings. The number of possible combinations depends on the aperture settings the camera can select, which depends on your lens.

Tap to adjust shutter speed Tap to adjust aperture

Shutter speed | Aperture

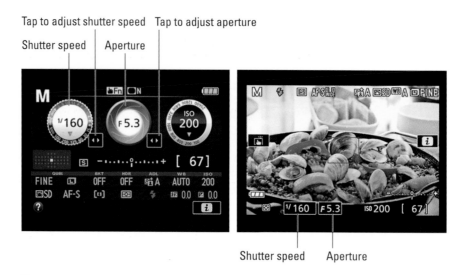

Shutter speed   Aperture

Figure 3-14: You can view the current f-stop and shutter speed on the Information display and Live View screen.

TIP

An asterisk (*) appears next to the P symbol in the upper-left corner of the Information and Live View displays if you adjust the aperture/shutter speed settings. You see a tiny P* symbol at the left end of the viewfinder display as well. To get back to the initial combo of shutter speed and aperture, rotate the Command dial until the asterisk disappears from the displays and the P* viewfinder symbol turns off.

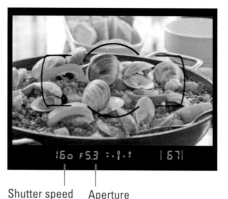

Shutter speed   Aperture

Figure 3-15: The settings also appear in the viewfinder.

✔ **S (shutter-priority autoexposure):** Your fastest option is to rotate the Command dial to set the shutter speed. As you do, the camera automatically adjusts the aperture as needed to maintain proper exposure.

You can also use the touchscreen to adjust the shutter speed, as follows:

- *Viewfinder photography:* First, tap the arrow box labeled on the left in Figure 3-16, which displays the arrows shown on the right in the figure. Tap *those* arrows to change the shutter speed and then tap the exit arrow (upper-right corner of the screen).

- *Live View photography:* Just tap the current shutter speed value to display the adjustment arrows. After setting the shutter speed, tap the exit arrow.

Tap to access shutter speed controls   Tap to lower/raise shutter speed

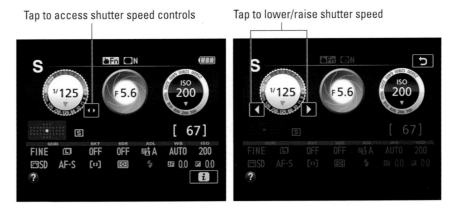

Figure 3-16: You can use these touchscreen controls to adjust shutter speed.

Available shutter speeds range from 30 seconds to 1/4000 second *except* when flash is enabled. When you use flash, the top shutter speed is 1/200 second; minimum shutter speeds vary depending on the exposure mode. (See Chapter 2 for flash details.) This limitation is due to the way the camera must time the flash with the opening of the shutter.

As the aperture shifts, so does depth of field — so even though you're working in shutter-priority mode, keep an eye on the f-stop, too, if depth of field is important to your photo. Also note that in extreme lighting conditions, the camera may not be able to adjust the aperture enough to produce a good exposure at the current shutter speed. So you may need to compromise on shutter speed or ISO.

✓ **A (aperture-priority autoexposure):** Again, you can change the f-stop setting by rotating the Command dial or by using the touchscreen. In A mode, the touchscreen controls appear under the aperture readout on the Information display, and you can simply tap the f-stop setting value on the Live View display. The camera automatically selects the appropriate shutter speed needed to expose the image at your chosen aperture.

The range of available f-stop settings depends on your lens. For zoom lenses, the range typically also changes as you zoom in and out. For example, a lens may offer a maximum aperture of f/3.5 when set to its widest angle (shortest focal length) but limit you to f/5.6 when you zoom in to a longer focal length. Check your lens manual for details on the minimum and maximum aperture settings.

The aperture symbol that surrounds the f-stop value in the Information display is designed to remind you what the f-stop setting does: The center of the graphic grows or shrinks as you change the f-stop value, indicating that the setting is opening or closing the aperture. Note that this graphic disappears if you switch from the default Information display style (called Graphic) to a simpler display (Classic). You adjust this setting via the Info Display Format option on the Setup menu; Chapter 10 has details.

When you raise the f-stop value, be careful that the shutter speed doesn't drop so low that you risk camera shake if you handhold the camera. And if your scene contains moving objects, make sure that the shutter speed the camera selects is fast enough to stop action (or slow enough to blur it, if that's your creative goal). These same warnings apply when you use P mode.

✔ **M (manual exposure):** Set aperture and shutter speed like so:

- *To adjust shutter speed:* Rotate the Command dial or use the touch-screen controls, just as you do in shutter-priority mode.

  In Manual mode, you can access two shutter speed settings not available in the other modes: Choose the value one notch past the slowest speed (30 seconds) to access the *Bulb* setting, which keeps the shutter open as long as the shutter button is pressed. If you use the ML-L3 wireless remote control unit, rotate the dial one more time to display the *Time* setting. When you select the Time setting, press the remote's shutter button once to begin the exposure and a second time to end it; maximum exposure time is 30 minutes. If you set the shutter speed to either of these options and then change the Mode dial to S, an alert appears in the Information and Live View displays to let you know that you can't use those options in S mode; you must shift back to M mode to take advantage of them.

- *To adjust aperture:* Press the Exposure Compensation button (on top of the camera) while rotating the Command dial. Notice the little aperture-like symbol that lies next to the button? That's your reminder of the button's role in setting the f-stop in M mode.

  Fortunately for those of us who have a hard time remembering our phone number, let alone which button to press to access the f-stop in Manual mode, the camera also provides touchscreen access to the setting. For viewfinder shooting, tap the arrow box under the f-stop readout to access the adjustment arrows; during Live View shooting, just tap the f-stop value at the bottom of the screen.

In P, S, or A mode, the settings that the camera selects are based on what it thinks is the proper exposure. If you don't agree, you can switch the camera to manual exposure mode and dial in the aperture and shutter speed that deliver the exposure you want. Or, if you want to stay in P, S, or A mode, you can tweak exposure using the features explained in the section "Solving Exposure Problems," later in this chapter.

Controlling ISO

The ISO setting adjusts the camera's sensitivity to light. A higher ISO enables you to use a faster shutter speed or a smaller aperture (higher f-stop number) because less light is needed to expose the image. But a higher ISO also increases the possibility of noise (refer to Figure 3-5).

You can't adjust ISO in Auto and Auto Flash Off exposure modes; the camera sets the ISO automatically. In any other exposure mode except Night Vision Effects mode, you can choose ISO values ranging from 100 to 25600. You also have the option of sticking with Auto ISO and letting the camera select the ISO it feels is appropriate for your chosen aperture and shutter speed.

To see the ISO setting, look in the Information and Live View displays, in the areas labeled in Figure 3-17. The viewfinder reports the ISO value only when the option is set to Auto. The value appears on the right end of the viewfinder, just to the left of the Shots Remaining value. Otherwise, the ISO area of the viewfinder is empty.

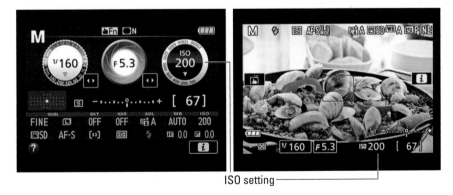

ISO setting

Figure 3-17: The ISO setting appears in the Information and Live View displays.

If you want to view the ISO setting in the viewfinder, you can tell the camera to display that number in the area normally reserved for the Shots Remaining value. Make the change via the ISO Display option, found in the Exposure section of the Custom Setting menu. Choose On to replace the Shots Remaining value with the ISO value. You can then refer to the Information and Live View displays to check the Shots Remaining value. (All figures and instructions in this book assume that you stick with the default arrangement.)

To adjust ISO, you have these options:

- ✔ **Fn (Function) button:** By default, pressing the Fn button (left front side of the camera) highlights the ISO setting in the displays. Hold the button while rotating the Command dial to change the setting.

- ✔ **Information display or Live View control strip:** You also can adjust the setting via the control strip, as illustrated in Figure 3-18. Press the *i* button or tap the onscreen *i* icon to access the strip.

- ✔ **Shooting menu:** Finally, you can change the setting via the ISO Sensitivity Settings option on the Shooting menu, shown on the left in Figure 3-19. After choosing that option, choose ISO Sensitivity on the screen shown on the right to display the menu of available ISO settings. (The other options you see in Figure 3-19 are available only in the P, S, A, and M modes.)

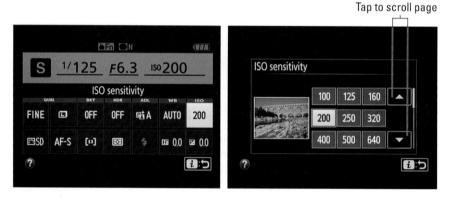

Figure 3-18: In the control strip, look for the ISO setting here.

So what's up with the special menu options provided for the P, S, A, and M modes? Well, in those modes, Auto ISO doesn't appear as an option when you select an ISO setting. But by way of the Shooting menu options, you can enable Auto ISO as a backup. Here's how it works: You dial in a specific ISO setting — say, ISO 100. If the camera decides that it can't properly expose the image at that ISO given the current aperture and shutter speed, it automatically adjusts ISO as necessary.

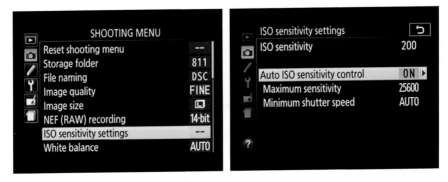

Figure 3-19: You can access advanced ISO options from the Shooting menu.

To enable this option, select ISO Sensitivity Settings on the Shooting menu, as shown on the left in Figure 3-19. On the next screen, turn the Auto ISO Sensitivity Control option to On. Next, use these two menu options to tell the camera when it should step in and offer ISO assistance:

⮞ **Maximum Sensitivity:** This option sets the highest ISO that the camera can use when it overrides the selected setting — a great feature because it enables you to decide how much noise potential you're willing to accept in order to get a good exposure. Even if the picture can't be properly exposed, the camera won't go any higher than the limit you set.

⮞ **Minimum Shutter Speed:** Set the minimum shutter speed at which the ISO override engages when you use the P and A exposure modes.

If you set this option to Auto, the camera selects the minimum shutter speed setting based on the focal length of your lens — the idea is that with a longer lens, you need a faster shutter speed to avoid the blur that camera shake can cause when you handhold the camera. You also have the option to select a specific shutter speed. However, ultimately, exposure trumps camera shake issues: If the camera can't expose the picture at what it thinks is a safe shutter speed for your lens focal length, it uses a slower speed.

When the camera is about to override your ISO setting, it alerts you by blinking the ISO Auto label in the viewfinder and in the Live View display. The message "ISO-A" blinks in the Information display as well. When you view your pictures in the monitor, the ISO value appears in red if you use certain playback display modes. (Chapter 8 has details.)

To disable Auto ISO override, set the Auto ISO Sensitivity Control option to Off.

Dampening noise

High ISO settings and long exposure times can result in *noise,* a defect that gives pictures a speckled look. To help solve the problem, your camera offers two noise-removal filters: *Long Exposure Noise Reduction,* which dampens the type of noise that occurs during long exposures; and *High ISO Noise Reduction,* designed to reduce the appearance of ISO-related noise. You enable both filters from the Shooting menu, as shown in the figures here.

If you turn on Long Exposure Noise Reduction, the camera applies the filter to pictures taken at shutter speeds of longer than 1 second. For High ISO Noise Reduction, you can choose from four settings. The High, Normal, and Low settings let you control the strength of the noise-removal effect. At the fourth setting, Off, the camera actually still applies a tiny amount of noise removal "as required." In other words, you can't really disable this function altogether. Nikon does promise that the amount of noise reduction at the Off setting is less than at the Low setting, so that's something.

Why would you want to turn off noise reduction anyway? Because enabling these features has a few disadvantages. First, the filters are applied after you take the picture, as the camera processes the image data. While the Long Exposure Noise Reduction filter is being applied, the message "Job Nr" appears in the viewfinder. The time needed to apply this filter can significantly slow your shooting speed — in fact, it can double the time the camera needs to record the file to the memory card.

Second, although filters that go after long-exposure noise work fairly well, those that attack high ISO noise work primarily by applying a slight blur to the image. Don't expect this process to totally eliminate noise, and do expect some resulting image softness. You may be able to get better results by using the blur tools or noise-removal filters found in many photo editors, because you can blur just the parts of the image where noise is most noticeable — usually in areas of flat color or little detail, such as skies.

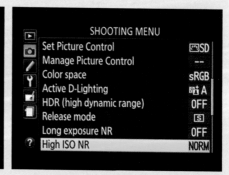

Solving Exposure Problems

Along with controls over aperture, shutter speed, and ISO, your camera offers a collection of tools designed to solve tricky exposure problems.

If the problem is underexposure due to a lack of ambient light, your camera's built-in flash is at the top of the list of exposure aids to consider. Chapter 2 explains how to get good flash results. But you also have several other exposure-correction features at your disposal, whether your subject appears under- or overexposed. The next several sections introduce you to these features. Also check out Chapter 11, which shows you how to tweak exposure of existing photos by applying tools found on the Retouch menu.

Applying Exposure Compensation

In the P, S, and A exposure modes, you have some input over exposure: In P mode, you can rotate the Command dial to choose from different combinations of aperture and shutter speed; in S mode, you can dial in the shutter speed; and in A mode, you can select the aperture setting. But because these are semiautomatic modes, the camera ultimately controls the final exposure. If your picture turns out too bright or too dark in P mode, you can't simply choose a different f-stop/shutter speed combo because they all deliver the same exposure — which is to say, the exposure that the camera has in mind. And changing the shutter speed in S mode or adjusting the f-stop in A mode won't help either because as soon as you change the setting that you're controlling, the camera automatically adjusts the other setting to produce the same exposure it initially delivered. What about changing the ISO? Nope, won't do the trick. The camera just recalculates the f-stop or shutter speed (or both) it needs to maintain the "proper" exposure at that ISO.

Not to worry: You actually do have final say over exposure in P, S, and A modes. The secret is Exposure Compensation, a feature that tells the camera to produce a brighter or darker exposure on your next shot, whether or not you change the aperture or shutter speed (or both, in P mode).

As an example of what Exposure Compensation can do, take a look at the first image in Figure 3-20. The initial exposure selected by the camera left the balloon too dark; I used Exposure Compensation to produce the brighter image on the right.

How the camera arrives at the brighter or darker image depends on the exposure mode: In A mode, the camera adjusts the shutter speed but leaves your selected f-stop in force. In S mode, the camera adjusts the f-stop and keeps its hands off the shutter speed control. In P, the camera decides whether to adjust aperture, shutter speed, or both. In all three modes, the camera may also adjust ISO if you enable Auto ISO Sensitivity Control. Keep in mind, though, that the camera can adjust f-stop only so much, according to the aperture range of your lens. And the range of shutter speeds, too, is limited by the camera itself. So there's no guarantee that the camera can actually deliver a better exposure when you dial in Exposure Compensation. If you reach the end of the f-stop or shutter speed range, you either have to adjust ISO or compromise on your selected f-stop or shutter speed.

EV 0.0   EV +1.0

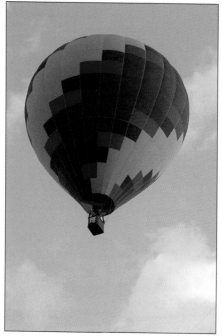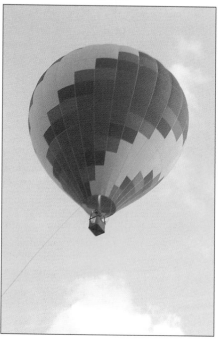

Figure 3-20: For a brighter exposure in P, S, or A mode, raise the Exposure Compensation value.

With that background out of the way, here are the details about this feature:

- ✔ **Exposure Compensation settings are stated in terms of EV numbers, as in EV +2.0.** Possible values range from EV +5.0 to EV –5.0. (*EV* stands for *exposure value.*) Each full number on the EV scale represents an exposure shift of one stop. A setting of EV 0.0 results in no exposure adjustment. For a brighter image, raise the Exposure Compensation value; for a darker image, lower the value. For my balloon image, I set the value to EV +1.0.

- ✔ **Where and how you check the current setting depends on the display, as follows:**

    - *Information display:* This one's straightforward: The setting appears in the area labeled on the left in Figure 3-21. In addition, the meter shows the amount of compensation being applied. In Figure 3-21, for example, the meter indicator appears one stop toward the positive end of the meter, reflecting the EV +1.0 setting.

- *Live View display:* If Exposure Compensation is turned on, you see the plus/minus symbol labeled on the right in the figure; otherwise, that area of the display appears empty.

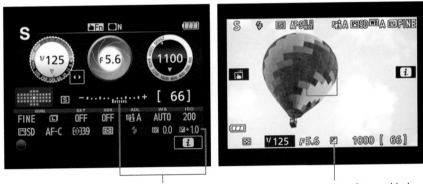

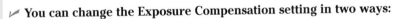

Exposure compensation amount   Exposure compensation enabled

Figure 3-21: These indicators tell you whether Exposure Compensation is enabled.

To view the selected adjustment amount in Live View mode, press the Exposure Compensation button. While the button is pressed, the EV value appears next to the plus/minus symbol.

- *Viewfinder:* The viewfinder also displays the plus/minus symbol only, but again, you can press the Exposure Compensation button to temporarily view the EV setting. Or just look at the exposure meter: As in the Information display, the exposure meter tells you how much exposure shift is in force.

✔ **You can change the Exposure Compensation setting in two ways:**

- *Press the Exposure Compensation button while rotating the Command dial.* Pressing the button automatically activates the setting, and you can spin the Command dial to enter the amount of adjustment you want to apply.

- *Use the control strip.* Press the *i* button or tap the *i* symbol on the touchscreen to activate the strip and then select the Exposure Compensation option to display the screen where you can set the amount of adjustment, as shown in Figure 3-22.

✔ **As you adjust the setting in Live View mode, the monitor brightness updates to show you how the change will affect exposure.** However — and this is a biggie, so stop texting and pay attention — the preview can only show an adjustment up to +/– EV 3.0, even though you can set the adjustment as high as +/– EV 5.0.

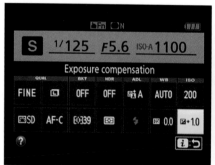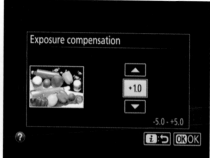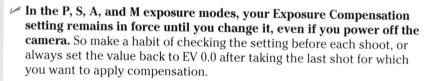

Figure 3-22: One way to adjust Exposure Compensation is via the control strip, as shown here.

 ✔ **You also can enable this feature in several Scene modes and Night Vision Effects mode.** Unlike some of the options I cover in this chapter, using Exposure Compensation isn't limited to the P, S, and A exposure modes. To check whether the feature is available for your selected mode, just look at the Information display or Live View display or press the Exposure Compensation button. If the option is off limits, the camera tells you so.

✔ **Exposure Compensation is also available for shooting movies.** Chapter 7 details the art of cinematography with your D5500.

 ✔ **In the P, S, A, and M exposure modes, your Exposure Compensation setting remains in force until you change it, even if you power off the camera.** So make a habit of checking the setting before each shoot, or always set the value back to EV 0.0 after taking the last shot for which you want to apply compensation.

For the Scene and Effects modes that allow you to set Exposure Compensation, the adjustment is reset to zero compensation when you turn the camera off or choose a different exposure mode.

✔ **When you use flash, the Exposure Compensation setting affects both background brightness and flash power.** But you can further modify the flash power through a related option, Flash Compensation. You can find out more about that feature at the end of Chapter 2.

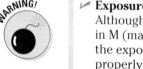 ✔ **Exposure Compensation affects the meter in M exposure mode.** Although the camera doesn't change your selected exposure settings in M (manual) exposure mode if Exposure Compensation is enabled, the exposure *meter* is affected: It indicates whether your shot will be properly exposed based on the Exposure Compensation setting. So if you don't realize that Exposure Compensation is enabled, you may mistakenly adjust your exposure settings when they're actually on target. This is yet another reason why it's best to always reset the Exposure Compensation setting back to EV 0.0 after you're done using the feature.

Expanding tonal range

A scene like the one in Figure 3-23 presents the classic photographer's challenge: Choosing exposure settings that capture the darkest parts of the subject appropriately causes the brightest areas to be overexposed. And if you instead *expose for the highlights* — that is, set the exposure settings to capture the brightest regions properly — darker areas are underexposed.

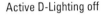 Active D-Lighting off   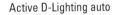 Active D-Lighting auto

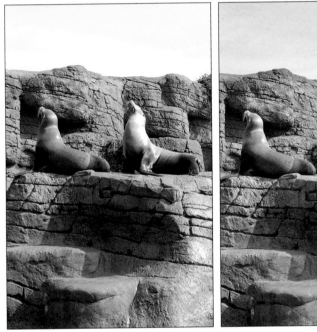

Figure 3-23: Active D-Lighting captured the shadows without blowing out the highlights.

In the past, you had to choose between favoring highlights or shadows. But with the D5500, you can expand *tonal range* — the range of brightness values in an image — through two features: Active D-Lighting and HDR (high dynamic range). The next two sections explain both options.

Applying Active D-Lighting

One way to cope with a high-contrast scene like the one in Figure 3-23 is to turn on Active D-Lighting. The *D* is a reference to *dynamic range,* the term used to describe the range of brightness values that an imaging device can capture. By turning on this feature, you enable the camera to produce an image with a slightly greater dynamic range than usual.

REMEMBER

Specifically, Active D-Lighting gives you a better chance of keeping highlights intact while better exposing the darkest areas. In my seal scene, Active D-Lighting produced a brighter rendition of the darkest parts of the rocks and the seals, for example, yet the color in the sky didn't get blown out, as it did when I captured the image with Active D-Lighting turned off. The highlights in the seal and in the rocks in the lower-right corner of the image also are toned down a tad in the Active D-Lighting version.

Active D-Lighting does its thing in two stages. First, it selects exposure settings that result in a slightly darker exposure than normal, which helps to retain highlight details. After you snap the photo, the camera brightens the darkest areas of the image to rescue shadow detail.

Symbols representing the current Active D-Lighting setting appear in the Information and Live View displays, in the areas labeled in Figure 3-24. The symbol that you see in the figures represents the Auto setting, which tells the camera to select the amount of exposure adjustment. I used this setting for my seal image.

Active D-Lighting setting   Active D-Lighting setting

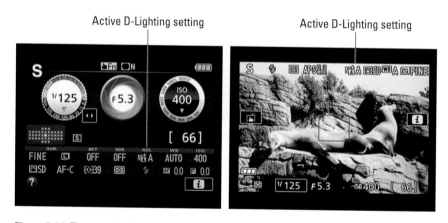

Figure 3-24: These symbols represent the Auto Active D-Lighting setting.

In Auto, Auto Flash Off, Scene, and Effects exposure modes, you're stuck with Auto Active D-Lighting; you can't disable the feature or vary the extent of the adjustment. In the P, S, A, and M modes, Auto is the default Active D-Lighting setting, but you can choose from five other settings: H* (extra high), H (high), N (normal), L (low), and Off.

TIP

I usually keep this option set to Off so that I can decide for myself whether I want any adjustment instead of having the camera apply it to every shot. Even with a high-contrast scene that's designed for the Active D-Lighting feature, you may decide that you prefer the "contrasty" look that results from disabling the option.

To select the setting you want to use, you can take two paths:

- ✔ **Control strip:** Press the *i* button or tap the *i* symbol in the display to activate the control strip, and then select the Active D-Lighting option, as shown on the left in Figure 3-25. You're escorted to the screen shown on the right in the figure, where you can specify the adjustment level.

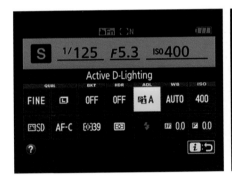 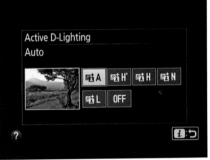

Figure 3-25: Press the *i* button to activate the control strip and adjust the Active D-Lighting setting.

- ✔ **Shooting menu:** You also can change the setting via the Shooting menu, as shown in Figure 3-26.

A few pointers about using Active D-Lighting:

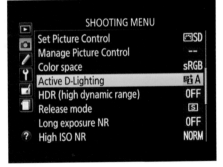

Figure 3-26: Or select the setting via the Shooting menu.

- ✔ You get the best Active D-Lighting results in matrix metering mode.

- ✔ Although Nikon doesn't recommend that you use Active D-Lighting in the M exposure mode, it's worth taking a test shot anyway if you can't get the results you like with the feature turned off. In M mode, the camera doesn't change the shutter speed or f-stop to achieve the darker exposure it needs for Active D-Lighting to work; instead, the meter readout guides you to select the right settings unless you have automatic ISO override enabled. In that case, the camera may instead adjust ISO to manipulate the exposure.

- ✔ If you're not sure whether the picture will benefit from Active D-Lighting, try Active D-Lighting bracketing, which automatically records the scene once with the feature disabled and once at a level you select. See the last section in this chapter for details.

If you opt out of Active D-Lighting, remember that the camera's Retouch menu offers a D-Lighting filter that applies a similar adjustment to existing pictures. See Chapter 11 for help.

Exploring high dynamic range (HDR) photography

In the past few years, many digital photographers have been experimenting with a technology called HDR photography. HDR stands for *high dynamic range* — again, dynamic range refers to the spectrum of brightness values that a camera or another imaging device can record.

The idea behind HDR is to capture the same shot multiple times, using different exposure settings for each image. You then use special imaging software, called *tone mapping software,* to combine the exposures in a way that uses specific brightness values from each shot. By using this process, you get a shot that contains a much higher dynamic range than the camera can capture in a single image.

The D5500 offers a feature that provides automated HDR photography. When you enable this option, the camera records two images, each at different exposure settings, and then does the tone-mapping manipulation for you to produce a single HDR image. This feature is available only in the P, S, A, and M exposure modes.

So how is HDR different from Active D-Lighting — other than the fact that it records two photos instead of manipulating a single capture? Well, with the HDR feature, you can request an exposure shift that results in up to three stops difference between the two photos. That enables you to create an image that has a broader dynamic range than you can get with Active D-Lighting.

Figure 3-27 shows an example of the type of results you can expect. In this scene, half of the area is in bright sunshine, and the other is in shadow. For the top-left photo in the figure, I exposed for the highlights, which left the right side of the scene too dark. For the top-right image, I set exposure for the shaded area, which blew out the highlights in the sunny areas. With the HDR feature, I was able to produce the bottom image in the figure. The shadows aren't completely eliminated, and some parts of the rose bush on the left side of the shot are a little brighter than I want, but on the whole, the camera balanced out the exposure fairly well.

Before you try the HDR feature, note these important points:

- Although the camera shoots two frames, you wind up with just a single HDR photo. You can't play back or access the original two shots.

- Because the camera is recording and merging two photos, the feature works well only on stationary subjects. If the subject is moving, it appears as two translucent forms in different areas in the merged frame.

✔ Use a tripod to make sure that you don't move the camera between shots. Otherwise, the merged shots may not align properly.

✔ You can't use the HDR feature if you set the Image Quality option to Raw (NEF). It works only for photos captured in the JPEG format. (Select the file format via the Image Quality setting; choose Fine for top picture quality.)

✔ When HDR is turned on, you can't use flash or the Continuous Release mode settings.

✔ You can choose from four levels of HDR exposure shift: Low, Normal, High, or Extra High. Choose Extra High for the 3-stop exposure maximum. I used this setting to produce the image in Figure 3-27. If you select Auto, the camera chooses what it considers the best adjustment.

✔ One clunky aspect of this tool: The camera disables HDR after your first two frames are captured and merged. That makes experimenting cumbersome because you have to continuously enable the feature each time you want to try different exposure settings or simply shoot another HDR frame. Annoying, to say the least.

Exposed for highlights

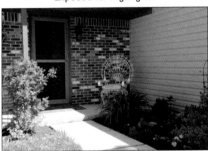

Exposed for shadows

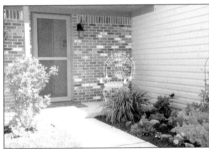

HDR, Extra high

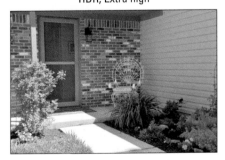

Figure 3-27: The HDR option enables you to produce an image with an even greater tonal range than Active D-Lighting.

I should also explain that if you want to produce the more-extreme type of HDR imagery that you see in photography magazines, you need to go beyond the two-frame, three-stop limitations of the in-camera HDR feature. To give you a point of comparison, Figure 3-28 shows an example I created by blending five frames with a variation of five stops between frames. The first two images show you the brightest and darkest exposures; the last image shows the HDR composite.

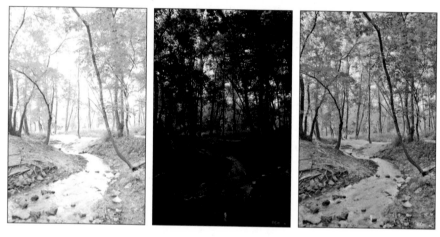

Figure 3-28: Using HDR software tools, I merged the brightest and darkest exposures (left and middle) along with several intermediate exposures, to produce the composite image (right).

On the other hand, the effect created by the camera's HDR tool looks more realistic than the one in Figure 3-28 because the tonal range isn't stretched to such an extent. When applied to its extreme limits, HDR produces something of a graphic-novel look. My example is pretty tame; some people might not even realize that any digital trickery has been involved. To me, it has the look of a hand-tinted photo.

And of course, even though the in-camera HDR tool may not be enough to produce the surreal HDR look that's all the rage these days, you can still use your D5500 for HDR work — you just have to adjust the exposure settings yourself between shots and then merge the frames using your own HDR software. You should also shoot the images in the Raw format because HDR tone-mapping tools work best on Raw images, which contain more bits of picture data than JPEG files.

All that said, the HDR feature is worth investigating when you're confronted with a high-contrast scene and you want to see how much you can broaden the dynamic range. Just take one shot with the feature enabled and a second with it turned off, and then compare the results to see which setting works best.

The Information display indicates the HDR setting in the area labeled in Figure 3-29. In the Live View display, the setting status appears in the area shown on the right in the figure, but this data appears only if you enable HDR. When the feature is turned off, that part of the Live View display is empty. To adjust the HDR setting, use these options:

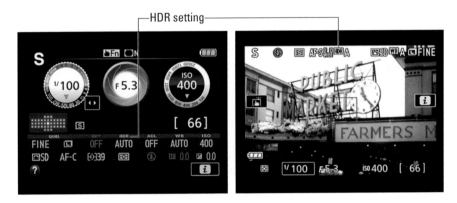

Figure 3-29: These symbols indicate the HDR setting.

✔ **Control strip:** The fastest way to enable HDR and choose the level of exposure shift is via the control strip, as illustrated in Figure 3-30. To take advantage of the control strip, press the *i* button or tap the onscreen *i* icon.

✔ **Shooting menu:** You also can set up your HDR shot via the Shooting menu, as shown in Figure 3-31.

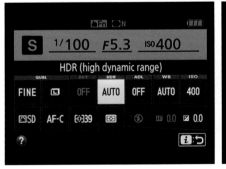
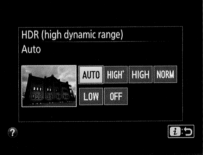

Figure 3-30: The fastest way to enable the HDR feature is via the control strip.

Either way, frame your subject a little loosely; the camera may need to trim away the edges of the frame in order to perfectly align the two shots in the HDR image. When you press the shutter button, the camera records two frames in quick succession and then creates the merged HDR image. The message "Job Hdr" appears in the viewfinder as this digital manipulation is being accomplished.

SHOOTING MENU	
Set Picture Control	SD
Manage Picture Control	--
Color space	sRGB
Active D-Lighting	OFF
HDR (high dynamic range)	AUTO
Release mode	S
Long exposure NR	OFF
High ISO NR	NORM

Figure 3-31: You also can enable HDR via the Shooting menu.

Eliminating vignetting

Because of some optical science principles that are too boring to explore, some lenses produce pictures that appear darker around the edges of the frame than in the center, even when the lighting is consistent throughout. This phenomenon goes by several names, but the two heard most often are *vignetting* and *light fall-off*. How much vignetting occurs depends on the lens, your aperture setting, and the lens focal length.

To help compensate for vignetting, your camera offers a Vignette Control feature, which adjusts image brightness around the edges of the frame. Figure 3-32 shows an example. In the left image, just a slight amount of light fall-off occurs at the corners, most noticeably at the top of the image. The right image shows the same scene with Vignette Control enabled.

Now, this "before" example hardly exhibits serious vignetting — it's likely that most people wouldn't even notice if it weren't shown next to the "after" example. But if you're a stickler for this sort of thing or your lens suffers from stronger vignetting, it's worth trying the feature. The adjustment is available in all your camera's exposure modes.

The only way to enable Vignette Control is via the Shooting menu, as shown on the left in Figure 3-33. You can choose from four settings, High, Normal, Low, and Off. (Normal is the default.)

When the feature is enabled, the Information display contains a symbol showing the setting at the top of the screen, as shown on the right in Figure 3-33. The Live View display doesn't offer any indication about the Vignette Control status.

Vignette control off   Vignette control, Normal setting

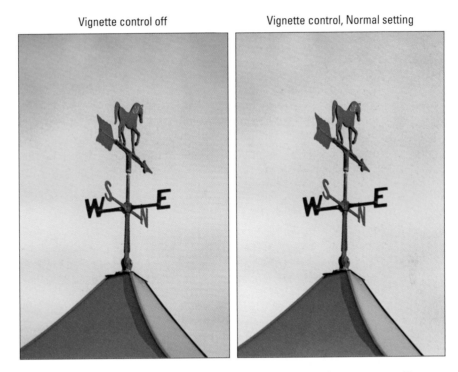

Figure 3-32: Vignette Control tries to correct the corner darkening that can occur with some lenses.

Vignette Control setting

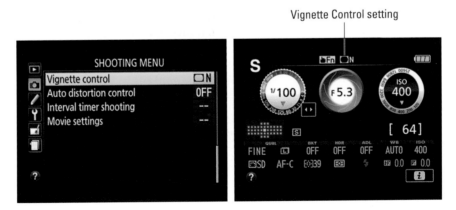

Figure 3-33: If you enable Vignette Control (left), a symbol indicating the setting appears in the Information display (right).

✔ **The correction is available only for still photos.** Sorry, video shooters; this feature doesn't apply in Movie mode.

✔ **Vignette Correction works only with certain lenses.** First, your lens must be Nikon Type G, E, or D (PC, or Perspective Control, lenses excluded). In addition, the feature works only with DX lenses, which are lenses specifically made for the size of the sensor used by the D5500. The feature doesn't work with FX lenses, which are designed for the larger sensors used in so-called *full-frame cameras.*

✔ **In some circumstances, the correction may produce increased noise at the corners of the photo.** This problem occurs because exposure adjustment can make noise more apparent.

Using autoexposure lock

To help ensure a proper exposure, your camera continually meters the light until the moment you depress the shutter button fully. In autoexposure modes, it also keeps adjusting exposure settings as needed to maintain a good exposure.

For most situations, this approach works great, resulting in the right settings for the light that's striking your subject at the moment you capture the image. But on occasion, you may want to lock in a certain combination of exposure settings. For example, perhaps you want your subject to appear at the far edge of the frame. If you were to use the normal shooting technique, you'd place the subject under a focus point, press the shutter button halfway to lock focus and set the initial exposure, and then reframe to your desired composition to take the shot. The problem is that exposure is then recalculated based on the new framing, which can leave your subject under- or overexposed.

The easiest way to lock in exposure settings is to switch to M (manual) exposure mode and use the f-stop, shutter speed, and ISO settings that work best for your subject. But if you prefer to stay with an autoexposure mode, you can press the AE-L/AF-L button to lock exposure before you reframe. This feature is known as *autoexposure lock,* or AE Lock for short. You can take advantage of AE Lock in any autoexposure mode except Auto or Auto Flash Off.

A few fine points about using this feature:

✔ **While AE Lock is in force, the letters AE-L appear in the displays.** Look for this indicator at the left end of the viewfinder; next to the Metering mode icon at the bottom of the Live View display; and just beneath the shutter speed setting in the Information display.

✔ **By default, focus is also locked when you press the button if you're using autofocusing.** You can change this behavior by customizing the AE-L/AF-L button function, as outlined in Chapter 10.

✏ **For the best results, pair this feature with the Spot Metering mode and autofocus settings that enable to you select a single focus point.** Then, if you frame your subject under that focus point, exposure is set and locked based on your subject. You can find out how to use Spot metering earlier in this chapter; see Chapter 4 for help with autofocus settings.

✏ **Be sure to keep holding the AE-L/AF-L button until you release the shutter button.** And if you want to use the same focus and exposure settings for your next shot, just keep the AE-L/AF-L button pressed.

Bracketing Exposures

Many photographers use *exposure bracketing* to ensure that at least one shot of a subject is properly exposed. *Bracketing* simply means to shoot the same subject multiple times, slightly varying the exposure settings for each image.

In the P, S, A, and M exposure modes, your camera offers *automatic bracketing.* When you enable this feature, your only job is to press the shutter button to record the shots; the camera automatically adjusts the exposure settings between each image. This feature is especially helpful in situations where you don't have time to review images and adjust exposure settings between shots. The D5500, however, takes things one step further than most cameras that offer automatic bracketing, enabling you to bracket not just basic exposure but also Active D-Lighting or white balance.

The camera records a three-shot series of bracketed images when you use the autoexposure and white-balance bracketing options. For Active D-Lighting, you get only two shots in the series: one with the feature turned off and one at the setting currently in force for the Active D-Lighting option. (See "Applying Active D-Lighting," earlier in this chapter, for details on changing that setting.)

Chapter 5 explains how to use the white-balance bracketing option. To try your hand at exposure or Active D-Lighting bracketing, follow these steps:

1. **Set your camera to the P, S, A, or M exposure mode.**

   You can't take advantage of the feature in any other mode.

2. **Display the Custom Setting menu, highlight Bracketing/Flash, and press OK.**

3. **Select Auto Bracketing Set, as shown on the left in Figure 3-34, and press OK.**

   You see the options shown on the right in the figure. This screen is where you tell the camera whether you want to bracket the exposure (AE), white balance (WB), or Active D-Lighting (ADL). Note that even though the first option is called AE (for autoexposure), it enables you to bracket exposure in M (manual exposure) mode just the same.

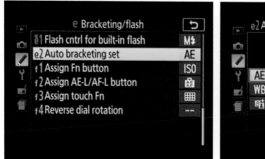
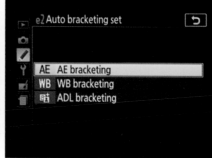

Figure 3-34: Before enabling auto bracketing, select the feature you want the camera to adjust between shots.

4. **Select the desired bracketing option and press OK.**

5. **Use the control strip to specify the bracketing increment.**

   After pressing the *i* button or tapping the *i* icon onscreen, select the BKT setting, as shown on the left in Figure 3-35. On the next screen, shown on the right in the figure, choose the desired amount of shift you want the camera to apply when taking your bracketed shots. The available settings depend on the feature you're bracketing, as follows:

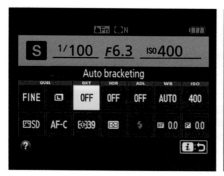
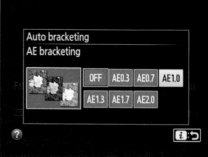

Figure 3-35: Set the bracketing amount from the control strip.

- *For exposure bracketing,* the settings control the amount of exposure shift between frames. The settings are based on Exposure Compensation values. For example, if you choose 0.7 for an auto-exposure bracketing set, the camera makes three exposures: one with exposure values as metered by the camera, one exposure with EV +0.7, and one exposure with EV –0.7 Your choices are from 0.3 EV to 2.0 EV. Choosing Off disables bracketing.

- *For Active D-Lighting bracketing,* you get only two options: ADL and Off. Select ADL. (This option is a little weird — if you select Off, you just disable bracketing.)

6. Return to shooting mode by pressing the shutter button halfway.

7. Shoot your first bracketed series.

Remember: For autoexposure bracketing, a series consists of three shots; for Active D-Lighting, two shots.

When bracketing is enabled, the Information and Live View displays offer a *bracketing indicator,* as shown in Figure 3-36. That's a technical way of saying, "Little bars appear under the meter, each one representing one shot in your bracketed series." The indicator updates after each picture to show you how many more shots are left in the series. For example, the middle bar represents your first shot; after you take your first picture, it disappears. You then see one or two bars — and thus, one or two shots left to shoot — depending on whether you're bracketing exposure or Active D-Lighting. A label on top of the meter reminds you which feature you're bracketing — AE-BKT (autoexposure) bracketing, in the figure.

8. To disable bracketing, repeat Step 5 and select Off from the second screen shown in Figure 3-35.

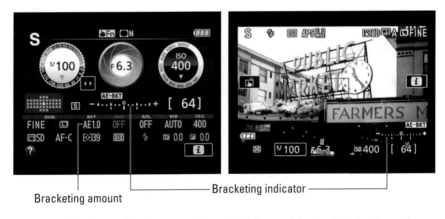

Bracketing amount — Bracketing indicator

Figure 3-36: The bars under the meter tell you which frame of the bracketed series you're about to shoot.

If you set the Release mode to Continuous Low or Continuous High, you can save yourself some button pressing: In those two Release modes, the camera records the entire bracketed series with one push of the shutter button. To change the Release mode, press the Release Mode button or select Release Mode from the Shooting menu. Remember, though, that you can't use flash in either Release mode. See Chapter 2 for more details about the Release mode setting.

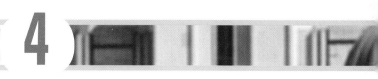

Controlling Focus and Depth of Field

In This Chapter

▶ Understanding autofocusing options

▶ Choosing a specific autofocusing point

▶ Tracking focus when shooting moving subjects

▶ Taking advantage of manual-focusing aids

▶ Using the touchscreen to set focus

▶ Manipulating depth of field

*T*o many people, the word *focus* has just one interpretation when applied to a photograph: Either the subject is in focus or it's blurry. But an artful photographer knows that there's more to focus than simply getting a sharp image of a subject. You also need to consider *depth of field,* or the distance over which other objects in the scene appear sharply focused. This chapter explains how to manipulate both aspects of an image.

The chapter begins with details of the focusing options available for viewfinder photography; following that, you can get help with focusing during Live View photography and movie recording. Just a word of warning: The two focusing systems are quite different, and mastering them takes time and practice. So don't think that you're not up for the challenge if everything doesn't sink in right away. If you start feeling overwhelmed, take a break and simplify things by following the steps laid out at the end of Chapter 1, which show you how to take a picture using the default autofocus settings and the Auto exposure mode. Then return another day to study the advanced focusing options discussed here.

Things get much easier (and more fun) at the end of the chapter, where I explain how to control depth of field. Thankfully, the concepts related to that subject apply no matter whether you're using the viewfinder, taking advantage of Live View photography, or shooting movies.

Exploring Standard Focusing Options (Viewfinder Photography)

In case you're the type who doesn't read chapter introductions (I bring this up only because I'm that type), I want to reiterate that the D5500 uses different focusing technologies depending on whether you're using the viewfinder or taking advantage of Live View. This part of the chapter deals with viewfinder photography. For help with the other half of the focusing equation, skip to the section "Focusing During Live View and Movie Shooting."

Mastering the D5500 focus system

Assuming that your lens supports autofocusing with the D5500, the first step in taking advantage of autofocusing is to set the lens focus method to auto. On most lenses, you find a switch with two settings: A (or AF) for autofocusing and M (or MF) for Manual focusing, as shown in Figure 4-1. Some lenses, though, sport a switch with a dual setting, such as AF/M, which enables you to use autofocusing initially but then fine-tune focusing by turning the lens focusing ring. On this type of lens, select the M (or MF) setting for manual-only focusing.

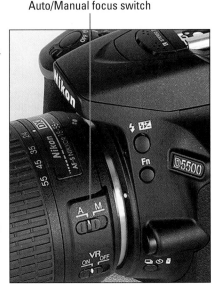

Auto/Manual focus switch

Figure 4-1: On this lens, as on many Nikon lenses, you set the switch to A for autofocusing and to M for manual focusing.

As for the camera, these settings determine focusing behavior:

- **Focus mode:** For autofocusing, you can set the camera to lock focus when you press the shutter button halfway; to adjust focus continually up to the moment you depress the button fully to take the picture; or to decide for you which option is best. You also get a setting that disables autofocusing so that you can focus manually.

- **AF-area mode:** This setting determines which focus points the camera uses to establish focus. You can tell the camera to select a point for you or to base focus on a point that you select.

You can view the current settings in the Information display, as shown in Figure 4-2. The symbols in the figure represent AF-A for the Focus mode and Auto Area for the AF-Area mode, which are the default settings for all exposure modes except for a few of the Scene modes. At these settings, the camera decides whether to lock focus when you press the shutter button halfway and also selects the focus point for you.

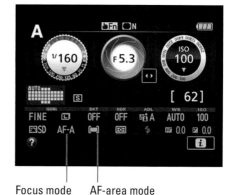

Focus mode   AF-area mode

Figure 4-2: The Focus mode and AF-area mode settings appear here.

The next several sections explain these settings, offer advice on which combination of settings work best for different subjects, and provide step-by-step focusing recipes for shooting stationary subjects and moving subjects.

Just a note before you dig in: When you use the Night Vision Effects mode, you can use autofocusing only in Live View mode. If you use the viewfinder, you're limited to manual focusing.

Changing the Focus mode setting

First up on your list of focus settings to investigate is the Focus mode. You get three settings for tweaking autofocusing behavior and one option for manual focusing.

Choose the Focus mode via the Information display control strip, as illustrated in Figure 4-3. *Remember:* To activate the control strip, press the *i* button or tap the *i* symbol on the display.

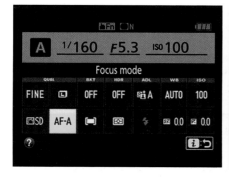
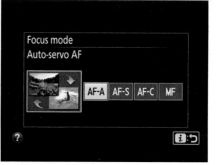

Figure 4-3: You can access all four Focus mode settings only in the P, S, A, and M exposure modes.

When the camera is in the P, S, A, or M exposure mode, you can choose from four options, which work as detailed in the following list; in other exposure modes, you can choose only the last two options (AF-A and MF). The exception, again, is the Night Vision Effects mode, which limits you to manual focusing when you use the viewfinder.

- ✔ **AF-S (single-servo autofocus):** Designed for shooting stationary subjects, this setting tells the camera to lock focus when you depress the shutter button halfway.

  In this mode, the camera won't release the shutter to take a picture until focus is achieved. If you can't get the camera to lock onto your focusing target, switching to manual focusing is the easiest solution. Also be sure that you're not too close to your subject; if you exceed the minimum focusing distance of the lens, you can't focus manually, either.

- ✔ **AF-C (continuous-servo autofocus):** Geared to photographing moving subjects, this mode causes the camera to adjust focus continuously while the shutter button is pressed halfway.

  By default, AF-C mode prevents you from taking a picture until focus is achieved, just like AF-S mode. But you can tell the camera to capture the shot at the instant you fully depress the shutter button, regardless of whether focus is set. Make the call via the AF-C Priority Selection option, found in the Autofocus section of the Custom Setting menu and shown in Figure 4-4. Focus is the default setting; choose Release to allow shutter release before focus is set.

  For the most part, I stick with Focus. Yes, I may miss a few shots waiting for the focus to occur, but if they're going to be out of focus, who cares? But when my subject is moving at a really rapid pace, I do unlock the shutter release. Although I may wind up with lots of wasted shots, I also increase the odds that I'll capture that split-second "highlight reel" moment. If the subject is slightly out of focus, I can probably retouch it enough to make it passable, especially if the picture content is truly special.

- ✔ **AF-A (auto-servo autofocus):** This mode, which is the default, gives the camera control over whether focus is locked when you press the shutter button halfway or continuously adjusted until you snap the picture. The camera makes the decision based on whether it detects motion in front of the lens. Either way, shutter release is prevented if the camera can't focus.

  AF-A mode works pretty well but can get confused sometimes. If your subject is motionless but other people are moving in the background, the camera may mistakenly switch to continuous autofocus. By the same token, if the subject is moving only slightly, the camera may not make the switch. So my advice is to choose AF-S or AF-C instead.

- ✔ **MF (manual focus):** Choose this setting to focus manually instead of using autofocus.

On Nikon AF-S lenses, including the 18–55mm lens featured in this book and the 18–140mm lens available in a bundle with the camera body, simply setting the switch on the lens to M automatically sets the Focus mode to MF. However, the opposite isn't true: Choosing MF as the Focus mode does not free the lens focusing ring so that you can set focus manually; you must set the lens switch to the M position. For other lenses, check the lens instruction manual for focusing details.

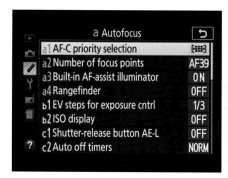
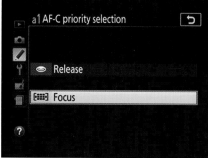

Figure 4-4: This setting controls whether you can take a picture before focus is achieved in the AF-C Focus mode.

Choosing an AF-area mode: One focus point or many?

The D5500 has 39 available autofocus points, which are located within the frame region indicated by the autofocus brackets in the viewfinder. Figure 4-5 shows you the approximate location of the individual points. (You don't actually see the points in the viewfinder; when you press the shutter button halfway, one or more points lights up, depending on your autofocusing settings.)

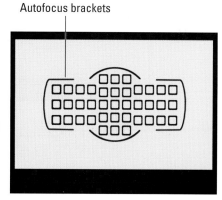

The AF-area mode tells the camera which autofocus points to consider when establishing focus. You have these choices:

Figure 4-5: The camera's 39 autofocus points are located within the portion of the frame surrounded by the AF-area brackets.

✔ **Single Point:** This mode is designed to quickly and easily lock focus on a still subject. You select a single focus point, and the camera bases focus on that point only. This option is best paired with the single-servo autofocus (AF-S) Focus mode, which is also geared to still subjects.

✔ **Dynamic Area:** Dynamic Area autofocusing is designed for capturing moving subjects. You select an initial focus point, but if your subject moves away from that point before you snap the picture, the camera looks to surrounding points for focusing information.

To use Dynamic Area autofocusing, you must set the Focus mode to AF-C or AF-A. In fact, the Dynamic Area options don't even appear when the Focus mode is set to AF-S.

You can choose from three Dynamic Area settings:

- *9-point Dynamic Area:* Rather than look at all 39 autofocus points, the camera takes focusing cues from your selected point plus the 8 surrounding points. If you choose the center focus point, for example, the points shown on the left in Figure 4-6 are active. This setting is ideal when you have a moment or two to compose your shot and your subject is moving in a predictable way, making it easy to reframe as needed to keep the subject within the 9-point area.

  This setting provides the fastest Dynamic Area autofocusing because the camera has to analyze the fewest number of autofocusing points.

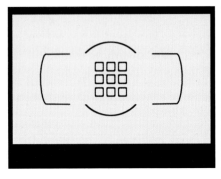
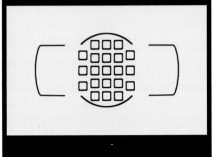

Figure 4-6: The camera considers these autofocus points when you select the center focus point and use the 9-point (left) and 21-point (right) Dynamic Area modes.

- *21-point Dynamic Area:* This mode uses your selected point plus the 20 surrounding points. The right screen in Figure 4-6 shows you which points are active if you select the center point. Obviously, this setting enables your subject to move a little farther afield from your selected focus point and still remain in the target zone. So it works better than 9-point mode when you can't quite predict the path your subject will take.

- *39-point Dynamic Area:* The camera makes use of the full complement of autofocus points. This mode is designed for subjects that are moving so rapidly that it's hard to keep them within the framing area of the 21-point or 9-point setting — a flock of birds, for example. The drawback to this setting is focusing time: With all 39 points on deck, the camera has to work a little harder to find a focus target.

✓ **3D Tracking:** This one is a variation of 39-point Dynamic Area autofocusing. As in that mode, you start by selecting a single focus point and then press the shutter button halfway to set focus. But the goal of the 3D Tracking mode is to maintain focus on your subject if you recompose the shot after you press the shutter button halfway to lock focus.

The problem with 3D Tracking is that the camera detects your subject by analyzing the colors of the object under your selected focus point. So if not much difference exists between the subject and its background, the camera can get fooled. And if your subject moves out of the frame, you must release the shutter button and reset focus by pressing it halfway again.

As with Dynamic Area mode, if you want to use 3D Tracking autofocus, you must set the Focus mode to AF-C or AF-A.

✓ **Auto Area:** At this setting, the camera automatically chooses which of the 39 focus points to use, usually locking on the object closest to the camera.

Frankly, I don't use Auto Area mode very often unless I'm handing the camera over to someone who's inexperienced and who wouldn't know how to use the other two modes. And with a camera that costs as much as the D5500, I can think of only a few people whom I'd even trust to hand it over *to.* ("Oh, I'm sorry, but I'm borrowing this from my boss and I *swore* I wouldn't let anyone else use it.") So I keep things nice and simple and stick with Single Point for still subjects and with one of the Dynamic Area modes for moving subjects.

You can select from the full complement of AF-area mode settings in all exposure modes *except* the Miniature and Night Vision Effects modes. Miniature mode always uses Single-Point mode, and autofocusing is off-limits altogether in Night Vision mode.

Here's how to dial in the AF-area setting you want to use and specify a focus point:

✓ **Selecting the AF-area mode setting:** Get the job done via the Information display control strip, as shown in Figure 4-7.

When you return to the Information display, notice the graphic labeled *Autofocus points symbol* in Figure 4-8. This symbol gives you information about which focus points are active. A solid gray square indicates the selected focus point. A fuzzy gray square indicates that the point is active, meaning that if the camera can't establish focus based on the selected point, it may consider the other active points. Any other points are inactive. In the figure, the symbol reflects the 9-point Dynamic Area setting, with the center point selected, for example.

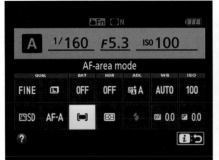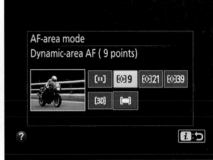

Figure 4-7: Select the AF-area mode setting via the Information display control strip.

✓ **Selecting a single focus point:** To choose a focus point in the Single Area, Dynamic Area, or 3D Tracking modes, look through the viewfinder and press the shutter button halfway and release it. The currently selected point flashes red and then turns black. For example, in Figure 4-9, the point directly over the top of the clock tower is selected. Use the Multi Selector to cycle through the available focus points until the one you want to use flashes red and then turns black. You also can use the Information display Focus points symbol (see Figure 4-8) to monitor the position of the focus point; again, the selected point appears solid.

Either way, you can quickly select the center focus point by pressing OK.

A few additional tips:

✓ **You can reduce the number of focus points available for selection from 39 to 11.** Why would you do this? Because it enables you to choose a focus point more quickly — you don't have to keep pressing the Multi Selector zillions

Autofocus points symbol

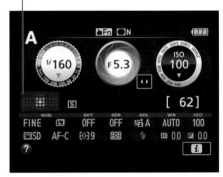

Figure 4-8: This symbol gives you more information about which autofocus points are active in the current AF-area mode.

Selected focus point

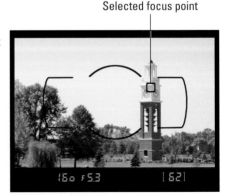

Figure 4-9: Use the Multi Selector to select the focus point that's over your subject.

of times to get to the one you want to use. Make the change via the Number of Focus Points option, found in the Autofocus section of the Custom Setting menu, as shown on the left in Figure 4-10. The right half of the figure shows you which autofocus points you can select at the reduced setting.

If you change the setting to 11, the Information display symbol that represents the active autofocus points changes to show the reduced number of selectable points.

✔ **The nine autofocus points at the center of the frame are more capable than others.** These points use *cross-type sensors,* which evaluate focus by analyzing both horizontal and vertical lines in the scene. The other points assess only horizontal lines. Cross-type sensors typically work better, especially in dim lighting, so if you're having trouble getting the camera to focus, select one of these focus points.

✔ **When you use spot metering, the camera bases exposure on the selected focus point.** The point you choose affects the way the camera calculates flash exposure as well. See Chapter 3 for details on spot metering; see Chapter 2 for help with flash photography.

✔ **In any exposure mode except P, S, A, or M, the camera resets the AF-area mode to the default setting if you change exposure modes.** So this setting is one that you need to check before every shoot if you aren't using the P, S, A, or M modes.

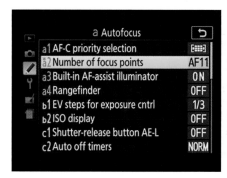
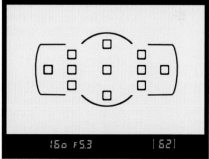

a Autofocus	↺
a1 AF-C priority selection	▦
a2 Number of focus points	AF11
a3 Built-in AF-assist illuminator	ON
a4 Rangefinder	OFF
b1 EV steps for exposure cntrl	1/3
b2 ISO display	OFF
c1 Shutter-release button AE-L	OFF
c2 Auto off timers	NORM

ISo F5.3   [62]

Figure 4-10: You can limit the number of focus points available for selection to the 11 shown here.

Choosing the right autofocus combo

You get the best autofocus results if you pair your chosen Focus mode with the most appropriate AF-area mode, because the two settings work in tandem. Here are the combinations I suggest:

✔ **For still subjects: AF-S and Single Point.** You select a focus point, and the camera locks focus on that point when you press the shutter button halfway. (It helps to remember the *s* factor: For *s*till subjects, *S*ingle Point and AF-*S*.)

✔ **For moving subjects: AF-C and 39-point Dynamic Area.** You still begin by selecting a focus point, but the camera adjusts focus as needed if your subject moves within the frame after you press the shutter button halfway to establish focus. (Think *motion, dynamic, continuous.*) Remember to reframe as needed to keep your subject within the boundaries of the autofocus points, though. And if you want speedier autofocusing, consider switching to 21-point or 9-point Dynamic Area mode — just remember that you need to keep your subject within that smaller portion of the frame for the focus adjustment to work properly.

The next two sections spell out the steps you use to set focus with both autofocus pairings.

Autofocusing with still subjects: AF-S + Single Point

For stationary subjects, the fastest, most precise autofocus option is to pair the AF-S (single-servo autofocus) Focus mode with the Single Point AF-area mode, as shown in Figure 4-11.

After selecting these options (via the Information display control strip), follow these steps to focus:

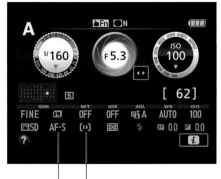

Focus mode   AF-area mode

Figure 4-11: Select these autofocus settings for stationary subjects.

1. **Looking through the viewfinder, use the Multi Selector to position the focus point over your subject.**

   The focus point is represented by a black rectangle within the AF-area brackets. You can get a look at one in Figure 4-12. The point also appears solid when you view the AF-point graphic on the Information display. (Refer to Figure 4-8.)

   If the focus point doesn't respond, press the shutter button halfway and release it to wake up the camera. Then try again.

2. **Press the shutter button halfway to set focus.**

   When focus is achieved, the camera displays a green focus light in the viewfinder (refer to

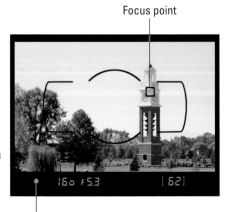

Focus point

Focus indicator light

Figure 4-12: The camera won't take the picture until focus is achieved and the green focus indicator lights up.

Figure 4-12). Unless you're using the Quiet Shutter release mode, you also hear a beep. (You can disable the sound through the Beep Options setting on the Setup menu.)

Focus remains locked as long as you keep the shutter button pressed halfway. If you're using autoexposure (any exposure mode but M), the initial exposure settings are also chosen at the moment you press the shutter button halfway, but they're adjusted as needed up to the time you take the shot.

3. Press the shutter button the rest of the way to take the shot.

If needed, you can position your subject outside a focus point. Just compose the scene initially so that your subject is under a point, press the shutter button halfway to lock focus, and then reframe. However, if you're using autoexposure, you may want to lock focus and exposure together before you reframe, by pressing the AE-L/AF-L button. Otherwise, exposure is adjusted to match the new framing, which may not work well for your subject. See Chapter 3 for more details about autoexposure lock.

Focusing on moving subjects: AF-C + Dynamic Area

To autofocus on a moving subject, select AF-C for the Focus mode and choose one of the Dynamic Area options for the AF-area mode. The earlier section "Choosing an AF-area mode: One focus point or many?" provides information to help you decide whether to use the 9-, 21-, or 39-point Dynamic Area setting.

The focusing process is the same as just outlined, with a couple exceptions:

✔ **When you press the shutter button halfway, the camera sets the initial focusing distance based on your selected autofocus point.** But if your subject moves from that point, the camera checks surrounding points for focus information.

✔ **Focus is adjusted as needed until you take the picture.** You see the green focus indicator light in the viewfinder, but it may flash on and off as focus is adjusted. The beep that you usually hear when using the AF-S Focus mode doesn't sound in AF-C mode, which is a Good Thing — otherwise, things could get pretty noisy because the beep would sound every time the camera adjusted focus.

✔ **Try to keep the subject under the selected focus point to increase the odds of good focus.** But as long as the subject falls within one of the other focus points (9, 21, or 39, depending on which Dynamic Area mode you selected), focus should be adjusted accordingly. Note that you don't see the focus point actually move in the viewfinder, but the focus tweak happens just the same. You can feel and hear the focus motor doing its thing, if you pay attention.

✔ **By default, the camera doesn't let you take the picture until focus is achieved.** To change this behavior, head for the AF-C Priority Selection option, found in the Autofocus section of the Custom Setting menu, and change the setting to Release.

Getting comfortable with continuous autofocusing takes some time, so it's a good idea to practice before you need to photograph an important event. After you get the hang of the AF-C/Dynamic Area system, though, I think you'll really like it.

On occasion, you may want to switch to Single Point AF-area mode when using continuous autofocusing. For example, if you're photographing a tuba player in a marching band, you want to be sure that the camera tracks focus on just that musician. With Dynamic Area, it is possible that the focus may drift to another nearby band member. The difficulty with the Single Point/ Dynamic Area pairing is that you must constantly reframe to keep your subject under the single point you selected. I like to use the center point with this setup; I find it more intuitive because I just reframe as needed to keep my subject in the center of the frame. (You can always crop your image to achieve a different composition after the shot.)

Using autofocus lock

When you set your camera's Focus mode to AF-C (continuous-servo autofocus), focusing is continually adjusted while you hold the shutter button halfway, so the focusing distance may change if the subject moves out of the active autofocus point or you reframe the shot before you take the picture. The same is true if you use AF-A mode (auto-servo autofocus) and the camera senses movement in front of the lens, in which case it operates as I just described. Either way, the upshot is that you can't control the exact focusing distance the camera ultimately uses.

Shutter speed and blurry photos

A poorly focused photo isn't always caused by the issues discussed in this chapter. Any movement of the camera or subject can also cause blur. Both of these problems are related to shutter speed, an exposure control that I cover in Chapter 3. Be sure to also visit Chapter 6, which provides some additional tips for capturing moving objects without blur.

Should you want to lock focus at a specific distance, you have the following options:

- ✔ **Focus manually.**

- ✔ **Change the Focus mode to AF-S (single-servo autofocus).** In this mode, focus is locked when you press and hold the shutter button halfway.

- ✔ **Lock focus with the AE-L/AF-L button.** First, set focus by pressing the shutter button halfway. When the focus is established at the distance you want, press and hold the AE-L/AF-L button. Focus remains set as long as you hold down the button.

  Keep in mind, though, that by default, pressing the AE-L/AF-L button also locks autoexposure. You can change this behavior, however, setting the button to lock just one or the other. Chapter 10 explains this option.

For my money, manual focusing is by far the easiest solution; the next section offers more advice on that topic.

Focusing manually

Some subjects confuse even the most sophisticated autofocusing systems, causing the camera's autofocus motor to spend a long time hunting for its focus point. Animals behind fences, reflective objects, water, and low-contrast subjects are just some of the autofocus troublemakers. Autofocus systems also struggle in dim lighting, although that difficulty is often offset by the AF-assist lamp, which shoots out a beam of light to help the camera find its focusing target.

When you encounter situations that cause an autofocus hang-up, you can try adjusting the autofocus options discussed earlier in this chapter. But often, it's easier and faster to switch to manual focusing. For the best results, follow these manual-focusing steps:

1. **Adjust the viewfinder to your eyesight.**

   If you don't adjust the viewfinder, scenes that are in focus may appear blurry and vice versa. If you haven't already done so, look through the viewfinder and rotate the little dial near its upper-right corner. As you do, the viewfinder data and the AF-area brackets become more or less sharp. (Press the shutter button halfway to wake up the meter if you don't see any data in the viewfinder.)

2. **Set the lens and camera to manual focusing.**

   First, move the focus-method switch on the lens to the manual position. The setting is usually marked M or MF.

Next, you need to set the camera to manual focusing by setting the Focus mode to MF. (Get the job done via the Information display control strip.) Note, though, that you can skip this step if you're using the 18–55mm or 18–140mm kit lens or certain other compatible lenses, because the camera automatically changes the Focus mode to MF as soon as you set the lens to manual focusing.

3. **Select a focus point.**

Use the same technique as when selecting a point during autofocusing: just press the Multi Selector right, left, up, or down until the point you want to use flashes red in the viewfinder or appears solid in the Information display focusing-point grid. (Refer to Figure 4-8.) Press OK to quickly select the center point.

During autofocusing, the selected focus point tells the camera what part of the frame to use when establishing focus. And technically speaking, you don't *have* to choose a focus point for manual focusing — the camera focuses according to the position you set by turning the focusing ring. However, choosing a focus point is still a good idea, for two reasons: First, even though you're focusing manually, the camera provides some feedback to let you know whether focus is correct, and that feedback is based on the selected focus point. Second, if you use spot metering, an exposure option covered in Chapter 3, exposure is based on the selected focus point.

4. **Frame the shot so that your subject is under the selected focus point.**

5. **Press and hold the shutter button halfway to initiate exposure metering.**

6. **Rotate the focusing ring on the lens to bring the subject into focus.**

When the camera thinks focus is set on the object under the focus point, the green focus lamp in the lower-left corner of the viewfinder lights, just as it does during autofocusing.

7. **Press the shutter button the rest of the way to take the shot.**

I know that when you first start working with an SLR-style camera, focusing manually is intimidating. But if you practice a little, you'll find that it's really no big deal and saves you the time and aggravation of trying to bend the autofocus system to your will when it has "issues."

In addition to the green focus lamp, your camera offers another manual focusing aid: You can swap out the viewfinder's exposure meter with a *rangefinder,* which uses a similar, meter-like display, as shown in Figure 4-13, to indicate whether focus is set on the object in the selected focus point. If bars appear to the left of the 0, as shown in the left example in Figure 4-13, focus is set in front of the subject; if the bars are to the right, as in the middle example, focus is slightly behind the subject. The more bars you see, the greater the focusing error. As you twist the focusing ring, the rangefinder updates to help you get focus on track. When you see a single bar on either side of the 0, you're good to go.

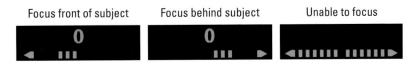

Figure 4-13: The rangefinder offers manual-focusing assistance.

Before I tell you how to activate this feature, I want to point out a few things:

- ✔ You can use the rangefinder in any exposure mode except M (manual exposure). In M mode, the viewfinder always displays the exposure meter.

- ✔ In the other exposure modes, you can continue to view the exposure meter in the Information display, even with the rangefinder enabled.

- ✔ Your lens must offer a maximum aperture of f/5.6 or lower.

- ✔ With subjects that confuse the camera's autofocus system, the rangefinder may not work well either; it's based on the same system. If the system can't find the focusing target, the rangefinder display appears as shown on the right in Figure 4-13.

- ✔ The rangefinder is automatically replaced by the normal exposure meter if you switch back to autofocusing, but reappears when you return to manual focus.

Personally, I leave the rangefinder off and just rely on the focus indicator light and my eyes to verify focus. I shoot in the S and A exposure modes frequently, and I find it a pain to monitor exposure in the Information display rather than in the viewfinder. But if you want to try the rangefinder, set the Mode dial to any setting but M and then head for the Autofocus submenu of the Custom Setting menu. Change the Rangefinder option from Off to On, as shown in Figure 4-14, to enable the feature.

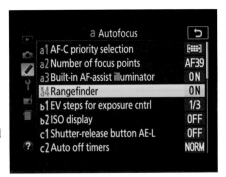

Figure 4-14: Enable the rangefinder via the Custom Setting menu.

Correcting lens distortion

When you shoot with a wide-angle lens, vertical structures sometimes appear to bend outward from the center of the image. This is known as *barrel distortion.* On the flip side of the coin, shooting with a telephoto lens can cause vertical structures to bow inward, which is known as *pincushion distortion.*

The Retouch menu offers a post-capture Distortion Control filter you can apply to try to correct both problems. But the D5500 also has an Auto Distortion Control feature that attempts to correct the image as you're shooting. It works with only certain types of lenses — specifically, those that Nikon classifies as type G, E, or D, excluding PC (perspective control), fisheye, and certain other lenses. To activate the option, just set Auto Distortion Control on the Shooting Menu to On, as shown here.

One caveat: Some of the area you see in the viewfinder may not be visible in your photo

because the anti-distortion manipulation requires some cropping of the scene. So frame your subject a little loosely when you enable Auto Distortion Control. Also, the feature isn't available for movie recording.

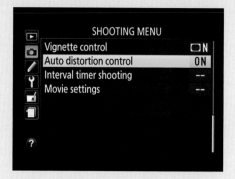

Focusing During Live View and Movie Shooting

As with viewfinder photography, you can opt for autofocusing or manual focusing during Live View and movie shooting, assuming that your lens supports autofocusing with the D5500. But focus options and techniques differ from those you use for viewfinder photography.

The next several sections detail Live View and movie focusing. It's important to understand, however, that the camera typically takes longer to autofocus in Live View mode than it does during viewfinder photography — the difference is because of the type of autofocusing the camera must use when in Live View. For the fastest autofocusing response during still photography, take the camera out of Live View mode. Unfortunately, Live View is the only game in town for movie recording; you can't use the viewfinder to frame movie shots. You also need to use Live View if you want to use autofocusing in the Night Vision Effects mode; otherwise, you must focus manually.

Tap to focus: Using the Touch Shutter

The easiest way to set focus in Live View and Movie mode is to use the *Touch Shutter,* which is a touchscreen feature than sets focus on the area of the monitor you tap. The *shutter* part of the name refers to the fact that you can also set the camera to take a single, still photo immediately after you lift your finger off the screen.

In my opinion, the touch-to-focus feature is pretty cool; the touch-to-shoot option, not so much. Why? Well, first off, when you're shooting outdoors in bright light, the monitor can wash out so much that it's difficult to see your subject clearly, let alone find the precise spot on the touchscreen to tap.

Secondly, the act of tapping the screen can cause camera shake that can blur your image, which happens if the camera moves during the exposure. I find it nearly impossible to get a shake-free shot using the Touch Shutter when handholding the camera. When you use a tripod, things become much easier, of course. In fact, assuming that you tap lightly (no poking or jabbing!), you may get a steadier shot and movie footage than when you use the shutter button to set focus.

Here's what you need to know to try the Touch Shutter:

- ✔ **Your lens must be set to autofocusing mode.** On the kit lenses sold with the D5500 (and many other Nikon lenses), just move the A/M switch to the A position. Perhaps one day, Nikon will develop a little mechanical hand that can reach out and turn the manual focusing ring for you after you tap, but for now, you can't use either touch shutter function (focusing or releasing the shutter) in manual focus mode.

- ✔ **Check the status of the Touch Controls option on the Setup menu.** You must select Enable to use the touchscreen during shooting or movie recording.

- ✔ **Tap the icon labeled in Figure 4-15 to toggle the image-capture function on and off.** When the word Off appears on the icon, as in the figure, your tap sets focus only. If you want the shutter to release after you set focus, tap the Touch Shutter icon again, so that you see just the little finger pressing the monitor.

Touch Shutter control

Focus achieved box

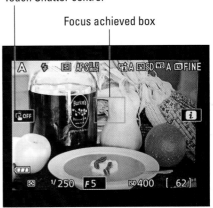

Figure 4-15: Tap the Touch Shutter icon to toggle the shutter-release feature on and off.

✔ **When the camera achieves focus, the focus box (refer to Figure 4-15) turns green.** You also hear the same beep that occurs when you focus using the shutter button. If you set the Focus mode to AF-S, focus is locked when you lift your finger from the screen. To reset focus before the shot, just tap again.

When you use the other Live View Focus mode, AF-F, (full-time servo autofocusing) the initial focusing distance is set after you tap, but the camera adjusts focus as necessary up until the time you take the picture or stop movie recording. You can tap at any time to reset the initial focusing distance.

✔ **To access the control strip while the Touch Shutter is enabled, press the *i* button rather than tapping the *i* symbol (right side of the screen).** If you don't tap directly on the right part of the *i* symbol, you set focus instead of activating the control strip.

✔ **The shutter-release function doesn't work during movie recording or when the Continuous Release Mode is selected.** Even if the Live View icon shows that the shutter-release function is enabled, tapping the screen only resets focus. If you want to take a still photo during movie recording, press and release the shutter button. Ditto for shooting a burst of frames when using the Continuous Release mode. (Chapter 2 discusses this and other Release Mode settings.) You get just a single photo for each touch even when Continuous Release is selected.

Understanding Live View autofocusing

Whether you're shooting stills or movies, you control the camera's Live View focusing performance through the same two settings as for viewfinder photography: Focus mode and AF-area mode. Again, the settings are different from those available for viewfinder photography, though; the next two sections provide details.

You can view the current settings at the top of the screen when you use the default Live View display mode, Show Photo Information, as shown in Figure 4-16, as well as in Show Movie Information mode. (Just press the Info button to change the display mode.)

Choosing a Focus mode

The Focus mode setting tells the camera whether you want the autofocus system to lock focus at the time you press the shutter button halfway (or tap the screen using the Touch Shutter function) or to continue to

Focus mode   AF-area mode

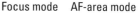

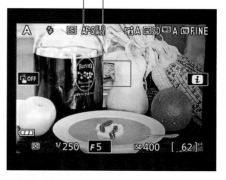

Figure 4-16: During Live View shooting, the Focus mode and AF-area mode settings appear here.

adjust focus until you take the picture or throughout movie recording. Or you can tell the camera that you prefer to focus manually. Choose the setting via the Live View control strip, as shown in Figure 4-17. (Press the *i* button or tap the onscreen *i* symbol to access the control strip.)

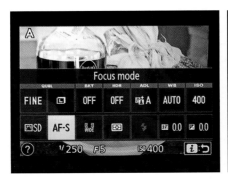 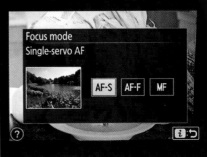

Figure 4-17: Adjust the Focus mode from the Live View control strip.

You get three Focus mode options, which work as follows:

- ✓ **AF-S (single-servo autofocus):** The camera locks focus when you press the shutter button halfway or, if you're using the Touch Shutter, when you lift your finger off the monitor. This focus setting is one of the few that works the same during Live View shooting as it does during viewfinder photography. Generally speaking, AF-S works best for focusing on still subjects.

  There's a hiccup in the touchscreen-focusing feature, however: Although focus will be locked when you lift your finger, the camera still goes through its autofocusing process when you press the shutter button to take the picture. Focus is reset when the button reaches the halfway point. Also remember that if the Touch Shutter feature is enabled, the camera records the shot when you lift your finger.

- ✓ **AF-F (full-time servo autofocus):** This option is available for all exposure modes except for the Effects modes Color Sketch, Toy Camera, and Miniature.

  The main purpose of AF-F is to enable continuous focus adjustment throughout a movie recording. To use this option, frame your subject within the Live View focus frame, which looks like a red box by default. (The appearance of the frame depends on your Auto Area mode; see the section, "Stepping through the autofocusing process," later in this chapter, for more information.) But instead of pressing the shutter button halfway or using the tap-to-focus Touch Shutter feature, keep your finger *off* the shutter button and monitor. Instead, just wait for the camera to lock onto the subject in the focus frame and then press the movie-record button to start recording. Focus is adjusted as needed if your subject moves through the frame or you pan the camera. If you decide to lock focus, press and hold the shutter button halfway down. As soon as you release the button, continuous autofocusing begins again. You also can tap the screen to refocus; keep your finger on the monitor to lock focus and lift your finger to restart continuous autofocusing.

Unfortunately, there's a downside that makes AF-F less than ideal. If you shoot a movie with sound recording enabled and use the internal microphone, the microphone may pick up the sound of the autofocus motor as it adjusts focus. So if pristine audio is your goal, use AF-S mode and lock focus before you begin recording, or abandon autofocus altogether and focus manually. As another option, you can attach an external microphone to the camera and place it far enough away that it doesn't pick up the camera sounds.

AF-F focusing works the same way for still photography. Focus is set when the focus frame turns green, but is adjusted as needed until you take the shot. Again, you can lock focus at any time by holding the shutter button halfway down or by keeping your finger on the monitor.

✓ **MF (manual focus):** Select this option to focus manually, by twisting the focusing ring on the lens.

With the 18–55mm and 18–140mm kit lenses and some other Nikon AF-S lenses, moving the switch on the lens to the manual-focusing position automatically selects the MF Focus mode setting. For other lenses, you need to select the Focus mode setting yourself.

Selecting the AF-area mode

Through the AF-area mode, you give the camera's autofocusing system instructions on what part of the frame contains your subject so that it can set the focusing distance correctly. For Live View photography and movie recording, the camera offers these settings:

✓ **Wide Area:** In this mode, the camera focuses on the area under a rectangular focusing frame. You can position the frame by tapping the screen or by using the Multi Selector. (Details on using this option and others are provided in the upcoming section "Stepping through the autofocusing process.")

✔ **Normal Area:** This mode works the same way as Wide Area autofocusing but uses a smaller focusing frame. The idea is to enable you to base focus on a very specific area. With such a small focusing frame, however, you can easily miss your focus target when handholding the camera. If you move the camera slightly as you're setting focus and the focusing frame shifts off your subject as a result, focus will be incorrect. For the best results, use a tripod in this mode.

✔ **Face Priority:** Designed for portrait shooting, this mode attempts to hunt down and focus on faces. Face Priority typically works only when your subjects are facing the camera, however. If the camera can't detect a face, you see a plain red focus frame, and things work as they do in Wide Area mode. In a group shot, the camera typically focuses on the closest face.

✔ **Subject Tracking:** This mode tracks a subject as it moves through the frame and is designed for focusing on a moving subject. But subject tracking isn't always as successful as you might hope. For a subject that occupies only a small part of the frame — say, a butterfly flitting through a garden — autofocus may lose its way. Ditto for subjects moving at a fast pace, subjects getting larger or smaller in the frame (when moving toward you and then away from you, for example), or scenes in which not much contrast exists between the subject and the background. Oh, and scenes in which there's a great deal of contrast can create problems, too. My take on this feature is that when the conditions are right, it works well, but otherwise the Wide Area setting gives you a better chance of keeping a moving subject in focus.

You can't adjust this option in Auto mode or Auto Flash Off mode. In those two modes, the camera insists on using Face Priority mode. Nor do you have control in the Miniature Effects mode, which always uses Wide Area focusing. Subject Tracking mode isn't available for the Night Vision, Toy, Color Sketch, and Selective Color Effects modes.

In other exposure modes, adjust the setting via the control strip, as shown in Figure 4-18, which shows Wide Area mode selected. Again, pressing the *i* button is the most surefire way to shift to the control strip when the touch shutter is enabled, but you also can tap on the *i* icon on the right side of the screen. (Be precise with where you tap, though, or the camera will think your tap is meant to set focus.)

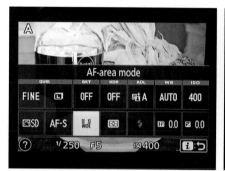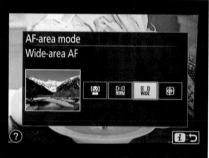

Figure 4-18: Live View and movie autofocusing offers these AF-area mode options.

Choosing the right Live View and movie focusing pairs

To recap, the way the camera sets focus during Live View and movie shooting depends on your Focus mode and AF-area mode settings. Until you get fully acquainted with the various combinations of Focus mode and AF-area mode settings and can make your own decisions about which pairings you like best, I recommend the following settings (assuming, of course, that the exposure mode you're using permits them):

- **For moving subjects:** Set the Focus mode to AF-F and the AF-area mode to Wide Area. You also can try the Subject Tracking AF-area mode, but see my comments in the preceding section regarding which subjects may not be well suited to that mode.

- **For stationary subjects:** Set the Focus mode to AF-S and the AF-area mode to Wide Area. Or, if you're shooting a portrait, give the Face Priority AF-area option a try.

- **For difficult-to-focus subjects:** If the camera has trouble finding the right focusing point when you use autofocus, don't spend too much time fiddling with the different autofocus settings. Just set the camera to manual focusing and set focus yourself. Remember that every lens has a minimum focusing distance, so if you can't focus automatically or manually, you may simply be too close to your subject.

Stepping through the autofocusing process

Having laid out all the whys and wherefores of the Live View autofocusing options, I offer the following summary of the steps involved in choosing the autofocus settings and then actually setting focus:

1. **Choose the Focus mode and AF-area mode.**

   You adjust both settings via the control strip, which you can access by pressing the *i* button or tapping the touchscreen's *i* icon (right side of the screen). Refer to Figures 4-17 and 4-18 if you need help locating the two options in the control strip. Remember that the camera doesn't let you access all settings in certain exposure modes; see the preceding sections for details on which modes permit which settings.

If you set the Focus mode to AF-F, the autofocus system perks up and initiates focusing immediately.

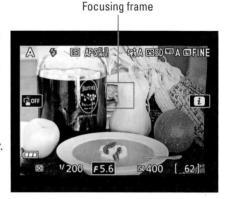

Focusing frame

Figure 4-19: The red box represents the focusing frame in Wide Area and Normal Area AF-Area modes.

2. **Locate the focus frame in the Live View display.**

The frame appearance depends on the AF-area mode:

- *Wide Area and Normal Area:* You see a red rectangular frame, as shown in Figure 4-19. (The figure shows the frame at the size it appears in Wide Area mode; it's smaller in Normal Area mode.)

- *Face Priority:* If the camera locates faces, you see a yellow focus frame around each one, as shown on the left in Figure 4-20. One frame sports corner brackets inside the frame — in the figure, it's the frame on the right. The brackets indicate the face that the camera will use to set focus — typically, the closest person.

 If you instead see a plain red frame, the camera can't detect a face and will set focus as it would if you were using Wide Area mode.

- *Subject Tracking:* A focusing frame like the one shown on the right in Figure 4-20 appears.

Selected face

Subject Tracking focus frame

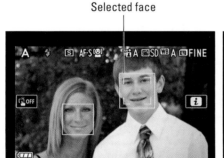 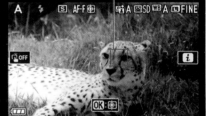

Figure 4-20: The focusing frame appears differently in Face Priority mode (left) and Subject Tracking mode (right).

In AF-F mode, the frame turns green when the object under the frame is in focus. The frame blinks any time focus is being reset.

3. Position the focusing frame over your subject.

For example, I moved the frame over the soup garnish in the left example in Figure 4-21.

You can use the Multi Selector to shift the focusing frame over your subject. Or, if the Touch Shutter's shooting function is disabled, you can tap to position the frame. (You see the word "Off" over the Touch Shutter icon, as shown in Figure 4-21.) If the shutter-release function is turned on, the camera takes the picture when you lift your finger.

A couple of tips for positioning the frame:

- *In Face Priority mode,* use the Multi Selector to move the box with the double yellow border — which indicates the final focusing point — from face to face in a group portrait. You also can tap the face — again, assuming that the shutter-release part of the Touch Shutter feature is disabled.

- *In Wide Area and Normal Area modes,* press OK to quickly move the focus point to the center of the frame.

Focusing frame   Focus achieved

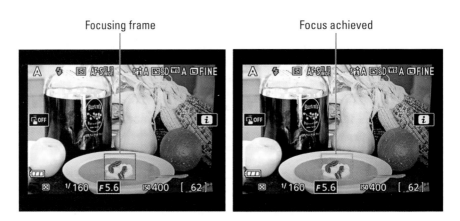

Figure 4-21: The focus frame turns green when focus is achieved.

4. In Subject Tracking AF-Area mode, press OK to initiate focus tracking.

If your subject moves, the focus frame moves with it. To stop tracking, press OK again. (You may need to take this step if your subject leaves the frame — press OK to stop tracking, reframe, and then press OK to start tracking again.)

You also can tap the OK symbol onscreen to start focusing. But on your second tap, which stops tracking, the camera will then take the picture if the shutter-release part of the Touch Shutter is enabled. If you turn off that function, tap the OK button to perform both initial focusing and to stop tracking.

5. **In AF-S Focus mode, press the shutter button halfway to initiate autofocusing.**

Why not use the Touch Shutter? Well, you can, and the focus will lock when you lift your finger off the screen. But then when you press the shutter button to take the picture, the camera sets focus again as soon as the button reaches the halfway point.

6. **Wait for the focus frame to turn green, signaling that focus has been set. (Refer to the right screen in Figure 4-21.)**

The appearance of the frame depends on the AF-Area mode; the figure shows it as it looks in Wide Area mode.

What happens next depends on the Focus mode:

- *AF-S:* You also hear a little beep (assuming that you didn't disable the beep, which you can do via the Beep Options setting on the Setup menu). Focus is locked as long as you keep the shutter button pressed halfway. If you used the touchscreen to set focus, the camera locks focus.

- *AF-F:* Focus is adjusted if the subject moves. The focus frame turns back to red (or yellow or white) if focus is lost; when the frame turns green and stops blinking, focus has been achieved again. You can lock focus by pressing the shutter button halfway. In most cases, the camera resets focus on your subject when you press the button, even if the focus frame is already green.

7. **(Optional) Press the Zoom In button to magnify the display to double-check focus.**

Each press gives you a closer look at the subject. A small thumbnail appears in the lower-right corner of the screen, with the yellow highlight box indicating the area that's being magnified, as shown in Figure 4-22. Press the Multi Selector to scroll the display if needed.

To reduce the magnification level, press the Zoom Out button. If you're not using Subject Tracking mode, you can also press OK to quickly return to normal magnification.

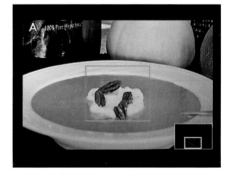

Figure 4-22: Press the Zoom In button to magnify the display and double-check focus.

Manual focusing during Live View and movie shooting

For manual focusing with the 18–55mm lens or a similarly featured Nikon lens (including the 18–140mm kit lens), just set the A/M switch to M. The camera automatically changes the Focus mode setting to MF (manual focus). For other lenses, refer to the lens instruction manual to find out how to set the lens to manual focusing. Then rotate the lens focusing ring to bring the scene into focus. But note a few quirks:

- ✔ Even with manual focusing, you still see the focusing frame; its appearance depends on the current AF-area mode setting. In Face Priority mode, the frame automatically jumps into place over a face if it detects one. And if you press OK when Subject Tracking mode is enabled, the camera tries to track the subject under the frame until you press OK again. I find these two behaviors irritating, so I always set the AF-area mode to Wide Area or Normal Area for manual focusing.

- ✔ The focusing frame doesn't turn green to indicate successful focusing as it does with autofocusing.

- ✔ You can press the Zoom In button to check focus in manual mode just as you can during autofocusing. Refer to Step 7 in the preceding section for details. Press the Zoom Out button to reduce the magnification level.

Manipulating Depth of Field

Getting familiar with the concept of depth of field is one of the biggest steps you can take to becoming a better photographer. I introduce you to depth of field in Chapter 3, but here's a quick recap:

- ✔ *Depth of field* refers to the distance over which objects in a photograph appear acceptably sharp.

- ✔ With a shallow, or small, depth of field, distant objects appear more softly focused than the main subject (assuming that you set focus on the main subject, of course).

- ✔ With a large depth of field, the zone of sharp focus extends to include objects at a distance from your subject.

Which arrangement works best depends on your creative vision and your subject. In portraits, for example, a classic technique is to use a short depth of field, as I did for the photo on the left in Figure 4-23. This approach increases emphasis on the subject while diminishing the impact of the

Shallow depth of field

Large depth of field

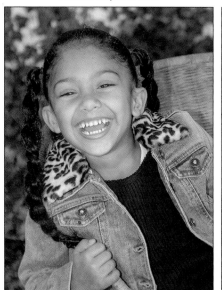 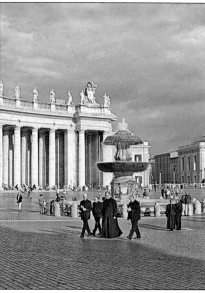

Figure 4-23: A shallow depth of field blurs the background (left); a large depth of field keeps both foreground and background in focus (right).

background. But for the photo shown on the right, I wanted to emphasize that the foreground figures were in St. Peter's Square, so I used a large depth of field, which kept the background buildings sharply focused and gave them equal weight in the scene.

REMEMBER

Depth of field depends on the aperture setting, lens focal length, and distance from the subject, as follows:

- ✔ **Aperture setting (f-stop):** The aperture is one of three main exposure settings, all explained fully in Chapter 3. Depth of field increases as you stop down the aperture (by choosing a higher f-stop number). For shallow depth of field, open the aperture (by choosing a lower f-stop number). Figure 4-24 offers an example; in the f/22 version on the left, focus is sharp all the way through the frame; in the f/2.8 version on the right, focus softens as the distance from the flag increases. I snapped both images using the same focal length and camera-to-subject distance, setting focus on the flag.

- ✔ **Lens focal length:** In lay terms, *focal length* determines what the lens "sees." As you increase focal length, measured in millimeters, the angle of view narrows, objects appear larger in the frame, and — the important

Aperture, f/22; Focal length, 93mm   Aperture, f/2.8; Focal length, 93mm

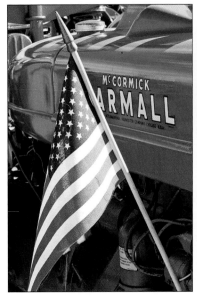 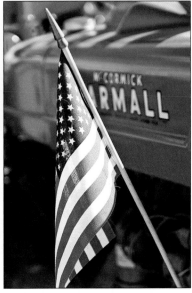

Figure 4-24: A lower f-stop number (wider aperture) decreases depth of field.

point for this discussion — depth of field decreases. Additionally, the spatial relationship of objects changes as you adjust focal length. As an example, Figure 4-25 compares the same scene shot at a focal length of 127 mm and 183 mm. I used the same aperture and camera-to-subject distance for each shot, setting focus on the parrot.

Whether you have any focal length flexibility depends on your lens: If you have a zoom lens, you can adjust the focal length by zooming in or out. If you have a prime lens — that is, not a zoom lens — the focal length is fixed, so scratch this means of manipulating depth of field.

For more details about focal length, flip to Chapter 1 and explore the sidebar related to that topic.

✓ **Camera-to-subject distance:** As you move the lens closer to your subject, depth of field decreases. This statement assumes that you don't zoom in or out to reframe the picture, thereby changing the focal length. If you do, depth of field is affected by both the camera position and focal length.

Aperture, f/5.6; focal length, 127mm

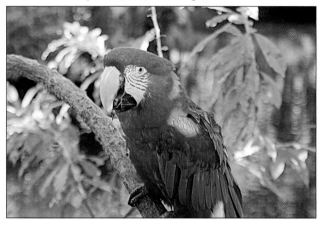

Aperture, f/5.6; focal length, 183mm

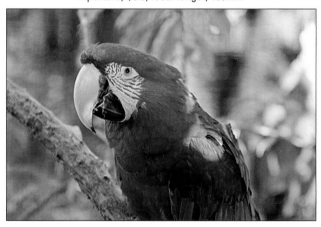

Figure 4-25: Zooming to a longer focal length also reduces depth of field.

Together, these three factors determine the maximum and minimum depth of field that you can achieve, as follows:

- **To produce the shallowest depth of field:** Open the aperture as wide as possible (the lowest f-stop number), zoom in to the maximum focal length of your lens, and get as close as possible to your subject.

- **To produce maximum depth of field:** Stop down the aperture to the highest possible f-stop number, zoom out to the shortest focal length (widest angle) your lens offers, and move farther from your subject.

A few final tips related to depth of field:

- ✔ **Aperture-priority autoexposure mode (A) enables you to easily control depth of field while enjoying exposure assistance from the camera.** In this mode, you rotate the Command dial to set the f-stop, and the camera selects the appropriate shutter speed to produce a good exposure. The range of available aperture settings depends on your lens.

- ✔ **For greater background blurring, move the subject farther from the background.** The extent to which background focus shifts as you adjust depth of field also is affected by the distance between the subject and the background.

- ✔ **In Live View mode, depth of field doesn't change in the preview as you change the f-stop setting.** The camera can't display the effect of aperture on depth of field properly because the aperture doesn't actually open or close until you take the photo. However, you can gauge the depth of field produced by the focal length and subject-to-camera distance in the preview.

Mastering Color Controls

Compared with understanding certain aspects of digital photography — resolution, aperture, shutter speed, and so on — making sense of your camera's color options is easy-breezy. First, color problems aren't all that common, and when they are, they're usually simple to fix with a quick shift of your camera's White Balance setting. And getting a grip on color requires learning only a couple of new terms, an unusual state of affairs for an endeavor that often seems more like high-tech science than art.

This chapter explains the aforementioned White Balance control along with other features that enable you to fine-tune the way your camera renders colors, whether you're shooting photos or recording movies.

Understanding the White Balance Setting

Every light source emits a particular color cast. The old-fashioned fluorescent lights found in most public restrooms, for example, put out a bluish-greenish light, which is why we all look sickly when we view our reflections in the mirrors in those restrooms. And if you think that your beloved looks especially attractive by candlelight, you aren't imagining it: Candlelight casts a warm, yellow-red glow that is flattering to the skin.

Science-y types measure the color of light, officially known as *color temperature,* on the Kelvin scale, which is named after its creator. You can see the Kelvin scale in Figure 5-1.

When photographers talk about "warm light" and "cool light," though, they aren't referring to the position on the Kelvin scale — or at least not in the way most people think of temperatures, with a higher number meaning hotter. Instead, the terms describe the visual appearance of the light. Warm light, produced by candles and incandescent lights, falls in the red-yellow spectrum at the bottom of the Kelvin scale; cool light, in the blue spectrum, appears in the upper part of the Kelvin scale.

8000	Snow, water, shade
	Overcast skies
	Flash
5000	Bright sunshine
	Fluorescent bulbs
	Tungsten lights
3000	Incandescent bulbs
2000	Candlelight

Figure 5-1: Each light source emits a specific color.

At any rate, most people don't notice these fluctuating colors of light, because human eyes automatically compensate for them. Except in extreme lighting conditions, we perceive a white tablecloth as white no matter whether it's lit by candlelight, fluorescent light, or daylight.

Similarly, a digital camera compensates for different colors of light through white balancing. Simply put, *white balancing* neutralizes light so that whites are always white, which in turn ensures that other colors are rendered accurately. If the camera senses warm light, it shifts colors slightly to the cool side of the color spectrum; in cool light, the camera shifts colors in the opposite direction.

The good news is that, as with your eyes, your camera's Auto White Balance setting tackles this process well in most situations, which means that you can usually ignore it and concentrate on other aspects of the picture. But if the scene is lit by two or more light sources that cast different colors, the white balance sensor can get confused, producing an unwanted color cast like the one you see in the left image in Figure 5-2.

I shot this image in my home studio — which is a fancy name for "guest bedroom" — using tungsten photo lights, which produce light with a color temperature similar to incandescent bulbs. The problem is that windows in the studio permit strong daylight to filter through. In Auto White Balance mode, the camera reacted to that daylight — which has a cool color cast — and applied too much warming, giving my original image a yellow tint. No problem: I switched the White Balance mode from Auto to the Incandescent setting. The image on the right in Figure 5-2 shows the corrected colors.

There's one problem with white balancing as it's implemented on your D5500, though: You can't make this kind of manual White Balance selection if you shoot in the fully automatic exposure modes. So if you spy color problems in your camera monitor, switch to P, S, A, or M exposure mode.

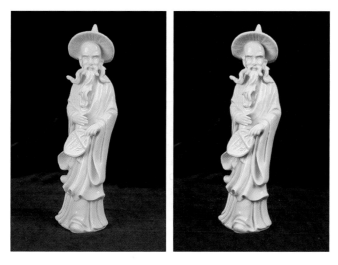

Figure 5-2: Multiple light sources resulted in a yellow color cast in Auto White Balance mode (left); switching to the Incandescent setting solved the problem (right).

The next section explains how to make a simple white balance correction; following that, you can explore advanced options.

Changing the White Balance setting

You can view the current White Balance setting in the Information and Live View displays, as shown in Figure 5-3. The icons in the figures represent the Auto setting; settings other than Auto are represented by the icons you see in Table 5-1.

White Balance setting

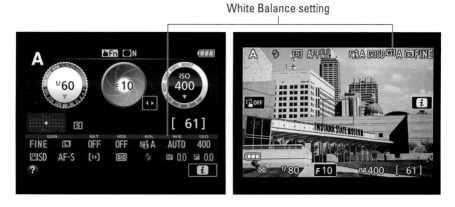

Figure 5-3: A symbol representing the current White Balance setting appears in the displays.

Table 5-1	Manual White Balance Settings
Symbol	*Light Source*
	Incandescent
	Fluorescent
	Direct sunlight
	Flash
	Cloudy
	Shade
PRE	Preset

In Live View mode, colors in the preview are rendered according to the current White Balance setting. If you're unsure of which setting to use, just experiment: After you adjust the setting, the preview updates to show you the effect on photo colors.

You can adjust the White Balance setting in two ways:

✔ **Control strip:** Activate the strip by pressing the *i* button or tapping the *i* icon on the display. Select the White Balance option, as shown on the left in Figure 5-4 to access the available settings, shown on the right.

✔ **Shooting menu:** You also can access the setting from the Shooting menu, as shown in Figure 5-5. After selecting a setting, press the OK button or tap the OK symbol, labeled in Figure 5-5. (You also can just tap your desired setting twice to return to the Shooting menu.)

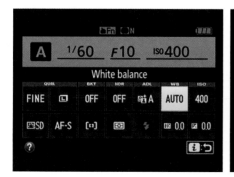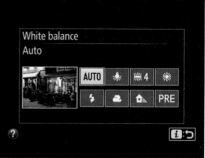

Figure 5-4: Select a White Balance setting by using the control strip.

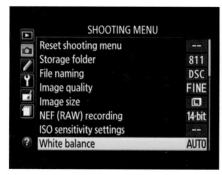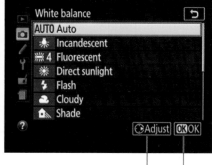

Tap to fine-tune setting

Tap to finalize your selection

Figure 5-5: To uncover more White Balance options, open the Shooting menu.

When you go the menu route, you can access the following advanced white balance features:

✔ **Fine-tune the settings.** If you choose any setting but Fluorescent, pressing the Multi Selector right or tapping the Adjust icon labeled in Figure 5-5 takes you to a screen where you can fine-tune the setting, a process I explain in the next section.

✔ **Select a specific type of fluorescent bulb.** When you choose Fluorescent from the menu, as shown on the left in Figure 5-6, you can select a specific type of bulb. The selection screen, shown on the right in the figure, appears automatically when you tap Fluorescent in the initial menu; you can also display the screen by pressing the Multi Selector right. Either way, select the option that most closely matches your bulbs and then press or tap OK. Or, to go to the fine-tuning screen, press the Multi Selector right or tap the Adjust icon.

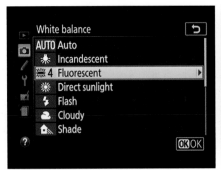 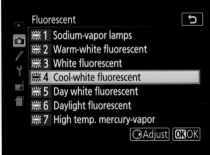

Figure 5-6: If you adjust the White Balance setting from the Shooting menu, you can select a specific type of fluorescent bulb.

> ✔ **Create a custom white balance preset.** Selecting the PRE option as the White Balance setting enables you to create and store a precise, customized White Balance setting, as explained in the upcoming section "Creating white balance presets." This feature provides the fastest way to achieve accurate colors when the scene is lit by multiple light sources that have differing color temperatures.

The selected White Balance setting remains in force for the P, S, A, and M exposure modes until you change it. Get in the habit of checking the setting before every shoot to make sure that you don't need to modify it. Otherwise, your pictures may take on an unwanted color cast due to an incorrect setting for the new lighting conditions.

Fine-tuning White Balance settings

You can fine-tune any White Balance setting except a custom preset that you create by using the PRE option. Make the adjustment as spelled out in these steps:

1. **Display the Shooting menu and select the White Balance option.**

   The menu of available settings appears.

2. **Highlight the White Balance setting you want to adjust.**

3. **Press the Multi Selector right or tap Adjust to display the fine-tuning screen, shown in Figure 5-7.**

   If you select Fluorescent, you first go to a screen where you select a specific type of bulb, as covered in the preceding section. After you highlight a bulb type, press the Multi Selector right or tap Adjust to get to the fine-tuning screen.

4. Fine-tune the setting by moving the adjustment marker in the color grid.

I labeled the marker in Figure 5-7. The grid is set up around two color pairs: Green and Magenta, represented by G and M; and Blue and Amber, represented by B and A. To adjust the White Balance setting, move the marker in the direction you want to shift colors. You can either tap inside the grid, tap the arrows on the sides of the grid, or press the Multi Selector to reposition the marker.

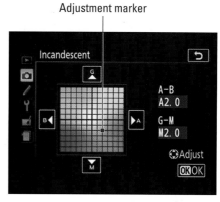

Adjustment marker

Figure 5-7: Move the black square around the color grid to fine-tune the selected White Balance setting.

As you move the marker, the A–B and G–M boxes on the right side of the screen show you the current amount of color shift. A value of 0 indicates the default amount of color compensation applied by the selected White Balance setting. In Figure 5-7, for example, I moved the marker two levels toward amber and two levels toward magenta to specify that I wanted colors to be a tad warmer.

5. Tap OK or press the OK button to complete the adjustment.

After you fine-tune a White Balance setting, an asterisk appears next to the icon representing the setting on the Shooting menu, as shown in Figure 5-8. You see an asterisk next to the White Balance setting in the Information and Live View displays as well.

Creating white balance presets

If none of the standard White Balance settings does the trick and you don't want to fool with fine-tuning them,

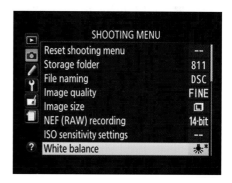

Figure 5-8: The asterisk next to the White Balance setting name indicates that you applied a fine-tuning adjustment.

take advantage of the PRE (Preset Manual) feature. This option enables you to do two things:

✔ Base white balance on a direct measurement of the actual lighting conditions.

✔ Match white balance to an existing photo.

Although you can create a preset using either method, you can store only one preset at a time. For example, if you create a preset based on lighting conditions on Monday and then decide on Tuesday to create a different one based on a photo, the light-based preset goes kaput.

The next two sections provide step-by-step instructions for creating both types of presets.

Setting white balance with direct measurement

To use this technique, you need a piece of card stock that's either neutral gray or absolute white — not eggshell white, sand white, or any other close-but-not-perfect white. (You can buy reference cards, made just for this purpose, in many camera stores for less than $20.)

Position the reference card so that it receives the same lighting you'll use for the photo. Then take these steps:

1. **Set the camera to the P, S, A, or M exposure mode.**

   If the exposure meter reports that the image will be under- or overexposed at the current exposure settings, make the necessary adjustments now. (Chapter 3 tells you how.) Otherwise, the camera can't create your preset.

2. **Frame your shot so that the reference card fills the viewfinder.**

   You must use the viewfinder to take the reference shot; you can't create a preset in Live View mode.

3. **From the Shooting menu, select White Balance and then select PRE Preset Manual, as shown on the left in Figure 5-9.**

4. **Press the Multi Selector right to display the screen shown on the right in Figure 5-9.**

   You also can get to this screen by tapping the PRE Preset Manual menu item (left side of the figure) two times.

5. **Select Measure, and press or tap OK.**

   A warning appears, asking you whether you want to overwrite existing data.

6. **Select Yes and press or tap OK.**

   You see a message telling you to take your picture. You have about 6 seconds to do so. (The letters *PRE* flash in the viewfinder and

Information display to let you know the camera is ready to record your white balance reference image.)

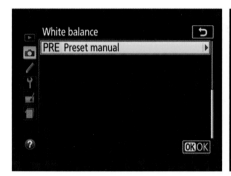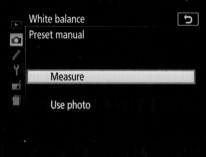

Figure 5-9: Select these options to set white balance by measuring a white or gray card.

7. **Take the reference shot.**

Your camera may have a hard time autofocusing because the reference card doesn't contain any contrast. To solve the problem, use manual focusing.

If the camera is successful at recording the white balance data, the letters *Gd* flash in the viewfinder and the message "Data Acquired" appears in the Information display. If the camera can't set the custom white balance, you instead see the message *No Gd* in the viewfinder, and a message in the Information display urges you to try again. Try adjusting the lighting before doing so.

You also can create a direct-measurement preset via the Information display. First, set the White Balance option to PRE. After you exit the menu or control strip and return to the Information display, press the OK button for a couple seconds until the letters *PRE* start to flash in the display. Then take your reference shot.

After you complete the process, the camera automatically sets the White Balance option to PRE so that you can begin using your preset. Your custom setting is stored in the camera until you override the setting with a new preset. Whenever you want to use the preset again, just choose PRE as the White Balance setting.

Matching white balance to an existing photo

Suppose that you're the marketing manager for a small business and one of your jobs is to shoot portraits of the company bigwigs for the annual report.

You build a small studio just for that purpose, complete with a couple of photography lights and a nice, conservative beige backdrop. Of course, the bigwigs can't all show up to get their pictures taken in the same month, let alone on the same day. But you have to make sure that the colors in that beige backdrop remain consistent for each shot, no matter how much time passes between photo sessions. This scenario is one possible use for a feature that enables you to create a White Balance preset based on an existing photo.

Two words of caution:

- ✔ Basing white balance on an existing photo works well only in strictly controlled lighting situations, where the color temperature of the lights is consistent from day to day. Otherwise, the White Balance setting that produces color accuracy when you shoot Big Boss Number One may add an ugly color cast to the one you snap of Big Boss Number Two.

- ✔ If you previously created a preset using the direct measurement option, you wipe out that preset when you base a preset on an existing photo.

With those caveats out of the way, follow these steps to create a preset based on a photo:

1. **Copy the picture that you want to use as the reference photo to your camera memory card, if it isn't already stored there.**

   You can copy the picture to the card using a card reader and whatever method you usually use to transfer files from one drive to another. Assuming that you're using the default folder names, copy the file to the 100D5500 folder, inside the main DCIM folder.

2. **Open the Shooting menu and select White Balance.**

3. **Select PRE Preset Manual and then press the Multi Selector right (or tap the PRE item on the screen one more time).**

   The screen shown on the left in Figure 5-10 appears.

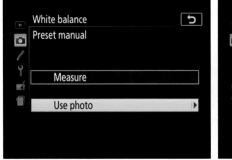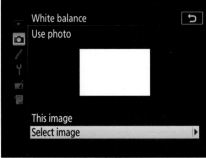

Figure 5-10: You can create a white balance preset based on a photo.

4. **Select Use Photo.**

   After you select the setting, the options shown on the right in Figure 5-10 appear. If you haven't yet used the photo option to store a preset, you see an empty white box in the middle of the screen, as shown in the figure. If you previously selected a photo to use as a preset reference, the thumbnail for that image appears instead.

5. **Choose Select Image and select the photo you want to use as the preset reference photo.**

   After you choose Select Image, select the folder that contains the image you want to use. Thumbnails of images in that folder then appear. Select the photo you want to use to return to the screen shown on the right in Figure 5-10. Your selected photo appears on the screen, and This Image appears highlighted.

6. **Tap the return arrow or press OK to set the preset white balance based on the selected photo.**

Whenever you want to base white balance on your selected photo, just set the White Balance setting to the PRE option.

Bracketing white balance

Chapter 3 introduces you to automatic exposure bracketing, which records the same image at different exposure settings or Active D-Lighting settings. You also can bracket white balance, creating a series of three images recorded at different white-balance settings.

Note the following details about this feature:

- **Bracketing is available only in the P, S, A, and M exposure modes.** Chapter 3 tells you how to use these exposure modes, if you haven't yet discovered them.

- **You must set the Image Quality option to one of the JPEG options (Fine, Normal, or Basic).** Why is the Raw (NEF) setting off limits? Because with Raw, white balance and other color settings aren't established until you process your images. So there's no reason to waste time bracketing white balance when you shoot Raw — you just adjust colors as you see fit during the Raw conversion process. (Chapter 9 shows you how to use the in-camera Raw converter.)

- **You can apply white balance bracketing only along the blue-to-amber axis of the color grid.** You can't shift colors along the green-to-magenta axis, as you can when tweaking a specific White Balance setting.

- **A single press of the shutter button creates all three images.** The camera captures the first photo at the selected White Balance setting and then creates two copies, one shifted toward amber and one toward blue.

✔ **You can shift colors from one to three steps between frames.** As an example of the maximum color shift you can achieve, refer to Figure 5-11, which I created using a three-step shift. As you can see, even at that "max" setting, the differences among the shots are subtle.

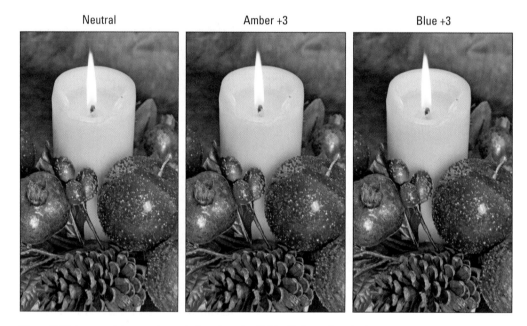

| Neutral | Amber +3 | Blue +3 |

Figure 5-11: I created three color variations by using White Balance bracketing.

To use White Balance bracketing, take these steps:

1. **Set the Auto Bracketing Set option on the Custom Setting menu to White Balance, as shown in Figure 5-12.**

   Look for the option in the Bracketing/Flash section of the Custom Setting menu.

2. **Enable bracketing and set the bracketing shift amount via the control strip, as shown in Figure 5-13.**

   As always, just press the *i* button to display the control strip.

   After you enable bracketing, the Information display shows bracketing indicators, as shown in Figure 5-14, reminding you that white balance bracketing is in force. The same indicator appears in the lower-right corner of the Live View display.

3. **To record the bracketed series, press the shutter button once.**

   The camera captures the first image at the current White Balance setting and then spends a few seconds creating two bracketed copies.

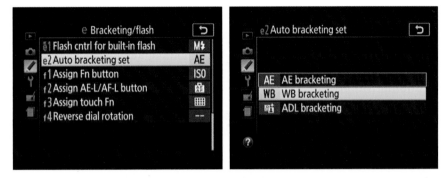

Figure 5-12: Tell the camera you want to bracket white balance by way of this Custom Setting menu option.

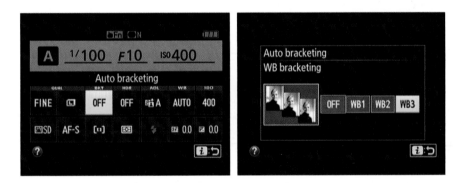

Figure 5-13: Enable bracketing and set the amount of color shift from the control strip.

4. **When you finish taking your bracketed shots, return to the control strip and turn off bracketing.**

   This step is important because the bracketing setting remains in effect even after you shut off the camera, and it's all too easy to overlook the fact that the feature is enabled when you head out for your next shoot.

If you view your photos in a playback mode that displays color data, the White Balance readout indicates which shots were shifted along the color axis. For the amber version, you see the letter *A;* for the blue version, *B.* Next

White Balance bracketing indicator

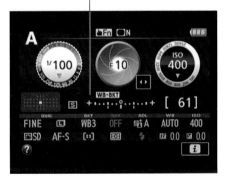

Figure 5-14: These markings remind you that white balance bracketing is enabled.

Choosing a color space: sRGB versus Adobe RGB

By default, your camera captures images using the *sRGB color space,* which refers to an industry-standard spectrum of colors. (The *s* is for *standard,* and the *RGB* is for *red, green, blue,* which are the primary colors in the digital color world.) This color space was created to help ensure color consistency as an image moves from camera (or scanner) to monitor and printer; the idea was to create a spectrum of colors that all devices can reproduce.

Because sRGB excludes some colors that *can* be reproduced in print and onscreen, at least by some devices, your camera also enables you to shoot in the Adobe RGB color space, which contains a larger spectrum of colors. You make the switch via the Color Space option on the Shooting menu.

Although using a larger color spectrum sounds like a no-brainer, choosing Adobe RGB isn't necessarily the right choice. Consider these factors when making your decision:

✔ Some colors in the Adobe RGB spectrum can't be reproduced in print; the printer substitutes the closest printable color, if necessary.

✔ If you print and share your photos without making any adjustments in your photo editor, sRGB is a better choice because most printers and web browsers are designed around that color space.

✔ To retain the original Adobe RGB colors when you work with your photos, your editing software must support that color space — not all programs do. You also must be willing to study the topic of digital color a little because you need to use specific software and printing settings to avoid mucking up the color works.

One final tip with regard to this option: The picture filename indicates which color space you used. Filenames of Adobe RGB images start with an underscore, as in _DSC0627.jpg. For pictures captured in sRGB, the underscore appears in the middle of the filename, as in DSC_0627.jpg.

to the letter, the value 1, 2, or 3 indicates the increment of color shift. For the neutral shot, the readout displays 0, 0. Chapter 8 shows you how to view this type of data during playback.

Taking a Quick Look at Picture Controls

When you capture photos using the JPEG Image Quality settings (Fine, Normal, or Basic), colors are also affected by the Picture Control setting. This option affects other picture characteristics that the camera tweaks when you shoot in the JPEG format, including contrast and sharpening.

Sharpening is a software process that boosts contrast in a special way to create the illusion of slightly sharper focus. Let me emphasize, "slightly sharper focus." Sharpening produces a subtle *tweak;* it's not a fix for poor focus.

In the P, S, A, and M exposure modes, you can choose from the following Picture Controls, represented on the menus and in the displays by the two-letter codes labeled in Figure 5-15. In other exposure modes, the camera selects the Picture Control setting.

Picture Control setting

Figure 5-15: This two-letter code represents the Picture Control setting.

- ✔ **Standard (SD):** The default setting, this option captures the image "normally" — that is, using the characteristics that Nikon offers up as suitable for the majority of subjects.

- ✔ **Neutral (NL):** At this setting, the camera doesn't enhance color, contrast, and sharpening as much as in the other modes. The setting is designed for people who want to precisely manipulate these picture characteristics in a photo editor. By not overworking colors, sharpening, and so on when producing your original file, the camera delivers an original that gives you more latitude in the digital darkroom.

- ✔ **Vivid (VI):** In this mode, the camera amps up color saturation, contrast, and sharpening.

- ✔ **Monochrome (MC):** This setting produces black-and-white photos. However, in the digital world, they're called *grayscale images* because a true black-and-white image contains only black and white, with no shades of gray.

  I'm not keen on creating grayscale images this way. I prefer to shoot in full color and then do my own grayscale conversion in my photo editor. That technique just gives you more control over the look of your black-and-white photos. Assuming that you work with a decent photo editor, you can control what original tones are emphasized in your grayscale version, for example. Additionally, keep in mind that you can always convert a color image to grayscale, but you can't go in the other direction. You can create a black-and-white copy of your color image directly in the camera, in fact; Chapter 11 shows you how.

✔ **Portrait (PT):** This mode tweaks colors and sharpening in a way that is designed to produce nice skin texture and pleasing skin tones. (If you shoot in the Portrait or Night Portrait Scene modes, the camera selects this Picture Control for you.)

✔ **Landscape (LS):** This mode emphasizes blues and greens. As you might expect, it's the mode used by the Landscape Scene mode.

✔ **Flat (FL):** A close cousin to the Neutral setting, the Flat setting produces, well, flat-looking images with little contrast or sharpness and reduced saturation. Like Neutral, this one is meant for photos that you plan to edit extensively to alter color, contrast, and sharpening. It's also especially useful to videographers who plan to do a lot of post-processing to their footage. Nikon claims that this mode holds onto the widest possible tonal range that the camera can capture in the JPEG format. (*Tonal range* refers to the range of brightness values in an image.)

The extent to which Picture Controls affect an image depends on the subject, but Figure 5-16 gives you a general idea of what to expect from the six full-color options. As you can see, Standard, Vivid, and Landscape produce pretty similar results, as do Portrait and Neutral. As for Flat — well, to my eye, that rendition *needs* extensive editing to bring it to life. (Again, I don't recommend using the Monochrome setting; instead, shoot in color and then create a black-and-white copy later.)

While you're new to the camera, I recommend sticking with the default Picture Control setting, Standard, which works well for most subjects. With all the other settings you have to worry about — f-stop, shutter speed, ISO, and all the rest — save experimenting with Picture Controls for a later day. In fact, if you really want to play with the characteristics that the Picture Control setting affects, you're better off shooting in the Raw (NEF) format and then making those adjustments as you process your Raw images. The camera tags the Raw file with whatever Picture Control is active when you take the shot, and that tag is used to render the image during playback mode. But the image adjustments are in no way set in stone, or even in sand — you can manipulate your photo at will during the image-processing stage.

For example, when you use the camera's built-in Raw processor, a feature I explain in Chapter 9, you can experiment with different Picture Control settings to see how each one affects the image. You have the same option when you process your Raw images using the free Nikon software Nikon ViewNX 2. That program's Raw converters, as well as those found in Adobe Photoshop and other third-party programs, offer other ways to fine-tune color, contrast, and sharpness as well.

If you do want to change the Picture Control setting, you can get the job done quickly via the control strip, as shown in Figure 5-17, or the Shooting menu, as shown in Figure 5-18.

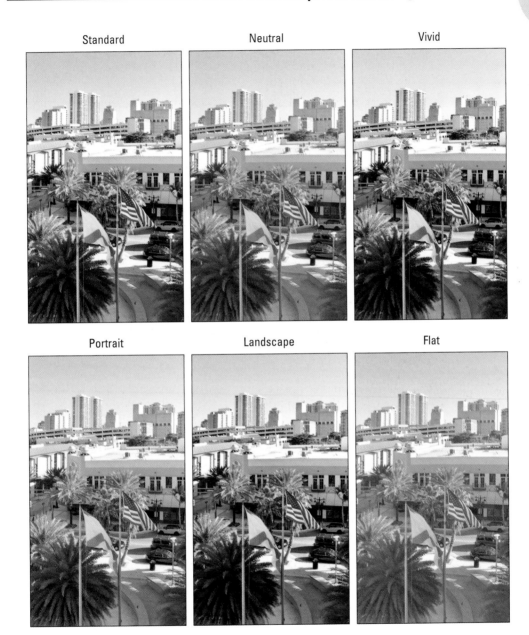

Standard   Neutral   Vivid

Portrait   Landscape   Flat

Figure 5-16: Picture controls apply preset adjustments to color, sharpening, and contrast to images you shoot in the JPEG file format.

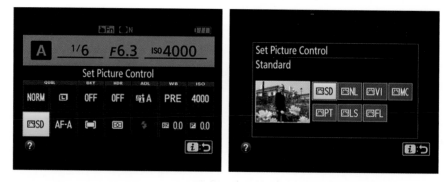

Figure 5-17: The fastest way to select a Picture Control is by using the control strip.

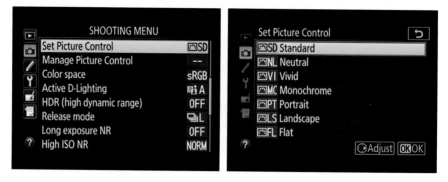

Figure 5-18: But the Shooting menu provides access to settings that let you tweak the results of each Picture Control.

Using the control strip is faster — just press the *i* button or tap the *i* icon on the monitor to bring up the strip — but the menu offers an option you can't get to from the strip: You can modify an existing Picture Control to increase or decrease color saturation, adjust the amount of sharpening, and so on. Press the Multi Selector right or tap the Adjust icon at the bottom of the screen shown on the right in Figure 5-18 to get to the options available for the current Picture Control.

To reserve page space in this book for functions that I believe are the most useful, I opted not to provide full details here about customizing Picture Controls. But you can find step-by-step instructions by going to the Extras page for this book at www.dummies.com/extras/nikon.

6

Putting It All Together

*E*arlier chapters of this book break down each and every picture-taking feature on your camera, describing in detail how the various controls affect exposure, picture quality, focus, color, and the like. This chapter pulls together all that information to help you set up your camera for specific types of photography.

Keep in mind, though, that there are no hard-and-fast rules for the "right way" to shoot a portrait, a landscape, or whatever. So feel free to wander off on your own, tweaking this exposure setting or adjusting that focus control, to discover your own creative vision. Experimentation is part of the fun of photography, after all — and thanks to your camera monitor and the Delete button, it's an easy, completely free proposition.

Recapping Basic Picture Settings

Your subject, creative goals, and lighting conditions determine which settings you should use for certain picture-taking options, such as aperture and shutter speed. I offer my take on those options throughout this chapter. But for many basic options, I recommend the same settings for almost every shooting scenario. Table 6-1 shows you those recommendations and also lists the chapter where you can find details about each setting.

Table 6-1	All-Purpose Picture-Taking Settings	
Option	**Recommended Setting**	**See This Chapter**
Active D-Lighting	Off	3
AF-area mode	Still subjects, Single Point; moving subjects, 9-, 21-, or 39-point Dynamic Area	4
Exposure mode	P, S, A, or M	3
Focus mode	For autofocusing on still subjects, AF-S; moving subjects, AF-C	4
Image Quality	JPEG Fine or Raw (NEF)	2
Image Size	Large or medium	2
ISO Sensitivity	100	3
Metering	Matrix	3
Release mode	Action photos: Continuous Low or High; all others: Single Frame	2
White Balance	Auto	5

One key point: The instructions in this chapter assume that you set the exposure mode to P, S, A, or M, as indicated in the table. These modes, detailed in Chapter 3, are the only ones that give you access to the entire cadre of camera features. In most cases, I recommend using S (shutter-priority autoexposure) when controlling motion blur is important, and A (aperture-priority autoexposure) when controlling depth of field is important. These two modes let you concentrate on one side of the exposure equation and let the camera handle the other. Of course, if you're comfortable making both the aperture and shutter speed decisions, you may prefer to work in M (manual) exposure mode instead. P (programmed autoexposure) is my last choice because it makes choosing a specific aperture or shutter speed more cumbersome.

Additionally, this chapter discusses choices for viewfinder photography. Although most picture settings work the same way during Live View photography as they do for viewfinder photography, the focusing process is quite different. For help with Live View focusing, visit Chapter 4.

Shooting Still Portraits

By *still portrait*, I mean that your subject isn't moving. For subjects who aren't keen on sitting still, skip to the next section and use the techniques given for action photography instead. Assuming that you do have a subject willing to pose, the classic portraiture approach is to keep the subject sharply focused while throwing the background into soft focus. This artistic choice emphasizes the subject and helps diminish the impact of any distracting background objects. The following steps show you how to achieve this look:

1. **Set the Mode dial to A (aperture-priority autoexposure) and select a low f-stop value.**

   A low f-stop setting opens the aperture, which not only allows more light to enter the camera but also shortens *depth of field,* or the distance over which focus appears sharp. So dialing in a low f-stop value is the first step in softening a portrait background. However, for a group portrait, don't go too low or else the depth of field may not be enough to keep everyone in the sharp-focus zone. Take test shots and inspect the results at different f-stops to find the right setting.

   Again, I recommend using aperture-priority mode when depth of field is a concern, because you can control the f-stop while relying on the camera to select the shutter speed. (You need to pay attention to shutter speed as well, however, to make sure that it's not so slow that movement of the subject or camera will blur the image.)

   You can monitor the current f-stop and shutter speed in the Information display and viewfinder, as shown in Figure 6-1. To adjust f-stop in A mode, rotate the Command dial or use the touchscreen controls (start by tapping the arrow box under the f-stop readout on the display).

Shutter speed   Aperture

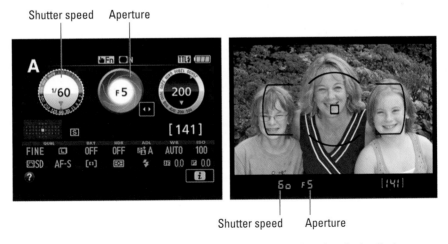

Shutter speed   Aperture

Figure 6-1: You can monitor aperture (f-stop) and shutter speed settings in the displays.

2. **To further soften the background, zoom in, get closer, and put more distance between the subject and background.**

   Zooming in to a longer focal length also reduces depth of field, as does moving physically closer to your subject. And the greater the distance between the subject and background, the more the background blurs. (A good rule is to place the subject at least an arm's length away from the background.)

   Avoid using a lens with a short focal length (a wide-angle lens) for portraits. They can cause features to appear distorted — sort of like how people look when you view them through the security peephole in a door. A lens with a focal length of 85–120mm is ideal for a classic head-and-shoulders portrait.

3. **Check composition.**

   Just two quick pointers on this topic:

   - *Consider the background.* Scan the entire frame, looking for background objects that may distract the eye from the subject. If necessary, reposition the subject against a more flattering backdrop.

   - *Frame the subject loosely to allow for later cropping to a variety of frame sizes.* Your camera produces images that have an aspect ratio of 3:2. That means your portrait perfectly fits a 4 x 6 print size but will require cropping to print at any other proportion, such as 5 x 7 or 8 x 10.

4. **For indoor portraits, shoot flash-free, if possible.**

   Shooting by available light rather than by flash produces softer illumination and avoids the problem of red-eye. To get enough light to go flash-free, turn on room lights or, during daylight, pose your subject next to a sunny window, as I did for the image in Figure 6-2.

   In the A exposure mode, simply keeping the built-in flash unit closed disables the flash. If flash is unavoidable, see my list of flash tips at the end of this step list to get better results.

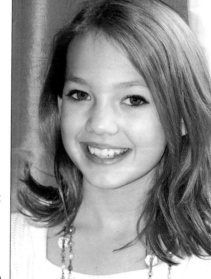

Figure 6-2: For more pleasing indoor portraits, shoot by available light instead of using flash.

5. For outdoor portraits, use a flash if possible.

Even in daylight, a flash adds a beneficial pop of light to subjects' faces, as illustrated in Figure 6-3. A flash is especially important when the background is brighter than the subjects, as in this example.

In the A exposure mode, press the Flash button on the side of the camera to raise the built-in flash. For daytime portraits, set the Flash mode to Fill Flash. (That's the regular, basic Flash mode.) For nighttime images, try red-eye reduction or slow-sync flash; again, see the flash tips at the end of these steps to use either mode most effectively.

By default, the top shutter speed for flash photography is 1/200 second, so in bright light, you may need to stop down the aperture to avoid overexposing the photo, as I did for the bottom image in Figure 6-3. Doing so, of course, brings the background into sharper focus, so if that creates an issue, move the subject into a shaded area instead.

No flash

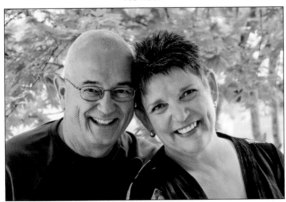

Fill flash

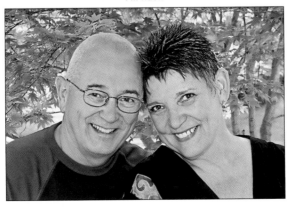

Figure 6-3: To properly illuminate the face in outdoor portraits, use flash.

6. **Press and hold the shutter button halfway to initiate exposure metering and autofocusing.**

   If the camera has trouble finding the correct focusing distance, you may be too close to your subject. Don't forget that you always have the option to focus manually, too (but the close-focusing distance doesn't change when you do so). See Chapter 4 for help with focusing.

7. **Press the shutter button the rest of the way to capture the image.**

When flash is unavoidable, try these tricks to produce better results:

✓ **Indoors, turn on as many room lights as possible.** With more ambient light, you reduce the flash power that's needed to expose the picture. Adding light also causes the pupils to constrict, further reducing the chances of red-eye. As an added benefit, the smaller pupil allows more of the subject's iris to be visible in the portrait, so you see more eye color.

✓ **Try using a Flash mode that enables red-eye reduction or slow-sync flash.** If you choose the first option, warn your subject to expect both a preliminary light from the AF-assist lamp, which constricts pupils, and the flash. And remember that slow-sync flash modes use a slower-than-normal shutter speed, which produces softer lighting and brighter backgrounds than normal flash. (Chapter 2 explains the various Flash modes.)

Take a look at Figure 6-4 for an example of how using slow-sync flash can improve an indoor portrait. When I used regular flash, the shutter speed was 1/60 second. At that speed, the camera has little time to soak up any ambient light. As a result, the scene is lit primarily by the flash. That caused two problems: The strong flash created some glare on the subject's skin, and the window panes and frame are much more prominent because of the contrast between them and the darker bushes outside the window. Although it was daylight when I took the picture, the skies were overcast, so at 1/60 second, the exterior appears dark.

In the slow-sync example, shot at 1/4 second, the exposure time was long enough to permit the ambient light to brighten the exteriors to the point that the window frame almost blends into the background. And because much less flash power was needed to expose the subject, the lighting is much more flattering. In this case, the bright background also helps to set the subject apart because of her dark hair and shirt. If the subject had been a pale blonde, this setup wouldn't have worked as well. Again, too, note the warming effect that can occur when you use Auto White Balance and shoot in a combination of flash and daylight.

Using a slower-than-normal shutter speed increases the risk of blur due to camera shake, so use a tripod or otherwise steady the camera. Remind your subjects to stay absolutely still, too, because they'll appear blurry if they move during the exposure. I was fortunate to have both a tripod and a cooperative subject for my examples, but I probably wouldn't opt for slow-sync for portraits of young children or pets.

Regular fill flash, 1/60 second   Slow-sync flash, 1/4 second

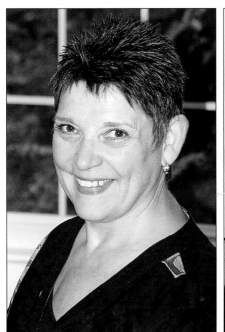 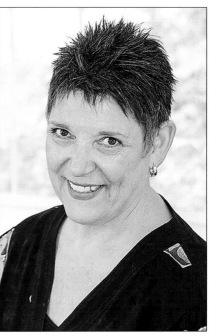

Figure 6-4: Slow-sync flash produces softer, more even lighting and brighter backgrounds.

✔ **For professional results, use an external flash with a rotating flash head.** Aim the flash head upward so that the flash light bounces off the ceiling and falls softly down onto the subject. External flashes can be pricey, but the results make the purchase worthwhile if you shoot lots of portraits. Compare the two portraits in Figure 6-5 for an illustration. In the first example, using the built-in flash resulted in strong shadowing behind the subject and harsh, concentrated light. To produce the better result on the right, I used a Nikon Speedlight external flash and bounced the light off the ceiling. I also moved the subject a few feet farther in front of the background to create more background blur.

Make sure that the ceiling or other surface you use to bounce the light is white; otherwise, the flash light will pick up the color of the surface and influence the color of your subject.

✔ **Invest in a flash diffuser to further soften the light.** A *diffuser* is simply a piece of translucent plastic or fabric that you place over the flash to soften and spread the light — much like how sheer curtains diffuse window light. Diffusers come in lots of different designs, including models that fit over the built-in flash.

✔ **Pay attention to white balance if your subject is lit by both flash and ambient light.** If you set the White Balance setting to Auto, as I recommend in Table 6-1, enabling flash tells the camera to warm colors to compensate for the cool light of a flash. If your subject is also lit by other light sources, such as sunlight, the result may be colors that are slightly warmer or cooler (more blue) than neutral. A warming effect typically looks nice in portraits, giving the skin a subtle glow. If you aren't happy with the result, see Chapter 5 to find out how to fine-tune white balance.

Direct flash Bounce flash

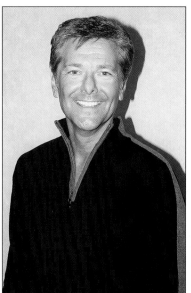 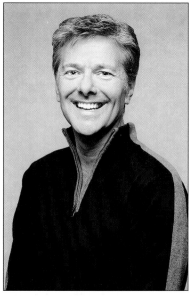

Figure 6-5: To eliminate harsh lighting and strong shadows (left), use bounce flash and move the subject farther from the background (right).

Capturing Action

Using a fast shutter speed is the key to capturing a blur-free shot of any moving subject, whether it's a flower in the breeze, a spinning Ferris wheel, or, as in the case of Figure 6-6, a racing cyclist.

Along with the basic capture settings outlined earlier, in Table 6-1, try the techniques in the following steps to photograph a subject in motion:

1. Set the Mode dial to S (shutter-priority autoexposure).

In this mode, you control the shutter speed, and the camera takes care of choosing an aperture setting that will produce a good exposure.

2. Select the shutter speed.

Refer to Figure 6-1 to locate shutter speed in the Information display and viewfinder. In S mode, you adjust shutter speed by rotating the Command dial or by using the touchscreen control found under the shutter-speed display in the Information screen.

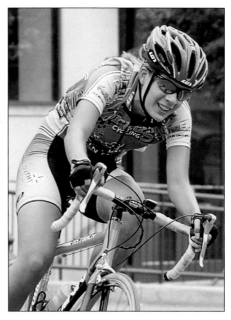

Figure 6-6: Use a high shutter speed to freeze motion.

What shutter speed should you choose? Well, it depends on the speed at which your subject is moving, so you need to experiment. But generally speaking, 1/320 second should be plenty for all but the fastest subjects (race cars, boats, and so on). For very slow subjects, you can even go as low as 1/250 or 1/125 second. My subject in Figure 6-6 zipped along at a pretty fast pace, so I set the shutter speed to 1/500 second. Remember, though, that when you increase shutter speed, the camera opens the aperture to maintain the same exposure. At low f-stop numbers, depth of field becomes shorter, so you have to be more careful to keep your subject within the sharp-focus zone as you compose and focus the shot.

You also can take an entirely different approach to capturing action: Rather than choose a fast shutter speed, select a speed slow enough to blur the moving objects, which can create a heightened sense of motion and, in scenes that feature very colorful subjects, cool abstract images. I took this approach when shooting the carnival ride featured in Figure 6-7, for example. For the left image, I set the shutter speed to 1/30 second; for the right version, I slowed things down to 1/5 second. In both cases, I used a tripod, but because nearly everything in the frame was moving, the entirety of both photos is blurry — the 1/5 second version is simply more blurry because of the slower shutter.

3. In dim lighting, raise the ISO setting, if necessary, to allow a fast shutter speed.

Unless you're shooting in bright daylight, you may not be able to use a fast shutter speed at a low ISO, even if the camera opens the aperture as far as possible. If auto ISO override is in force, ISO may go up automatically when you increase the shutter speed — Chapter 3 has details on that feature. Raising the ISO does increase the possibility of noise, so you have to decide whether a noisy shot is better than a blurry shot.

1/30 second   1/5 second

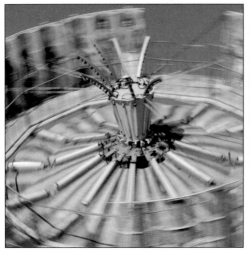 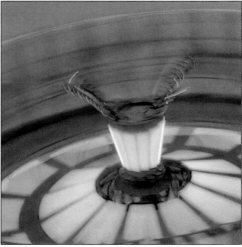

Figure 6-7: Using a shutter speed slow enough to blur moving objects can be a fun creative choice, too.

Why not add flash to brighten the scene? Well, adding flash is tricky for action shots, unfortunately. First, the flash needs time to recycle between shots, which slows the capture rate. Second, the built-in flash has limited range, so don't waste your time if your subject isn't close by. And third, remember that the fastest shutter speed you can use with flash is 1/200 second by default, which may not be high enough to capture a quickly moving subject without blur.

4. **For rapid-fire shooting, set the Release mode to Continuous Low or Continuous High.**

   In both modes, you can capture multiple images with a single press of the shutter button. Continuous Low captures up to 3 frames per second (fps), and Continuous High bumps the frame rate up to about 5 fps. As long as you hold down the button, the camera continues to record images. Here again, though, you need to go flash-free; otherwise, you get one shot per press of the shutter button, just as in Single Frame release mode.

5. **Select speed-oriented focusing options.**

   For fastest shooting, try manual focusing: It eliminates the time the camera needs to lock focus when you use autofocusing. If you use auto-focus, select these two autofocus settings for best performance:

   • Set the AF-area mode to one of the Dynamic Area settings. Chapter 4 has information to help you decide whether the 9-point, 21-point, or 39-point Dynamic Area setting is best for your subject.

   • Set the Autofocus mode to AF-C (continuous-servo autofocus).

You can adjust both focus settings via the control strip; press the *i* button or tap the onscreen *i* icon to activate the strip. The focus settings are found adjacent to each other on the second row of the strip. Be sure to set the switch on your lens to the autofocus position, too.

At these settings, the camera sets focus initially on your selected focus point but then looks to the surrounding points for focusing information if your subject moves away from the selected point. Focus is adjusted continuously until you take the shot.

6. Compose the subject to allow for movement across the frame.

Frame your shot a little wider than you normally might so that you lessen the risk that your subject will move out of the frame before you record the image. You can always crop to a tighter composition later. (I used this approach for my cyclist image — the original shot includes a lot of background that I later cropped away.) It's also a good idea to leave more room in front of the subject than behind it. This makes it obvious that your subject is going somewhere.

Using these techniques should give you a better chance of capturing any fast-moving subject, but action-shooting strategies also are helpful for shooting candid portraits of kids and pets. Even if they aren't currently running, leaping, or otherwise cavorting, snapping a shot before they do move is often tough. So if an interaction catches your eye, set your camera into action mode and fire off a series of shots as fast as you can.

Capturing Scenic Vistas

Providing specific capture settings for landscape photography is tricky because there's no single best approach to capturing a beautiful stretch of countryside, a city skyline, or another vast subject. Most people prefer using a wide-angle lens, for example, to incorporate a large area of the landscape into the scene, but if you're far away from your subject, you may like the results you get from a telephoto or medium-angle lens. When shooting the scene in Figure 6-8, for example, I had to position myself across the street from the buildings, so I captured the shot using a focal length of 82mm. And consider depth of field: One person's idea of a super cityscape might be to keep all buildings in the scene sharply focused, but another photographer might prefer to shoot the same scene so that a foreground building is sharply focused while the others are less so, thus drawing the eye to that first building.

I can, however, offer a few tips to help you photograph a landscape the way *you* see it:

✓ **Shoot in aperture-priority autoexposure mode (A) so that you can control depth of field.** If you want extreme depth of field so that both near

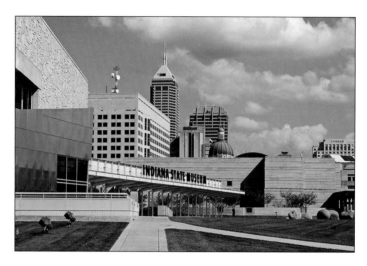

Figure 6-8: Use a high f-stop value to keep the foreground and background sharply focused.

and distant objects are sharply focused (refer to Figure 6-8), select a high f-stop value. I used an aperture of f/18 for this shot. For short depth of field, use a low value.

✔ **If the exposure requires a slow shutter speed, use a tripod to avoid blurring.** The downside to a high f-stop is that you may need a slower shutter speed to produce a good exposure. If the shutter speed drops below what you can comfortably handhold, use a tripod to avoid picture-blurring camera shake.

✔ **For dramatic waterfall shots, consider using a slow shutter to create that "misty" look.** The slow shutter blurs the water, giving it a soft, romantic appearance, as shown in Figure 6-9. Again, use a tripod to ensure that the rest of the scene doesn't also blur due to camera shake. Shutter speed for the image in Figure 6-9 was 1/5 second.

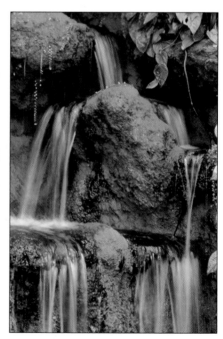

Figure 6-9: For misty waterfalls, use a slow shutter speed and a tripod.

In very bright light, you may overexpose the image at a very slow shutter, even if you stop the aperture all the way down and select the camera's lowest ISO setting. As a solution, consider investing in a *neutral density filter* for your lens. This type of filter works something like sunglasses for your camera: It simply reduces the amount of light that passes through the lens, without affecting image colors, so that you can use a slower shutter than would otherwise be possible.

✔ **At sunrise or sunset, base exposure on the sky.** The foreground will be dark, but you can usually brighten it in a photo editor, if needed. If you base exposure on the foreground, on the other hand, the sky will become so bright that all the color will be washed out — a problem you usually can't fix after the fact. You can also invest in a *graduated neutral-density filter,* which is clear on one side and dark on the other. You orient the filter so that the dark half falls over the sky and the clear side falls over the dimly lit portion of the scene. This setup enables you to better expose the foreground without blowing out the sky colors.

Also experiment with the Active D-Lighting and HDR features that I cover in Chapter 3; both are designed to create images that contain a greater range of brightness values than is normally possible.

✔ **For cool nighttime city pics, experiment with slow shutter speeds.** Assuming that cars or other vehicles with their lights on are moving through the scene, the result is neon trails of light like those you see in the foreground of the image in Figure 6-10. Shutter speed for this image was about 10 seconds.

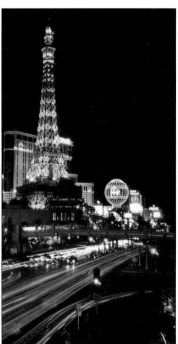

Rather than change the shutter speed manually between each shot, try *Bulb* mode. Available only in M (manual) exposure mode, this option records an image for as long as you hold down the shutter button. So just take a series of images, holding down the button for different lengths of time for each shot. In Bulb mode, you also can exceed the standard maximum exposure time of 30 seconds.

✔ **For the best lighting, shoot during the** *magic hours.* That's the term photographers use for early morning and late afternoon, when the light cast by the sun is soft and warm, giving everything that beautiful, gently warmed look.

Figure 6-10: Using a slow shutter speed creates neon light trails in nighttime city street scenes.

Can't wait for the perfect light? Tweak your camera's White Balance setting, using the instructions laid out in Chapter 5, to simulate the color of magic-hour light.

✔ **In tricky light, bracket exposures.** *Bracketing* simply means to take the same picture at several different exposure settings to increase the odds that at least one of them will capture the scene the way you envision. Bracketing is especially a good idea in difficult lighting situations, such as sunrise and sunset. Chapter 3 shows you how to make bracketing easier by using automatic exposure bracketing.

✔ **For wide-angle landscape shots, try including a person in the frame.** By comparing the size of the person with the surrounding landscape, the viewer gets a better idea of the vastness of the setting.

Capturing Dynamic Close-Ups

For great close-up shots, try these techniques:

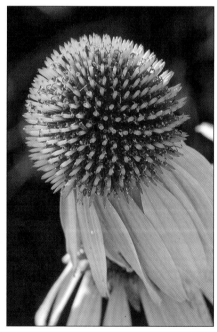

Figure 6-11: Shallow depth of field is a classic technique for close-up floral images.

✔ **Check your lens manual to find out its minimum close-focusing distance.** How "up close and personal" you can get to your subject depends on your lens, not on the camera body.

✔ **Take control over depth of field by setting the camera mode to A (aperture-priority autoexposure) mode.** Whether you want a shallow, medium, or extreme depth of field depends on the point of your photo. In classic nature photography, for example, the artistic tradition is a very shallow depth of field, as shown in Figure 6-11, and requires an open aperture (low f-stop value). If you want the viewer to be able to clearly see all details throughout the frame — for example, you're shooting a product shot for a sales catalog — you need to go in the other direction, stopping down the aperture as far as possible.

✔ **Remember that depth of field decreases when you zoom in or move closer to your subject.** Go back to that product shot: If you need depth of field beyond what you can achieve with the aperture setting, you may need to back away, zoom out, or both. (You can always crop your image to show just the parts of the subject that you want to feature.)

✓ **When shooting flowers and other nature scenes outdoors, pay attention to shutter speed, too.** Even a slight breeze may cause your subject to move, causing blurring at slow shutter speeds.

✓ **Use flash for better outdoor lighting.** Just as with portraits, a tiny bit of flash typically improves close-ups when the sun is the primary light source. Again, though, keep in mind that the maximum shutter speed possible when you use the built-in flash is 1/200 second. So in very bright light, you may need to use a high f-stop setting to avoid overexposing the picture. You can also adjust the flash output via the Flash Compensation control. Chapter 2 offers details.

✓ **When shooting indoors, try not to use flash as the primary light source.** Because you're shooting at close range, the light from your flash may be too harsh even at a low Flash Compensation setting. If flash is inevitable, turn on as many room lights as possible to reduce the flash power that's needed — even a shop light from a hardware store can do in a pinch as a lighting source. (Remember that if you have multiple light sources, though, you may need to tweak the White Balance setting.)

✓ **To get really close to your subject, invest in a macro lens or a set of diopters.** A true macro lens, which enables you to get really, really close to your subjects, is an expensive proposition; prices range from a few hundred to a couple thousand dollars. If you enjoy capturing the tiny details in life, though, it's worth the investment.

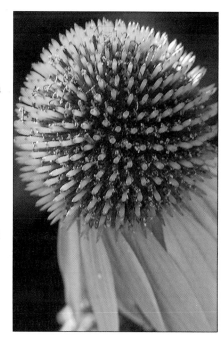

Nikon has a great guide to its macro lenses — officially titled *Micro-Nikkor Lenses* — at its www.nikonusa.com website, if you're ready to start shopping.

For a less expensive way to go, you can spend about $40 for a set of *diopters,* which are sort of like reading glasses that you screw onto your existing lens. Diopters come in several strengths — +1, +2, +4, and so on — with a higher number indicating a greater magnifying power. I took this approach to capture the extreme close-up in Figure 6-12, attaching a +2 diopter to my lens.

Figure 6-12: To extend your lens's close-focus capability, you can add magnifying diopters.

The downside of using a diopter, sadly, is that it typically produces images that are very soft around the edges, a problem that doesn't occur with a good macro lens.

Coping with Special Situations

A few subjects and shooting situations pose some additional challenges not already covered in earlier sections. To close this chapter, here's a quick list of ideas for tackling a variety of common tough-shot photos:

✓ **Shooting fireworks:** First off, use a tripod; fireworks require a long exposure, and trying to handhold your camera simply won't work. If using a zoom lens, zoom out to the shortest focal length (widest angle). Switch to manual focusing and set focus at infinity (the farthest focus point possible on your lens). Set the exposure mode to manual, choose a relatively high f-stop setting — say, f/16 or so — and start at a shutter speed of 1 to 5 seconds. From there, it's simply a matter of experimenting with different shutter speeds. Also play with the timing of the shutter release, starting some exposures at the moment the fireworks are shot up, some at the moment they burst open, and so on. For the example featured in Figure 6-13, I used a shutter speed of about 5 seconds and began the exposure as the rocket was going up — that's what creates the "corkscrew" of light that rises up through the frame.

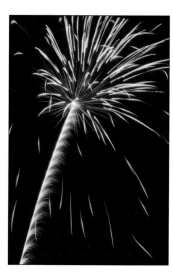

Figure 6-13: A shutter speed of 5 seconds captured this fireworks shot.

Be especially gentle when you press the shutter button — with a very slow shutter, you can easily create enough camera movement to blur the image. If you purchased the accessory remote control for your camera, this is a good situation in which to use it.

✓ **Shooting through glass:** To capture subjects that are behind glass, such as animals at a zoo, you can try a couple of tricks. First, set your camera to manual focusing — the glass barrier can give the autofocus mechanism fits. Disable the flash to avoid creating any unwanted reflections, too. Then, if you can get close enough, your best odds are to put the lens right up to the glass. (Be careful not to scratch your lens.) If you must stand farther away, try to position your lens at a 90-degree angle to the glass. I used this approach in Figure 6-14.

✓ **Shooting out a car window:** Set the camera to shutter-priority autoexposure or manual mode and dial in a fast shutter speed to compensate for the movement of the car. Also turn on Vibration Reduction, if your lens offers it. Oh, and keep a tight grip on your camera.

✓ **Shooting in strong backlighting:** When the light behind your subject is very strong, the result is often an underexposed subject. You can try using flash to better expose the subject, assuming that you're shooting in an exposure mode that permits flash. The Active D-Lighting feature covered in Chapter 3 can also help brighten your subject without blowing out highlights. And don't forget that your camera has a built-in HDR (high dynamic range) mode, which blends two exposures to include more shadows and highlights in the scene. (Chapter 3 has examples.)

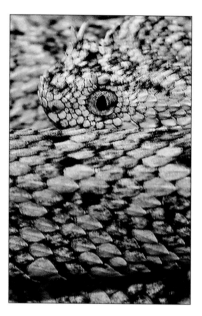

Figure 6-14: To photograph subjects that are behind glass, use manual focusing and disable flash.

For another creative choice, you can purposely underexpose the subject to create a silhouette effect, as shown in Figure 6-15. Base the exposure on the brightest areas of the background so that the darker areas of the frame remain dark.

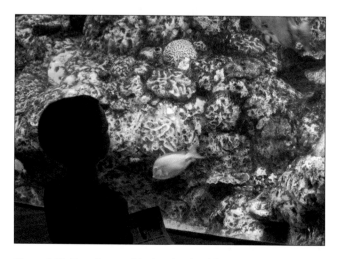

Figure 6-15: Experiment with shooting backlit subjects in silhouette.

Shooting, Viewing, and Trimming Movies

*I*n addition to being a stellar still-photography camera, your D5500 enables you to record HD (high-definition) movies. This chapter tells you everything you need to know to take advantage of the movie-recording options.

Check that: This chapter tells you *almost* everything about movie recording. What's missing here is detailed information about focusing, which works the same way for movie shooting as it does when you use Live View to shoot a still photo. Rather than cover the subject twice, I detail your focusing options in Chapter 4 and provide just a basic recap in these pages.

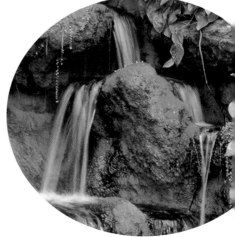

Also be sure to visit the end of Chapter 1, which lists precautions to take while Live View is engaged whether you're shooting stills or movies. (To answer your question: No, you can't use the viewfinder for movie recording; Live View is your only option.)

For even more insights into recording movies with a dSLR, hop online and check out Nikon Cinema, at `cinema.nikonusa.com`.

Shooting Movies Using the Default Settings

Video enthusiasts will appreciate the fact that the D5500 enables you to tweak a variety of movie-recording settings. But if you're not up to sorting through those options, just use the default settings. (You can restore the critical defaults by opening the Shooting menu and choosing Reset Shooting Menu.) At these settings, you get a full HD movie with sound enabled.

Movies are created in the MOV format, which means you can play them on your computer using most video-playback programs. You also can view movies in Nikon ViewNX 2, the free software provided with your camera. If you want to view your movies on a TV, see the end of Chapter 8 to find out how to connect your camera to your set.

The following steps show you how to record a movie using autofocusing. If you prefer manual focusing, just bypass the autofocusing instructions (again, you can find specifics on manual focusing during Live View in Chapter 4):

1. **Set the Mode dial on top of the camera to Auto.**

   In this mode, the camera takes care of most movie settings for you, including ones that affect exposure and color.

2. **Set the lens to autofocus mode.**

   Depending on your lens, you accomplish this by setting the lens switch to A, AF, or AF/M (auto with manual focus override). See your lens manual for help if you're unsure.

   Movie-record button

3. **Engage Live View by rotating the Live View switch, shown in Figure 7-1, toward the back of the camera.**

   The viewfinder goes dark, and your subject appears on the monitor.

4. **Press the Info button until the display is set to Show Movie Indicators view, as shown in Figure 7-2.**

   Later sections decode the various bits of data; for now, just pay attention to the available recording time readout, labeled in the figure. At the default settings, your movie can be 20 minutes long, but that number presumes that your memory

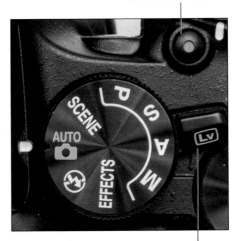

Live View switch

Figure 7-1: Rotate the Live View switch to toggle between Live View and viewfinder photography.

card has enough space on it to hold the entire movie. The maximum file size for a movie is 4GB (gigabytes).

If the upper-left corner of the screen displays the letters *REC* with a slash through them, something is amiss: That's the camera's way of telling you that movie recording isn't possible. You see this symbol if no memory card is inserted or the card is full, for example.

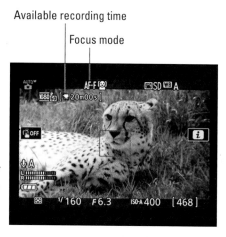

Figure 7-2: Press the Info button to cycle through the Live View display modes until you see these movie-recording symbols.

The picture-taking function of the Touch Shutter does not work during movie recording. (You see the word "Off" on the Touch Shutter icon on the right side of the screen, and tapping the icon does not enable the shutter-release option as it does during still shooting.) However, you can still use the touch screen to set focus and change camera settings.

5. **Set the Focus mode to AF-S or AF-F.**

The right choice depends on two factors: whether you're shooting a moving subject or a stationary one and whether you require pristine audio. Here's what you need to know to make the call:

- *AF-S:* Choose this option if you expect your subject to remain the same distance from the camera throughout the movie — for example, if you're recording a piano performance. (Think AF-*S,* for *stationary.*) To set focus quickly, tap the screen on the spot you want to be in focus. Or press the shutter button halfway and then lift your finger off the shutter button. For movies, focus remains set at the current distance throughout your recording unless you tap the screen or press the shutter button halfway again to reset focus.

- *AF-F:* This setting produces full-time, continuous autofocusing, with the camera adjusting focus as your subject moves or you pan the camera to follow the action. Focusing starts immediately after you set the Focus mode to AF-F. To lock focus, tap the screen or press the shutter button halfway. When you release the button or lift your finger from the screen, continuous autofocusing resumes. (In this case, using the shutter button to lock focus is easier than keeping your finger on the screen.)

Although AF-F autofocusing is best for tracking moving subjects, the built-in microphone sometimes picks up the sound of the focusing motor. To avoid this issue, you can attach an external microphone and place it far enough from the camera body that it can't hear the focus motor. The only other solutions are to switch to AF-S mode and lock in focus before you begin recording or to use manual focusing.

You can see the current Focus mode setting at the top of the monitor, as shown in Figure 7-2. To change the setting, use the control strip, as shown in Figure 7-3. *Remember:* Press the *i* button or tap the onscreen *i* symbol to bring up the control strip.

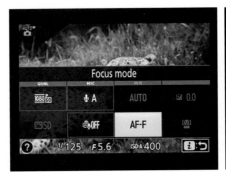 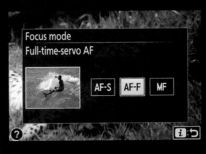

Figure 7-3: Set the Focus mode via the control strip.

6. **Compose your initial shot in the monitor.**

The shaded areas at the top and bottom of the monitor indicate the boundaries of the default frame size, 1920 x 1080 pixels, which produces a 16:9 aspect ratio.

7. **If necessary, move the focusing frame over your subject.**

By default, the camera uses the Face-Priority AF-area mode, which means that if your scene contains a face, the focusing system automatically focuses on that portion of the frame. In this scenario, you see a yellow focus frame over the face. When the scene contains more than one face, you see multiple frames; the one with the interior corner markings indicates the face chosen as the focus point. You can use the Multi Selector or tap the screen to move the frame over a different face.

If the camera doesn't detect a face, it instead uses the Wide Area AF-area mode, and the focus frame appears as a red rectangle (refer to Figure 7-2). Again, use the touchscreen or Multi Selector to move the frame over your subject.

8. **Focus the shot.**

Again, with AF-F focusing, you don't need to do anything; just wait for the focusing frame to turn green, indicating that initial focus is set. If you use the touchscreen to set focus in the AF-S mode, focus is locked as soon as you lift your finger from the screen. Again, the focus frame turns green when focus is achieved. To use the shutter button to focus, press the shutter button halfway until focus is achieved. You can then take your finger off the shutter button, if you want.

9. **To begin recording, press the red movie-record button on top of the camera (refer to Figure 7-1).**

   Most shooting data disappears from the screen, and a red Rec symbol flashes in the upper center, as shown in Figure 7-4. As recording progresses, the area labeled *Remaining recording time* in the figure shows you how many more minutes of video you can record.

10. **To stop recording, press the movie-record button again.**

    Your movie is recorded to the memory card.

Two quick tips to add to these basics:

- ✔ **Declutter the display by pressing the Info button.** The display changes to the Hide Indicators display mode, shown in Figure 7-5. In this mode, four white horizontal marks appear to indicate the 16:9 movie-framing area; I labeled one of the marks in the figure. Press Info again to display a grid over the scene. Here's an important caveat, though: In these display modes, pressing the *i* button brings up the control strip for still photography. To view the movie version, you must use the Show Movie Indicators display.

- ✔ **You can stop recording and capture a still image in one fell swoop.** Just press and hold the shutter button until you hear the shutter release. The number found within the brackets in the lower-right corner of the screen indicates how many still photos you can fit in the empty card space if you stop recording. As each second of recording ticks by and card space is depleted, the value that indicates the number of remaining still shots drops. For another option, you can save a single frame of your movie as a still photo. The last section of this chapter tells you how.

Remaining recording time

Recording symbol

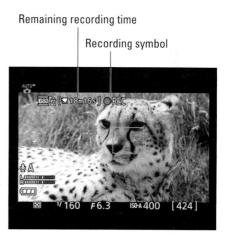

Figure 7-4: The red Rec symbol flashes while recording is in progress.

16:9 movie framing indicator

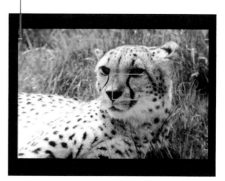

Figure 7-5: Press the Info button to hide most of the onscreen data.

Adjusting Video Settings

When you're ready to take more control over your movies, start by exploring the video settings detailed in the next three sections.

Choosing the video mode (NTSC or PAL)

The first option to consider is Video Mode, found on the Setup menu and shown in Figure 7-6. This setting determines whether movies adhere to the NTSC or PAL video standard. *NTSC* is used in North America; *PAL* is used in Europe and certain other countries. (Don't worry about what NTSC and PAL mean — they're just acronyms for the names of the standards.)

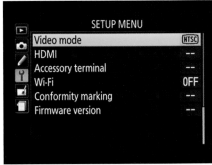

Figure 7-6: Set the video mode to the standard — NTSC or PAL — that's used in your country.

Your camera should already be set to match the country in which it was purchased, but it never hurts to check, especially because your decision affects your choice of movie frame rates, explained next. In fact, when you change the Video Mode setting, the camera displays a brief message alerting you to this fact.

Understanding the Frame Size/Frame Rate options

This setting determines the *resolution,* or frame size, of your movie, as well as the number of frames per second (fps), both of which affect video quality.

One way to access the setting is via the Movie Settings option on the Shooting menu, as shown in Figure 7-7. After you select the Frame Size/Frame Rate option, you see the settings screen shown in Figure 7-8.

If you're a digital video expert, these options probably make perfect sense to you; take your pick and move on. If you're new to video, here's the information you need to decode the settings:

- ✓ **Frame size:** The first pair of values shown for each Frame Size/Frame Rate setting indicates the number of pixels used to create the movie frame. In the world of HDTV, 1920 x 1080 pixels is considered *Full HD,* whereas 1280 x 720 is known as *Standard HD* and produces slightly lesser quality than Full HD (although I suspect few people can determine the difference). Both options result in a frame with a 16:9 aspect ratio.

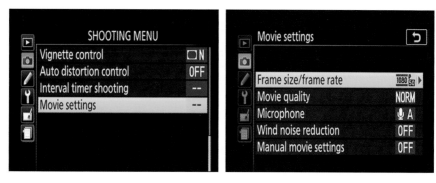

Figure 7-7: You can access the Frame Size/Frame Rate option via the Movie Settings option on the Shooting menu.

Selecting the last option on the list steps the frame size down to 640 x 424 pixels, which translates to a regular definition (that is, not a high-def) movie. This setting also produces a movie that has an approximate aspect ratio of 3:2 rather than the HD 16:9 format. This smaller resolution can be useful for online videos.

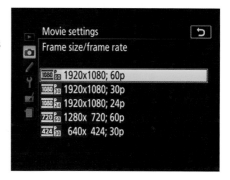

Figure 7-8: These options appear when NTSC is selected as the video mode.

✔ **Frame rate (fps):** The value immediately following the frame size indicates the *frame rate.* This value, measured in *frames per second* (fps), determines the smoothness of the playback.

Your options here depend on whether you select NTSC or PAL as the video standard. Assuming NTSC as the video standard, the following frame rates are available:

- *24:* This frame rate is the standard for motion pictures, giving your videos a softer, more movie-like look.

- *30:* This setting is the standard for most network broadcast TV and produces a crisper picture than the 24 fps setting.

- *60:* This option is often used for shooting video that will be played back in slow motion. With more frames per second, the video is smoother when you slow down the movie playback.

For PAL video, you can choose from 24, 25 (the PAL television broadcast standard), or 50 fps.

✔ **p:** The *p* that follows all the settings refers to *progressive video,* which is one of two technologies used to record the lines of pixels that make up a digital video frame. The other technology is *interlaced video.* With interlaced video, a single frame is split into odd and even *fields,* or lines of pixels. The data from the odd lines is recorded first, followed rapidly by the data from the even lines — so rapidly, in fact, that the picture appears seamless during playback. With progressive video, all the lines are pulled out of the magic video hat in sequential order, in a single pass.

Your camera offers only progressive video, but don't fret: Progressive, the newer technology, delivers smoother, cleaner footage than interlaced video when you're shooting fast motion or panning the camera. In other words, you can now forget about that *p* in the setting name until you want to impress your friends during the next discussion of digital video. Say, "Oh, your camera can do 60 fps only as interlaced video? Mine offers 60 fps progressive."

Two more notes about this setting:

✔ **Viewing the current setting:** See the little symbols appearing to the left of each setting in Figure 7-8? They're used in the monitor to indicate each setting, as shown in Figure 7-9. The first number specifies the vertical pixel count of the frame size; the *p* indicates progressive video, and the other number tells you the frame rate.

Frame Size/Frame Rate

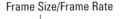

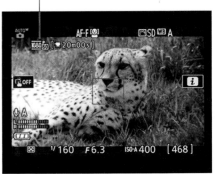

Figure 7-9: This data represents the current Frame Size/Frame Rate.

✔ **Changing the setting via the control strip:** You also can adjust the Frame Size/Frame Rate option by using the control strip, as shown in Figure 7-10. In this case, the available Frame Size/Frame Rate settings are presented together with the Movie Quality option, which I explain in the next section. (Otherwise, you select the Quality setting separately via the Movie Settings menu option.)

Together, these two settings affect the maximum length of the movie you can record. The gray box labeled *Maximum movie length* in Figure 7-10 updates to show you that length for the current combination of frame size/frame rate and movie quality. See the sidebar "Maximum recording times," later in this chapter, for a rundown of how many minutes of footage you can record at each combo.

Maximum movie length

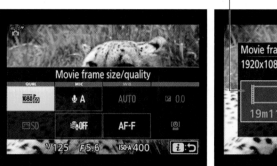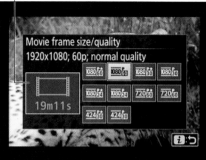

Figure 7-10: From the control strip, you select the Frame Size/Frame Rate and Movie Quality settings together.

Selecting the Movie Quality option

Next up on the list of video settings to digest is the aforementioned Movie Quality option. This setting determines how much compression is applied to the video file, which in turn affects the *bit rate,* or how much data is used to represent 1 second of video, measured in Mbps (megabits per second). You get just two choices: High and Normal (the default). The High setting results in a higher bit rate, which means better quality and larger files. Normal produces a lower bit rate and smaller files.

Because bit rate affects the size of the video file, it also determines the maximum length of the video clip you can create each time you press the movie-record button. Again, the sidebar "Maximum recording times" tells you the record-time limits at each combination of Movie Quality and Frame Size/ Frame Rate setting.

As with the Frame Size/Frame Rate setting, you can select the Movie Quality setting via the Movie Settings option on the Shooting menu, as shown in Figure 7-11. Or you can use the control strip to select both the Frame Size/ Frame Rate and Movie Quality setting together, as illustrated in Figure 7-10, in the preceding section.

One last tip about this setting: In the control strip and Live View display, a star appears with the Frame Size/Frame Rate setting when you select the High bit rate, as shown in Figure 7-12. No star means that the option is set to Normal.

Movie Quality setting

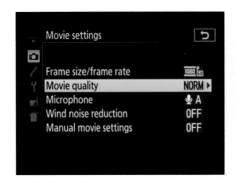

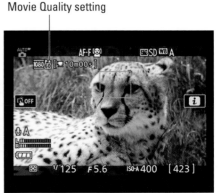

Figure 7-11: This option determines the movie bit rate, which affects playback quality and file size.

Figure 7-12: The tiny star indicates the High Movie Quality setting; the star disappears when you select the Normal setting.

Maximum recording times

The maximum recording time of a single video clip depends on the Frame Size/Frame Rate and Movie Quality options, as outlined here. Note that 60p, 30p, and 24p are the available Frame Size/Frame Rate settings when the Video Mode option is set to NTSC; when that option is set to PAL, available settings are 50, 25, and 24.

Frame Size	FPS	Quality	Maximum Movie Length
1920 x 1080	60, 50	High	10 minutes
		Normal	20 minutes
1920 x 1080	30, 25, 24	High	20 minutes
		Normal	29 minutes, 59 seconds
1280 x 720	60, 50	High	20 minutes
		Normal	29 minutes, 59 seconds
640 x 424	30, 25	High	29 minutes, 59 seconds
		Normal	29 minutes, 59 seconds

Controlling Audio

You can record sound using the camera's built-in microphone, labeled on the left in Figure 7-13, or attach an external microphone such as the Nikon ME-1 to the jack labeled on the right in the figure. During on-camera playback, sound comes from the speaker, labeled on the left in the figure.

Speaker   Built-in microphone   Microphone jack

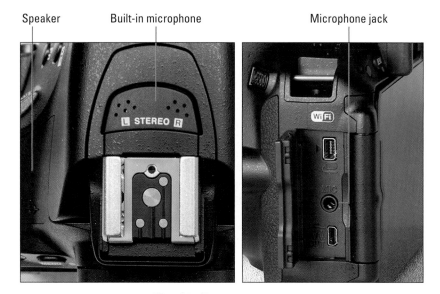

Figure 7-13: You can record audio with the internal microphone (left) or plug in an external microphone (right).

If you use the built-in mic, you can adjust two audio settings, Microphone and Wind Noise Reduction, explained in the next two sections. For an external mic, only the Microphone setting applies.

Choosing the Microphone setting (volume control)

The most critical audio-recording control is the Microphone setting, which affects sound volume. You have three options:

✓ **Auto Sensitivity:** The camera automatically adjusts the volume according to the level of the ambient noise. This setting is the default.

✓ **Manual Sensitivity:** You specify the volume level, with settings ranging from 1 to 20.

✓ **Microphone Off:** Choose this setting to record a movie with no sound or when you're using an off-camera microphone and you don't want the camera itself to record audio.

Symbols representing the current setting appear in the display, as shown in Figure 7-14. The microphone symbol indicates that audio recording is enabled; the letter *A* next-door indicates the Auto Sensitivity option. If you set the camera to Manual Sensitivity, your selected volume level appears instead.

Beneath those symbols, you see two horizontal bars that indicate the volume level of the left and right audio channels that are recorded when you use a stereo microphone. (The built-in mic offers stereo recording.) For monaural recording, both bars reflect the same data.

Audio levels are measured in decibels (dB), and levels on the volume meter range from –40 (very, very soft) to 0 (as loud as can be measured digitally). Ideally, sound should peak consistently in the –12 range. The indicators on the meter turn yellow in this range, as shown in Figure 7-14. If the sound level is too high, the bar at the end of the meter turns red — a warning that audio may be distorted.

Microphone setting/volume meter

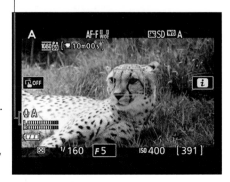

Figure 7-14: These symbols indicate the current Microphone setting and volume level.

To adjust the Microphone setting, you can go two routes:

- **Control strip:** Tap the *i* symbol on the Live View display or press the *i* button to display the control strip. Select the Microphone setting, as shown on the left in Figure 7-15, to display the second screen in the figure. Again, you see the volume meter plus symbols representing the Auto, Manual, and Off settings, as labeled in the figure.

  If you choose Manual, as shown in the figure, set the volume by using the touchscreen controls (the yellow triangles above and below the volume box) or by pressing the Multi Selector up and down.

Volume meter   Auto   Manual   Off

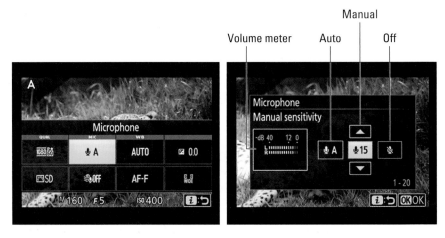

Figure 7-15: You can adjust the Microphone setting from the control strip.

✓ **Shooting menu:** Choose Movie Settings from the menu and then select Microphone, as shown on the left in Figure 7-16. You then see the second screen in the figure, where you can select the Microphone setting you want to use.

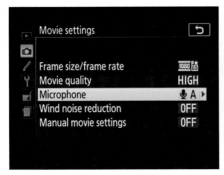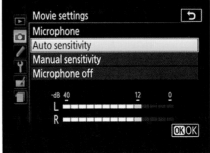

Figure 7-16: You also can access the Microphone option via the Movie Settings option on the Shooting menu.

Either way, choose the Microphone setting *before* starting the recording; you can't change it while recording is in progress.

Reducing wind noise

Ever seen a newscaster out in the field, carrying a microphone that looks like it's covered with a big piece of foam? That foam thing is a wind filter. It's designed to lessen the sounds that the wind makes when it hits the microphone.

You can enable a digital version of the same thing via the Wind Noise Reduction option. Essentially, the filter works by reducing the volume of noises that are similar to those made by wind. The problem is that some noises *not* made by wind can also be muffled when the filter is enabled. So when you're indoors or shooting on a still day, keep this option set to Off, as it is by default. Also note that when you use an external microphone, the Wind Filter feature has no effect.

To turn Wind Noise Reduction on or off, use the control strip, as shown in Figure 7-17. Or visit the Shooting menu, open the Movie Settings screen, and choose Wind Noise Reduction.

When the feature is enabled, the symbol labeled on the right in Figure 7-17 appears with the other microphone settings. The symbol disappears with Wind Noise Reduction turned off.

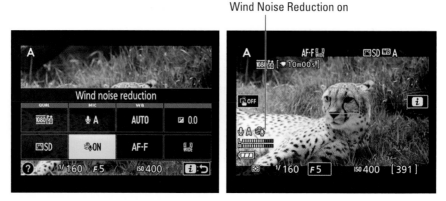

Figure 7-17: You can access the Wind Noise Reduction setting via the control strip, as shown on the left; the symbol labeled on the right appears when the feature is turned on.

Exploring Other Recording Options

In addition to settings reviewed in the preceding sections, you can control a few other aspects of your cinematic effort. The following list runs through these options; Figure 7-18 labels the symbols that represent these settings in the display.

✔ **Exposure mode:** You can record movies in any exposure mode (Auto, Scene modes, Effects modes, P, M, and so on). As with still photography, your choice determines which camera settings you can access. (The Movie Settings menu options are available in all modes, however.)

✔ **Exposure settings:** The aperture (f-stop), shutter speed, ISO, Metering mode, and Exposure Compensation settings, all labeled in Figure 7-18, determine movie exposure. In the P, S, A, and M modes, as well as in Night Vision Effects mode, you have some control over all these options except Metering mode; the camera always uses Matrix metering for movie recording. See the next section for details on adjusting exposure. For all other exposure modes, the camera handles exposure automatically.

✔ **Focus options:** Your options are the same as for Live View still photography, detailed in Chapter 4. As a quick recap, you adjust autofocusing behavior through Focus mode and AF-area mode; look for the current settings in the spots labeled in Figure 7-18.

   • _Focus mode:_ Choose AF-S to lock focus when you press the shutter button halfway; choose AF-F for continuous autofocusing. See the first section of this chapter for details about how each option works for movie recording. For manual focusing, choose MF.

   • _AF-area mode:_ You can choose from Face Priority, Wide Area, Normal Area, or Subject Tracking. The default setting is Face

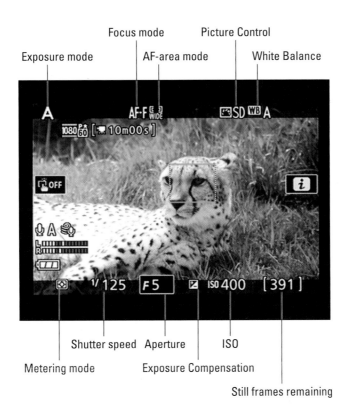

Figure 7-18: Here's your road map to other major settings you can monitor in the Show Movie Indicators display mode.

Priority; if the camera doesn't detect a face in the frame, it automatically uses Wide Area focusing instead. With any of these modes, you start by moving the focusing frame over your subject. How things work from there depends on the specific mode; again, Chapter 4 provides step-by-step instructions.

 Adjust both settings via the control strip; press the *i* button or tap the screen *i* symbol to bring up the strip.

✓ **White Balance and Picture Control:** The colors in your movie are rendered according to the current White Balance and Picture Control settings, both detailed in Chapter 5. However, you have control over these options only when the Mode dial is set to P, S, A, or M. The current settings appear in the areas labeled in Figure 7-18; you can adjust both options either via the Shooting menu or the control strip.

 Want to record a black-and-white movie? Select Monochrome as the Picture Control. Instant *film noir.*

Manipulating Movie Exposure

Normally, the camera automatically adjusts exposure during movie recording. Exposure is calculated using Matrix (whole frame) metering, regardless of which Metering mode setting is selected. But in a few exposure modes, you can adjust exposure by changing the following settings:

- ✔ **Shutter speed and ISO:** Both options are set by the camera by default. But if you enable the Manual Movie Settings option on the Movie Settings menu, as shown in Figure 7-19, you can control both settings. (Look for the current settings in the areas labeled in Figure 7-18.) This path is one for experienced videographers, however. If you fit that category, here are a few things you need to know:

  - *Exposure mode:* You must set the Mode dial to M (manual exposure), and you must set the aperture (f-stop setting) as well as the shutter speed and ISO to dial in the correct exposure.

    To set the f-stop in M mode while the Manual Movie Settings option is enabled, you must exit Live View mode. Then adjust the aperture via the onscreen controls (start by tapping the arrow box under the aperture symbol). You also can just press the Exposure Compensation button while rotating the Command dial to set shutter speed. Rotate the Live View switch to return to Live View mode.

  - *Shutter speed:* You can select shutter speeds as high as 1/4000 second. The slowest shutter speed depends on your chosen frame rate. For 24p, 25p, and 30p, you can drop as low as 1/30 second; for 50p, 1/50 second; and for 60p, 1/60 second. To set the shutter speed in M mode, you can use the touchscreen controls (start by tapping the shutter speed box) or by rotating the Command dial. (Remember that which frame rates are available depends on whether the Video Mode option on the Setup menu is set to NTSC or PAL.)

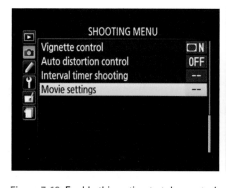
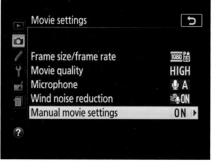

Figure 7-19: Enable this option to take control over movie exposure.

If you choose a shutter speed outside the stated ranges, the camera slaps your hand and chooses the closest in-range setting automatically.

- *ISO:* You can set the ISO value as low as 100 or as high as 25600. Note that Auto ISO Sensitivity control doesn't work when the Manual Movie Settings option is enabled; the camera sticks with your selected setting regardless of whether you enable Auto ISO — and, more importantly, regardless of whether your selected setting produces an under- or overexposed movie.

  To adjust ISO quickly, press the Fn button while rotating the Command dial. You can also select the ISO value via the ISO Sensitivity settings option on the Shooting menu or by using the Live View control strip

✔ **Aperture (f-stop):** You can adjust the f-stop *before* (but not during) recording if you set the Mode dial to A (aperture-priority autoexposure) or M (manual exposure). This option enables you to control depth of field in your movies; Chapter 3 explains the aperture setting's role in depth of field.

In A mode, rotate the Command dial or use the touchscreen to change the f-stop (just tap the f-stop value at the bottom of the display to access the setting). Again, in M mode, first exit Live View mode and then press and hold the Exposure Compensation button while rotating the dial; rotate the Live View switch again to return to the movie screen. In either case, remember that the live preview doesn't indicate the depth of field that your f-stop setting will produce — the camera can't provide this feedback because the aperture doesn't actually open to your selected setting until you start recording.

✔ **Exposure Compensation:** Exposure Compensation, detailed in Chapter 3, enables you to override the camera's autoexposure decisions, asking for a brighter or darker picture. You can apply this adjustment for movies when you use the following exposure modes: P, S, A, or M; any Scene mode; or the Night Vision Effects mode. However, you're limited to an adjustment range of EV +3.0 to –3.0 rather than the usual five steps that are possible during normal photography. Note that the display shows the plus/minus symbol you see in Figure 7-18 only when Exposure Compensation is in force.

To adjust the setting, use the control strip item highlighted in Figure 7-20. In any exposure mode except M, you also can press and hold the Exposure

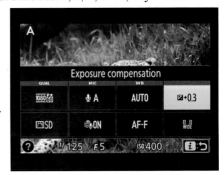

Figure 7-20: You can apply Exposure Compensation for movie shooting when you use certain exposure modes.

Compensation button while rotating the Command dial. (That button/ dial combo adjusts the aperture when you use the M exposure mode.)

Just to head off any possible confusion: For viewfinder photography, Exposure Compensation isn't needed in M exposure mode; if you want a brighter or darker exposure, you just change the aperture, shutter speed, or ISO Sensitivity settings. But because the camera doesn't give you control over shutter speed or ISO during movie recording — *unless you enable Manual Movie Settings* — you need some way to tell the camera that you want a brighter or darker picture in M mode, and Exposure Compensation is it.

✔ **Autoexposure lock:** In any exposure mode except Auto or Auto Flash Off, you can lock exposure at the current settings by pressing and holding the AE-L/AF-L button. Chapter 3 also tells you more about autoexposure lock.

Screening Your Movies

To play your movie, press the Playback button. In single-image playback mode, you can spot a movie file by looking for the little movie camera icon in the upper-left corner of the screen, as shown in Figure 7-21. A honking big "play" arrow also appears in the middle of the screen in the default playback display mode and in some other display modes. (Press the Multi Selector up/down to change the display mode.) The default display mode also shows other movie-related data, including the Frame Size, Frame Rate, and Movie Quality setting. (Remember: A star next to the Frame Rate value means that you set the Movie Quality option to High.)

To start playback, tap the play arrow or tap the OK/Play box at the bottom of the screen. Or, if the touchscreen is disabled, press the OK button.

In the thumbnail and Calendar playback modes, both described in Chapter 8, you see little dots along the edges of image thumbnails to represent movie files. Tap the thumbnail or press OK to shift to single-image view and then start playback as I just described.

After playback begins, you see the data labeled in Figure 7-22. The progress bar and Time Elapsed value show you how much of the movie has played so far; you can also see the total movie length.

You can control playback as follows:

✔ **Exit playback:** Press the Multi Selector up, tap the return arrow in the upper-right corner of the screen, or press the Playback button again.

✔ **Pause/resume playback:** If the touchscreen is enabled, tap the display once to pause; tap again to resume playback. You also can press the

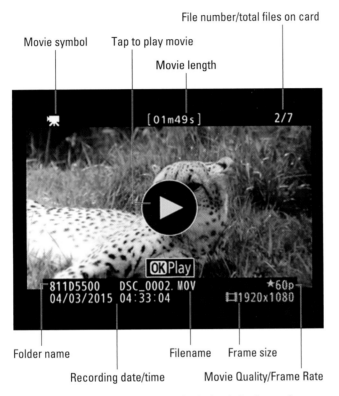

Figure 7-21: When you use the default playback display mode, you see this movie data on the screen.

Multi Selector down to pause playback and press OK to resume playback. (That white circle labeled Playback control symbols in the figure is designed to remind you of the Multi Selector's movie-playback role.)

- **Fast-forward/rewind:** Press the Multi Selector right or left to fast-forward or rewind the movie, respectively. Press again to double the fast-forward or rewind speed; keep pressing to increase the speed. Hold down the button to fast-forward or rewind all the way to the end or beginning of the movie.

  You also can tap on the progress bar to advance or rewind the movie to the spot you tap.

- **Forward/rewind 10 seconds:** Rotate the Command dial to the right to jump 10 seconds forward through the movie; rotate to the left to jump back 10 seconds. Again, note the little wheel symbol in the lower-left corner of the frame: That's your reminder to use the Command dial to perform 10-second jumps through the movie. The camera pauses playback after every jump; tap the screen or press OK to resume playback.

?

✔ **Advance frame by frame:** First press the Multi Selector down or tap the screen to pause playback. Then press the Multi Selector right to advance one frame; press left to go back one frame.

✔ **Adjust playback volume:** See the markings labeled *Volume controls* in Figure 7-22? They remind you that you can press the Zoom In button to increase volume and press the Zoom Out button to lower it. The number value tells you the current volume level (10, in the figure). You also can tap the symbols to adjust volume, but I find it difficult to tap just the right spot. And if you miss the tap target, the camera pauses the movie.

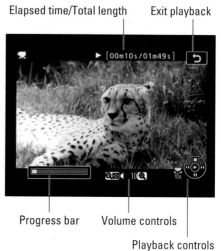

Elapsed time/Total length   Exit playback

Progress bar   Volume controls

Playback controls

Figure 7-22: The icons at the bottom of the screen remind you which buttons to use to control playback.

Trimming Movies

You can do some limited movie editing in camera. I emphasize: *limited* editing. You can trim frames from the start of a movie and clip off frames from the end, and that's it.

To eliminate frames from the start of a movie, take these steps:

1. **Display your movie in single-image view.**

2. **Tap the playback icon or press OK to begin playback.**

3. **When you reach the first frame you want to keep, pause the movie by tapping the screen or pressing the Multi Selector down.**

   The onscreen display updates to show you the controls that appear on the left in Figure 7-23.

4. **Press the *i* button or tap the *i* symbol at the bottom of the screen.**

   You see the menu options shown on the right in Figure 7-23.

5. **Select Choose Start/End Point.**

   You see the options shown in Figure 7-24.

6. **Select Start Point.**

   You're returned to the playback screen, which now sports a couple additional symbols. First, you see two yellow markers on

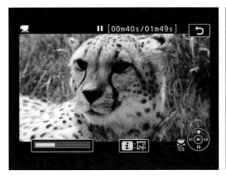 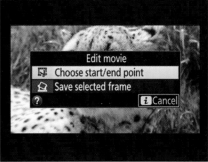

Figure 7-23: With the movie paused, press the *i* button or tap the *i* symbol to access the movie-editing screens.

the progress bar at the bottom of the screen. The left marker indicates the start point; the right marker, the end point. You also see an AE-L/AF-L symbol. (More about both these controls later.)

7. **Press the Multi Selector up or tap the scissors symbol (lower-right corner of the frame) to lop off all frames that came before the current frame.**

Now you see the options shown in Figure 7-25. To preview the movie, select Preview and press OK; after the preview plays, you're returned to the menu screen.

8. **To preserve your original movie and save the trimmed one as a new file, choose Save as New File and press OK.**

Alternatively, you can opt to overwrite the existing file, but you can't get the original file back if you do.

A message appears, telling you that the trimmed movie is being saved. During playback, edited files are indicated by a little scissors icon that appears in the upper-left corner of the screen, as shown in Figure 7-26.

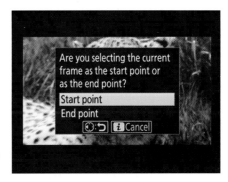

Figure 7-24: To trim frames from the beginning of a movie, select the Start Point option.

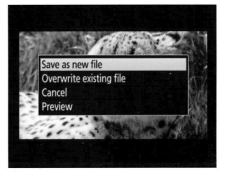

Figure 7-25: Choose Save as New File to avoid overwriting the original movie file.

To instead trim footage from the end of a film, follow the same steps but this time pause playback on the last frame you want to keep in Step 3. Then, in Step 6, select Choose End Point instead of Choose Start Point.

Trimmed movie symbol

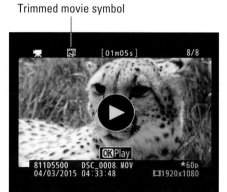

 You can trim an already trimmed movie, by the way. So you can go through the steps once to set a new start point and a second time to set a new end point. Or, if you prefer, you can trim files from both the beginning and end of a movie in one pass. After you take Step 6, press the AE-L/AF-L button or tap the corresponding icon at the bottom of the screen. The

Figure 7-26: The scissors symbol tells you that you're looking at a trimmed movie.

marker at the right end of the progress bar turns yellow, indicating that you can now rewind the movie to the frame that you want to use as the end of the video. You can keep tapping or pressing the AE-L/AF-L control to toggle between the start/end point controls on the progress bar. To finalize the edit, press the Multi Selector up or tap the scissors symbol.

Saving a Movie Frame As a Still Image

 You can save a frame of the movie as a still photo. Here's how:

1. **Begin playing your movie.**

2. **When you reach the frame you want to capture, pause playback.**

   You can tap the screen or press the Multi Selector down to pause the movie.

 3. **Press the *i* button or tap the onscreen *i* symbol to bring up the Edit Movie screen, shown in Figure 7-27.**

4. **Choose Save Selected Frame.**

   The frame appears on the monitor.

5. **Press the Multi Selector up or tap the scissors symbol in the lower-right corner of the screen.**

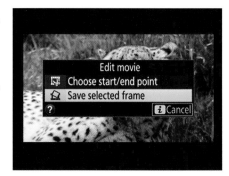

Figure 7-27: This option lets you save a single frame as a JPEG image.

6. On the confirmation screen that appears, select Yes.

Your frame is saved as a JPEG photo.

Remember a few things about pictures you create this way:

- When you view the image, it's marked with a little scissors icon in the upper-left corner. (It looks just like the one labeled in Figure 7-26.)

- The resolution of the picture depends on the resolution of the movie: For example, if the movie resolution is 1920 x 1080, your picture resolution is 1920 x 1080.

- You can't apply editing features from the Retouch menu to the file, and neither can you view all the shooting data that's normally associated with a JPEG picture.

Before you begin movie playback, you also can press the *i* button to display a mini-menu that contains the Edit Movie option. Select that option to access the Edit Movie screen (the one shown on the right in Figure 7-23). After choosing the editing function you want to use, press OK to start playback and proceed as outlined in the steps here and in the preceding section.

Part III
After the Shot

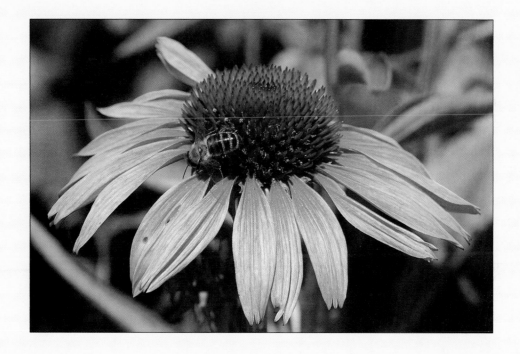

Discover five easy composition tricks you can use to shoot more captivating photos at www.dummies.com/extras/nikon.

In this part . . .

- Get the details on picture playback, including how to customize playback screens.

- Erase files you don't want and protect the ones you like from being accidentally deleted.

- Assign ratings to picture and movie files.

- Download files from the camera to the computer.

- Convert Raw (NEF) images using the in-camera converter and the one found in Nikon ViewNX 2.

- Prepare photos for online sharing.

- Transfer photos to a smartphone or other smart device via the built-in Wi-Fi feature.

8

Playback Mode: Viewing Your Photos

In This Chapter

▷ Exploring picture playback functions

▷ Deciphering the picture information displays

▷ Understanding histograms

▷ Viewing pictures and movies on a television

*W*ithout question, my favorite thing about digital photography is being able to view my pictures the instant after I shoot them. No more guessing whether I captured the image or need to try again, as in the film days; no more wasting money on developing pictures that stink.

Seeing your pictures is just the start of the things you can do when you switch your camera to playback mode, though. You also can review settings you used to take the picture, display graphics that alert you to exposure problems, and magnify a photo to check details. This chapter introduces you to these playback features and also explains how to connect your camera to a television for playback.

Note: Some information in this chapter applies only to still photographs; if a feature also works for movie files, I spell that out. For the basics of movie playback, see the end of Chapter 7.

Adjusting Playback Timing Options

By default, the camera displays your photo for 4 seconds immediately after it finishes recording the picture data to the memory card. This feature is called Image Review.

To take a longer look, press the Playback button to set the camera to playback mode. Your photo then appears for 5 minutes, after which the monitor goes to sleep if you don't press any buttons. (This auto shutdown is a Good Thing because the monitor is a major drain on the camera battery.)

If necessary, you can adjust the playback and Image Review duration from the Custom Settings menu. (Note that whatever setting you use for playback shutoff also affects the auto shutdown of menu displays.) To access the relevant settings, select the Timers/AE Lock menu option on the Custom Setting menu and then choose Auto Off Timers to display the screen you see on the left in Figure 8-1.

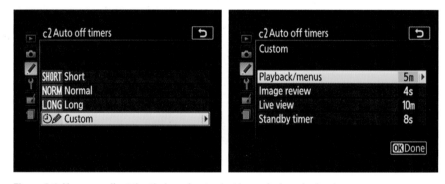

Figure 8-1: You can adjust the timing of auto shutdown during playback.

 You're offered these three general settings: Short, Normal (the default), and Long. But these settings apply a set of timing options to the Live View display and exposure meter display as well as to the playback/menus and Image Review displays. I suggest that you select Custom, as shown on the left in the figure, to display the screen shown on the right. You then can set the Playback/Menus timing and Image Review timing separately. (Chapter 10 goes into more detail about the automatic shutdown options.)

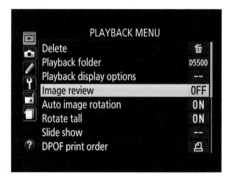

Figure 8-2: To disable Image Review, set this option to Off.

To turn off Image Review altogether, head for the Playback menu and set that option to Off, as shown in Figure 8-2.

Choosing Which Images to View

Your camera organizes pictures automatically into folders that are assigned generic names: 100D5500, 101D5500, and so on. You can see the name of the current folder by looking at the Storage Folder option on the Shooting menu. (The default folder name appears on this menu as simply *100*.) You also can create custom folders by using the process outlined in Chapter 10. Which folders' photos appear during playback depends on the Playback Folder option on the Playback menu, shown in Figure 8-3.

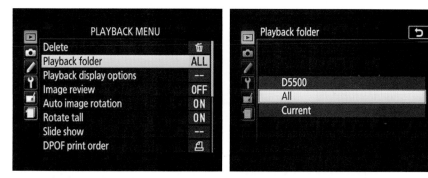

Figure 8-3: If your memory card contains multiple image folders, specify which folder you want to view.

You probably don't have to worry about this setting — all your photos likely are contained in one folder, and the camera selects that folder by default. But if you use a gargantuan memory card that contains zillions of images (and therefore may contain multiple folders), if you created custom folders, or if your card contains pictures taken on another Nikon camera, specify which folder you want to view by choosing one of the following options:

- ✓ **D5500:** All pictures taken with the D5500 are viewable, regardless of which folder they call home.

- ✓ **Current:** This setting is the default; the camera displays images contained in the folder selected as the Storage Folder option on the Shooting menu. Again, unless your card contains multiple folders, all your pictures are in that folder.

- ✓ **All:** This setting displays all pictures in all folders, even those you took with another camera, as long as the photos are in an image format that the camera recognizes.

Enabling Automatic Picture Rotation

When you take a picture, the camera can record the image *orientation* — whether you held the camera normally, creating a horizontally oriented image, or turned the camera on its side to shoot a vertically oriented photo. During playback, the camera can then read the orientation data and automatically rotate the image so that it appears in the upright position, as shown on the left in Figure 8-4. The image is also automatically rotated when you view it in Nikon ViewNX 2 and other photo programs that can interpret the data. If you disable rotation, vertically oriented pictures appear sideways, as shown on the right in Figure 8-4.

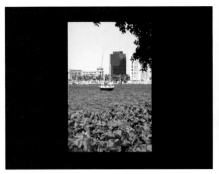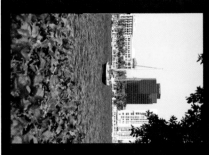

Figure 8-4: You can display vertically oriented pictures in their upright position (left) or sideways (right).

Photographers use the term *portrait orientation* to refer to vertically oriented pictures and *landscape orientation* to refer to horizontally oriented pictures. The terms stem from the traditional way that people and places are captured in paintings and photographs — portraits, vertically; landscapes, horizontally.

Set up your rotation preferences by using the following Playback menu options, both shown in Figure 8-5:

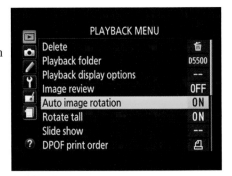

Figure 8-5: Visit the Playback menu to enable or disable image rotation.

- ✔ **Auto Image Rotation:** This option (highlighted in the figure) determines whether the orientation data is included in the picture file. The default setting is On.

- ✔ **Rotate Tall:** Found just below the Auto Image Rotation setting, this option controls whether the camera pays attention to the orientation data. This one is also enabled by default.

Regardless of these settings, your pictures aren't rotated during the instant-review period. Nor are movie files rotated.

Viewing Images in Playback Mode

My guess is that you've already figured out the basics of picture playback. But you may not be familiar with all the tricks you can use when viewing your images, such as zooming in on an image for a close-up check or displaying multiple image thumbnails at a time. The next four sections introduce you to basic options; the later section "Viewing Picture Data" explains how to modify and understand the data that appears with photos during playback.

To use touchscreen controls during playback, set the Touch Controls option on the Setup menu to Enable or Playback Only. (The Playback Only setting disables touch operations during shooting.) If you're used to viewing photos on a smartphone or tablet, most of the touchscreen gestures will be familiar; if you need a primer in touchscreen terminology, see Chapter 1.

Displaying photos one at a time (single-frame playback)

For normal playback — that is, to see each photo one at a time, as shown in Figure 8-6 — take these steps:

1. **Press the Playback button, labeled in Figure 8-6.**

   The camera displays the last picture you took, along with some picture data, such as the filename of the photo and the date it was taken, as shown in the figure.

2. **To scroll through your pictures, swipe a finger across the touchscreen, rotate the Command dial, or press the Multi Selector right or left.**

   I labeled the Command dial and Multi Selector in the figure. To view the next picture using the touchscreen, swipe your finger from right to left across the screen. Swipe from the left to go back one picture.

   In single-frame playback view, you can magnify or reduce the display size by pinching outward or inward, respectively. You also can press the Zoom In and Zoom Out buttons, both labeled in Figure 8-6. The upcoming section "Zooming in for a closer view" talks more about this feature.

   If the picture's a loser, press the Delete button, also labeled in the figure. A confirmation screen appears; press the button a second time to erase the file. (See the next chapter for other ways to delete photos.)

3. **To return to picture-taking mode, press the Playback button again or press the shutter button halfway and then release it.**

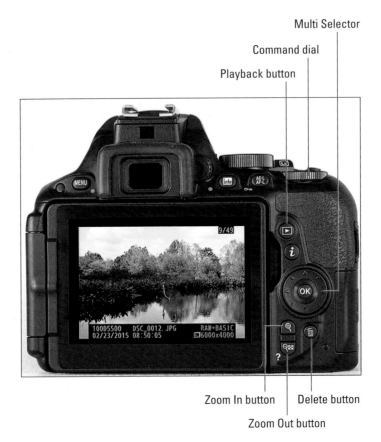

Figure 8-6: These buttons play the largest roles in picture playback.

Viewing multiple images at a time (thumbnails view)

Along with viewing images one at a time, you can display 4 or 12 thumbnails, as shown in Figure 8-7, or even a whopping 80 thumbnails.

Use these techniques to change to thumbnails view and navigate your photos:

✔ **Display thumbnails.** If the touchscreen is enabled, pinch in: That is, put your thumb and a finger on opposite corners of the monitor and drag both toward the center of the screen. You also can press the Zoom Out button (refer to Figure 8-6).

Selected photo

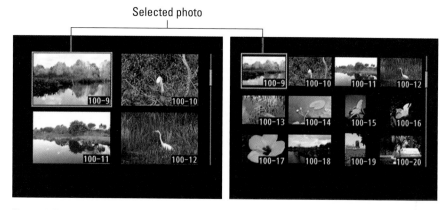

Figure 8-7: You can view multiple image thumbnails at a time.

Either way, your first pinch or press of the Zoom Out button cycles from single-picture view to 4-thumbnail view; keep pinching or pressing to shift to 12-picture view and then to 80 thumbnail view. One more pinch or press takes you to Calendar view, a nifty feature explained in the next section.

✔ **Display fewer thumbnails.** For touchscreen operation, pinch out: Place thumb and forefinger in the center of the screen and drag both toward the edge of the monitor. If you prefer, you can press the Zoom In button instead. Each pinch or press shifts you one step closer to full-frame view.

✔ **Scroll to the next screen of thumbnails.** Drag a finger up or down the screen or press the Multi Selector up and down.

✔ **Select an image.** To perform certain playback functions while in thumbnails view, such as deleting a photo or protecting it, you first need to select an image. A yellow box surrounds the selected image (refer to Figure 8-7). To select a different image, just tap its thumbnail. Or rotate the Command dial or use the Multi Selector to move the highlight box over the image. (This process works differently in Calendar view; again, see the next section for help.)

✔ **Shift directly from any thumbnails display to single-image view.** Select the photo you want to view and then tap its thumbnail or press OK.

Displaying photos in Calendar view

In Calendar view, you see a little calendar on the screen, as shown on the left in Figure 8-8. By selecting a date on the calendar, you can quickly navigate to all pictures you shot on that day. A thumbnail-free date indicates that your memory card doesn't contain any photos from that day.

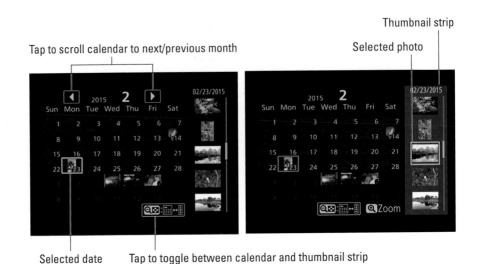

Thumbnail strip

Tap to scroll calendar to next/previous month

Selected photo

Selected date   Tap to toggle between calendar and thumbnail strip

Figure 8-8: Calendar view makes it easy to view all photos shot on a particular day.

Here's how to take advantage of Calendar view:

1. **Pinch in (on the touchscreen) or press the Zoom Out button as needed to cycle through the Thumbnail display modes until you reach Calendar view.**

   If you're viewing images in full-frame view, for example, you need to pinch or press four times to get to Calendar view.

2. **Select the date on which you shot the images you want to see.**

   A yellow box highlights the currently selected date. In Figure 8-8, for example, February 23 is selected. To select a different date, tap it in the calendar display or move the highlight box over it by using the Multi Selector or rotating the Command dial.

   The number of the month appears at the top of the screen. To quickly scroll to a different month, tap one of the arrows on either side of the number. You also can use the Command dial or Multi Selector to travel from one month to the next.

   After you select a date, the right side of the screen displays thumbnails of pictures taken on that date.

3. **To view all thumbnails from the selected date, tap the Zoom Out icon at the bottom of the screen, press the Zoom Out button, or press OK.**

   The Zoom Out icon is the one labeled "Tap to toggle . . . " in Figure 8-8. The thumbnail strip becomes active (refer to the right side of Figure 8-8), and you can scroll through the thumbnails by using the touchscreen, Command dial, or Multi Selector. The currently selected image is highlighted by a yellow box.

4. To temporarily display a larger view of the selected thumbnail, hold down the Zoom In button.

In the zoomed view, the image filename appears under the larger preview, as shown in Figure 8-9. When you release the Zoom In button, the large preview disappears, and the calendar display shown on the right in Figure 8-8 comes back into view. (There is no touchscreen option to perform this function.)

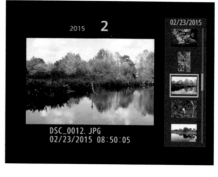

Figure 8-9: Highlight a photo in the thumbnail strip and press the Zoom In button to temporarily display it at a larger size.

5. To jump from the thumbnail strip back to the calendar so that you can select a different date, tap the Zoom Out icon or press the Zoom Out button again.

You can keep pressing the button or tapping the icon to jump between the calendar and the thumbnail strip as much as you want.

6. To exit the thumbnail strip and view the selected image in single-image view, tap the thumbnail or press OK.

If the calendar page is currently active instead of the thumbnail strip, press OK twice (the first press takes you to the thumbnail strip).

After Step 6, you can return immediately to Calendar view by pressing the OK button but only if you don't scroll to the next or previous picture first. Otherwise, you have to cycle through all the thumbnail views to get to Calendar view.

Zooming in for a closer view

When you display a photo in single-frame view, as shown on the left in Figure 8-10, you can magnify it to get a close-up look at important details, as shown on the right. Here's the scoop:

🖙 **Zoom in.** Pinch out on the touchscreen or press the Zoom In button. You can magnify the image to a maximum of 13 to 33 times its original display size, depending on the picture resolution (Image Size). Just keep pressing the button or pinching out until you reach the magnification you want.

🖙 **Zoom out.** To zoom out to a reduced magnification, pinch in or press the Zoom Out button.

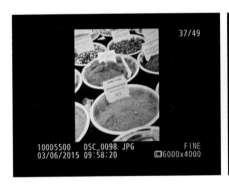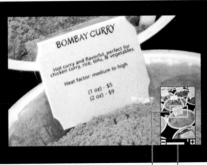

Magnified area

Magnification level

Figure 8-10: When viewing images in single-frame view (left), pinch out or press the Zoom In button to magnify the picture (right).

✔ **View another part of the magnified picture.** When an image is magnified, a thumbnail showing the entire image appears briefly in the lower-right corner of the monitor (refer to the right side of Figure 8-10). The yellow outline in the thumbnail indicates the area that's consuming the rest of the monitor space. To scroll the display and view a different portion of the image, you can use the Multi Selector or just drag your finger across the screen.

The bar at the bottom of the navigation window gives you an indication of the magnification level; the closer the white bar gets to the right end of the bar, the greater the magnification level.

After a few seconds, the navigation thumbnail disappears; just tap the screen or press the Multi Selector in any direction to redisplay it.

✔ **Inspect faces.** Try this trick to inspect each face in a group shot: First, magnify the image. The picture-in-picture thumbnail displays a white border around each detected face. (Typically, subjects must be facing the camera for faces to be detected.) An *i* symbol that sports a face and the word On also appears in the lower-left corner of the screen, as shown on the left in Figure 8-11.

Next, press the *i* button or tap that On symbol. A second symbol, decorated with a face and a Multi Selector symbol then appears, as shown on the right in the figure. You can tap that symbol or press the Multi Selector right or left to jump from face to face. Press OK to fill the frame with the selected face. Press the *i* button or tap the *i* symbol (now labeled Off) to turn the face-inspection feature off and return to the normal playback zoom behavior. (Like the navigation box, these icons disappear pretty quickly; just tap anywhere on the screen to redisplay them.)

✔ **View more images at the same magnification.** Here's another neat trick: While the display is zoomed, rotate the Command dial to display the same area of the next photo at the same magnification. So if you shot the same subject several times, you can easily check to see how a particular detail appears in each one.

✔ **Return to full-frame view.** You can switch from any magnification level to full-screen view by pressing OK.

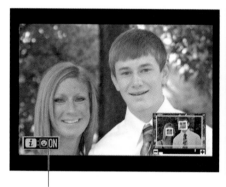 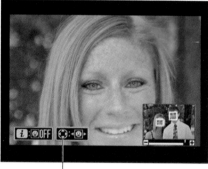

Tap to turn on face-inspection feature   Tap to toggle between faces

Figure 8-11: After magnifying a group portrait, you can tap these icons to closely inspect each face in the picture.

Viewing Picture Data

In single-picture view, you can choose from the six display modes shown in Figure 8-12. By default, however, only the File Information display is available.

To use any other display options, you must enable them from the Playback menu, by following these steps:

1. **Open the Playback menu and choose Playback Display Options, as shown on the left in Figure 8-13.**

   A menu listing all hidden display modes appears, as shown on the right in the figure. A check mark in the box next to a display mode means that the mode is enabled.

2. **To toggle a display mode on or off, tap it.**

   You also can highlight the mode and then press the Multi Selector right or tap the Select box at the bottom of the screen. Notice that the File Information option is missing from the menu — you can't disable this display mode.

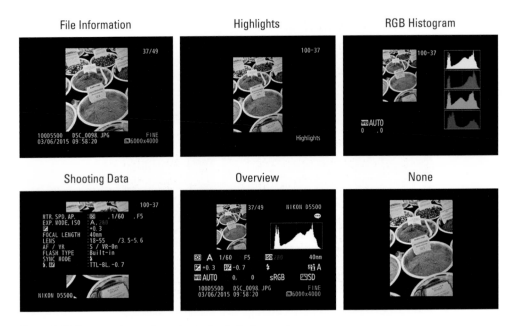

File Information   Highlights   RGB Histogram

Shooting Data   Overview   None

Figure 8-12: You can choose from six playback display modes.

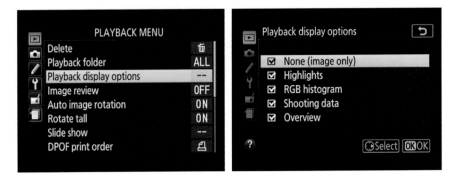

Figure 8-13: You enable and disable display modes via the Playback menu.

3. After turning on the options you want to use, tap or press OK.

After enabling the additional display modes and returning to playback mode, press the Multi Selector up or down to cycle from one display to the next.

The next several sections explain exactly what details you can glean from each display mode, save for the image-only mode. I present them here in the order they appear if you cycle through the modes by pressing the Multi Selector down. You can spin through the modes in the other direction by pressing the Multi Selector up.

File Information mode

In the File Information display mode, the monitor displays the data shown in Figure 8-14. Here's the key to what information appears, starting at the top of the screen and working down:

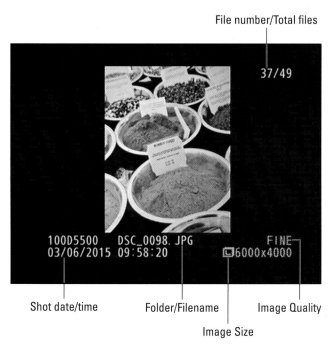

File number/Total files

37/49

100D5500 DSC_0098.JPG FINE
03/06/2015 09:58:20 6000x4000

Shot date/time   Folder/Filename   Image Quality

Image Size

Figure 8-14: In File Information mode, you can view these bits of data.

- **File number/Total files:** The first value indicates the number of the currently displayed photo; the second tells you the total number of files in the same folder.

- **Folder name:** Folders are named automatically by the camera unless you create custom folders, a trick you can explore in Chapter 10. The first camera-created folder is 100D5500. Each folder can contain up to 999 images; when you exceed that limit, or the last photo you stored in that folder had the file number 9,999, the camera creates a new folder and assigns the next folder number: 101D5500, 102D5500, and so on.

- **Filename:** The camera also automatically names your files. Filenames end with a 3-letter code that represents the file format, which is either JPG (for JPEG) or NEF (for Raw) for still photos. Chapter 2 discusses these formats. If you record a movie, the file extension is MOV; if you create a dust-off reference image file, an advanced feature designed for use with Nikon Capture NX 2, the camera instead uses the extension NDF. (Because this software must be purchased separately, I don't cover it in this book.)

The first four characters of filenames also can vary as follows:

- *DSC_:* You captured the photo in the default Color Space, sRGB. This setting is the best choice for most people, for reasons you can explore in Chapter 5.

- *_DSC:* If you change the Color Space setting to Adobe RGB, the underscore character comes first.

Each image is also assigned a 4-digit file number, starting with 0001. When you reach image 9999, the file numbering restarts at 0001, and the new images go into a new folder to prevent any possibility of overwriting the existing image files. For more information about file numbering, see the Chapter 1 section that discusses the File Number Sequence option, found on the Custom Setting menu. (I recommend keeping this option turned on.)

✔ **Date and Time:** Just below the folder and filename info, you see the date and time that you took the picture. Of course, the accuracy of this data depends on whether you set the camera's date and time values correctly, which you do via the Time Zone and Date option on the Setup menu.

✔ **Image Quality:** Here you can see which Image Quality setting you used when taking the picture. Again, Chapter 2 has details, but the short story is this: Fine, Normal, and Basic are the three JPEG recording options, with Fine representing the highest JPEG quality. Raw refers to the Nikon Raw format, NEF (for Nikon Electronic Format). If you captured the picture in both formats, you see Raw+Fine (or Normal or Basic). Only one thumbnail appears to represent each file.

✔ **Image Size:** This value tells you the image resolution, or pixel count. See Chapter 2 to find out about resolution.

Figure 8-15 shows you some additional symbols that appear when you use certain after-the-shot camera features, as follows:

✔ **Rating symbol:** Chapter 9 explains how you can rate a picture or movie, assigning it one to five stars or, if you're totally disgusted with the file, labeling it with a trash can so that you can easily locate it to delete it. The rating shown in Figure 8-15 indicates a five-star photo, for example. (I grade on a curve.) If you don't assign any rating, this area of the playback screen appears empty.

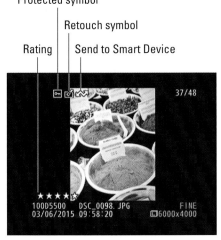

Figure 8-15: These symbols appear only if you use the related playback and retouching features.

- **Protected symbol:** The key icon indicates that you used the file-protection feature to prevent the image or movie from being erased when you use the camera's Delete function. See the next chapter to find out more. (*Note:* Formatting your memory card, a topic discussed in Chapter 1, *does* erase even protected pictures.) Again, this area appears empty if you didn't apply protection.

- **Retouch symbol:** This icon appears on images that you created by applying one of the Retouch menu features to a picture. (The camera preserves the original and applies your alterations to a copy of the file.) Chapter 11 explains this feature and other Retouch menu options. See Chapter 7 for help with the movie-editing function found on the menu; for edited movies, you see a little scissors icon instead of the Retouch symbol shown in the figure.

- **Send to Smart Device symbol:** After you tag a photo for Wi-Fi transfer to a smartphone or tablet, this symbol appears. Chapter 9 explains the Wi-Fi feature. (You can't transfer movies via Wi-Fi.)

Highlights (blinkies) mode

One of the most difficult problems to correct in a photo-editing program is known as *blown highlights* in some circles and *clipped highlights* in others. In plain English, both terms mean that *highlights* — the brightest areas of the image — are so overexposed that areas that should include a variety of light shades are instead totally white. For example, in a cloud image, pixels that should be light to very light gray become white due to overexposure, resulting in a loss of detail in those clouds.

Highlights display mode alerts you to clipped highlights by blinking the affected pixels on and off. But just because you see the flashing alerts doesn't mean that you should adjust exposure — the decision depends on where the alerts occur and how the rest of the image is exposed. If your subject appears fine and the blinkies are in the background, don't worry about it. If you adjust exposure to get rid of the blown highlights, your subject will then be underexposed. In other words, sometimes you simply can't avoid a few clipped highlights when the scene includes a broad range of brightness values.

Like all playback display modes except File Information, Highlights mode is disabled by default. Follow the instructions in the "Viewing Picture Data" section, earlier in this chapter, to enable it. You can get a look at the Highlights display in Figure 8-12; there's not much to it except the label Highlights at the bottom of the screen and the number of files/total number of files at the top. The rating, retouch, protected, and send-to-smart device markings also appear if you used those features. (Refer to Figure 8-15.)

RGB Histogram mode

Press the Multi Selector down to shift from Highlights mode to RGB Histogram mode, which displays your image as shown in Figure 8-16. Again, you can view your picture in this mode only if you enable it via the Display Mode option on the Playback menu. (See "Viewing Picture Data," earlier in this chapter, for help.)

Underneath the image thumbnail, you see just a few pieces of data. As with File Information mode, you see the Protected, Retouch, Rating, and Send to Smart Device icons if you used those features. Beneath that, you see the White Balance settings used for the shot. In the figure, the data shows that the picture was captured using the Auto White Balance with

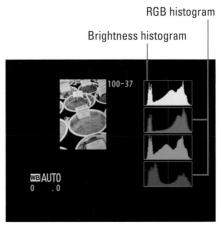

RGB histogram

Brightness histogram

Figure 8-16: RGB Histogram mode presents exposure and color information in chart-like fashion.

zero adjustment along the blue-to-amber axis and zero adjustment along the green-to-magenta axis. (Chapter 5 details White Balance options.) At the top of the display, you see the File number/Total files data, also part of the standard File Information display data.

The keys to this display mode, though, are those chart-like thingies called *histograms.* You get two types of histograms: The top one is a Brightness histogram; the three others are known collectively as an RGB (red, green, blue) histogram.

The next two sections explain what you can discern from the histograms. But first, here's a cool trick to remember: If you press the Zoom In button in this display mode, you can zoom the thumbnail to a magnified view. The histograms then update to reflect only the magnified area of the photo. Use the Multi Selector or drag in the image thumbnail to scroll the display to see other areas of the picture. To return to the regular view and once again see the whole-image histogram, press OK.

Reading a Brightness histogram

You can get an idea of image exposure by viewing your photo on the camera monitor and by looking at the blinkies in Highlight mode. But the Brightness histogram provides a way to gauge exposure that's a little more detailed.

A Brightness histogram indicates the distribution of shadows, highlights, and *midtones* (areas of medium brightness) in an image. Figure 8-17 shows you the histogram for the spice photo featured in Figure 8-16.

The horizontal axis of the histogram represents the possible picture brightness values — the maximum *tonal range,* in photography-speak — from the darkest shadows on the left to the brightest highlights on the right. And the vertical axis shows you how many pixels fall at a particular brightness value. A spike indicates a heavy concentration of pixels at that brightness value.

Shadows   Highlights

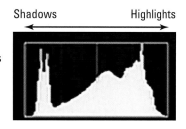

Figure 8-17: The Brightness histogram indicates tonal range, from shadows on the left to highlights on the right.

Keep in mind that there is no "perfect" histogram that you should try to achieve. Instead, interpret the histogram with respect to the distribution of shadows, highlights, and midtones that comprise your subject. You wouldn't expect to see lots of shadows, for example, in a photo of a polar bear walking on a snowy landscape. Pay attention, however, if you see a very high concentration of pixels at the far right or left end of the histogram, which can indicate a seriously overexposed or underexposed image, respectively.

When shooting subjects that contain a significant amount of white, I usually underexpose the photo just a hair. That way, I make sure that I don't blow out highlights. In such cases, the histogram may show no or few pixels at the right end of the scale. Again, though, you have to read the histogram with an eye toward getting the exposure of the main subject correct. Had I increased exposure enough to grow the highlights pixel population for my spice photo, I could easily have created blown highlights in the silver edges of the spice bowls.

Less   More
Saturated   Saturated

Understanding RGB histograms

When you view your images in RGB Histogram display mode, you see two histograms: the Brightness histogram, covered in the preceding section, and an RGB histogram. Figure 8-18 shows you the RGB histogram for the spice photo.

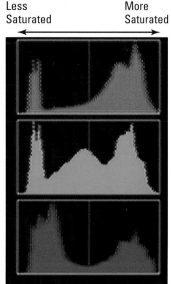

To make sense of an RGB histogram, you first need to know that digital images are known as *RGB images* because they're created from three primary colors of light: red, green, and blue. Whereas the Brightness histogram reflects the brightness of all three color channels rolled into one, RGB histograms let you view the values for each channel.

Figure 8-18: The RGB histogram can indicate problems with color saturation.

When you look at the brightness data for a single channel, though, you glean information about color saturation rather than image brightness. (*Saturation* refers to the purity of a color; a fully saturated color contains no black or white.) I don't have space in this book to provide a full lesson in RGB color theory, but the short story is that when you mix red, green, and blue light, and each component is at maximum brightness, you create white. Zero brightness in all three channels creates black. If you have maximum red and no blue or green, though, you have fully saturated red. If you mix two channels at maximum brightness, you also create full saturation. For example, maximum red and blue produce fully saturated magenta. And, wherever colors are fully saturated, you can lose picture detail. For example, a rose petal that should have a range of tones from medium to dark red may instead be a flat blob of pure red.

The upshot is that if all the pixels for one or two channels are slammed to the right end of the histogram, you may be losing picture detail because of overly saturated colors. If all three channels show a heavy pixel population at the right end of the histogram, you may have blown highlights — again, because the maximum levels of red, green, and blue create white. Either way, you may want to adjust the exposure settings and try again.

A savvy RGB histogram reader can also spot color balance issues by looking at the pixel values. But frankly, color balance problems are fairly easy to notice just by looking at the image on the camera monitor. See Chapter 5 to find out how to correct any color problems that you spot during picture playback.

Shooting Data display mode

Before you can access Shooting Data mode, you must enable it via the Playback Display Options setting on the Playback menu. See the earlier section "Viewing Picture Data" for details. After turning on the option, press the Multi Selector down to shift from RGB Histogram mode to Shooting Data mode.

In this mode, you can view up to five screens of information, which you flip through by pressing the Multi Selector up and down. Figure 8-19 shows just the first two screens of data.

Most of the data you see won't make sense until you explore Chapters 3 through 5, which explain the exposure, color, and focusing settings available on your camera. But I want to call your attention to a few facts now:

- ✔ The upper-left corner of the monitor shows the Protected, Retouch, and Send to Smart Device icons, if you used these features. If you assigned a rating to the file, the rating appears in the lower-left corner. Otherwise, these areas are empty, as in the figures. (Refer to Figure 8-15 to see each of these icons.)

- ✔ The current file number and total number of files appear in the upper-right corner of the display.

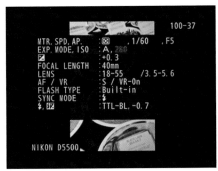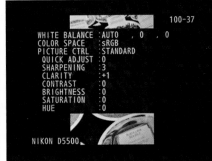

Figure 8-19: Here you see two of the Shooting Data screens.

✔ The Comment item, which is the final item on the third screen, contains a value if you use the Image Comment feature on the Setup menu. I cover this option in Chapter 10 also.

✔ If the ISO value on Shooting Data Page 1 appears in red (refer to the left screen in Figure 8-19), the camera overrode the ISO Sensitivity setting that you selected in order to produce a good exposure. This shift occurs only if you enable automatic ISO adjustment in the P, S, A, and M exposure modes; see Chapter 3 for details.

✔ The fifth data screen appears only if you attach the optional GPS unit to the camera. The GPS location data appears on this screen.

Overview mode

In this mode, the playback screen contains a small image thumbnail along with scads of shooting data — although not quite as much as Shooting Data mode — plus a Brightness histogram. Figure 8-20 offers a look.

The earlier section "Reading a Brightness histogram" tells you what to make of that part of the screen. Just above the histogram, you see the Protected, Retouch, and Send to Smart Device symbols, if you used those features, and the File number/Total files data appears at the upper-right corner of the image thumbnail. If you used the Rating feature, the rating appears under the thumbnail. (Again, refer to Figure 8-15 to see these miscellaneous symbols.)

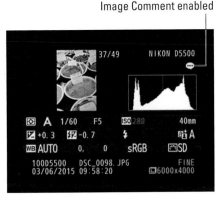

Figure 8-20: In Overview mode, you can view your picture along with the major camera settings you used to take the picture.

One more tiny symbol to notice: The speech bubble just above the histogram indicates that you enabled the Image Comment feature (Chapter 10). To actually read the comment, you need to go to the fourth data screen shown in Shooting Data display mode.

To sort out the maze of other information, the following list breaks down the five rows that appear under the thumbnail and histogram. In the accompanying figures as well as in Figure 8-20, I include all possible data simply for the purpose of illustration; if any of the items don't appear on your screen, it simply means that the relevant feature wasn't enabled when you captured the shot. Also note that if you're looking at a movie file, the screen shows only the third row of data, and the histogram represents the exposure of the first frame of the movie.

 ✔ **Row 1:** This row shows the exposure settings labeled in Figure 8-21, along with the focal length of the lens you used to take the shot. As in Shooting Data mode, the ISO value appears red (as in the figure) if you enabled auto ISO override in the P, S, A, or M exposure modes and the camera adjusted the ISO for you.

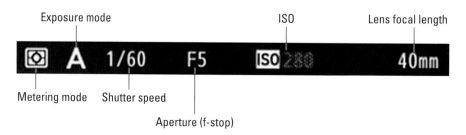

Figure 8-21: Here you can inspect major exposure settings along with the lens focal length.

 ✔ **Row 2:** This row contains a few additional exposure settings, labeled in Figure 8-22. See Chapter 3 for explanations of all these settings except Flash Compensation and Flash Mode, which I cover in Chapter 2.

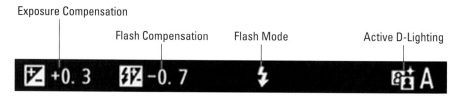

Figure 8-22: This row contains additional exposure information.

↙ **Row 3:** Items on this row, labeled in Figure 8-23, pertain to color options you can explore in Chapter 5.

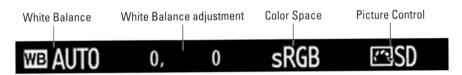

White Balance   White Balance adjustment   Color Space   Picture Control

Figure 8-23: Look at this row for details about color settings.

↙ **Rows 4 and 5:** The final two rows of data (refer to Figure 8-20) show the same information you get in File Information mode, explained earlier in this chapter.

Viewing Your Photos on a Television

Your camera is equipped with a feature that allows you to play your pictures and movies on a television screen. In fact, you have three playback options:

↙ **Regular (standard definition) video playback:** Haven't made the leap yet to HDTV? No worries: You can set the camera to send a regular standard-definition audio and video signal to the TV. The cable you need is even provided in the camera box. Look for the cable that has yellow, red, and white plugs at one end.

↙ **HDMI playback:** If you have a high-definition television, you need to purchase an HDMI cable to connect the camera and television. You need a Type C mini-pin HD cable; prices start at about $20. Nikon doesn't make its own cable, so just look for a quality third-party version.

By default, the camera decides the proper HD video resolution to send to the TV after you connect the two devices. But you have the option of setting a specific resolution as well. To do so, select HDMI from the Setup menu, press OK, and select Output Resolution, as shown in Figure 8-24. Press the Multi Selector right or tap Output Resolution to access the available settings.

↙ **For HDMI CEC TV sets:** If your television is compatible with HDMI CEC, your D5500 enables you to use the buttons on the TV's remote control to perform the functions of the OK button and Multi Selector during full-frame picture playback and slide shows. To make this feature work, you must enable it via the Setup menu. Again, start with the HDMI option, but this time, select Device Control and set the option to On.

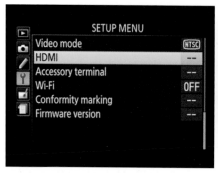
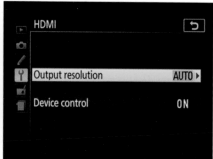

Figure 8-24: Select options for HD playback here.

You need to make one final preflight check before connecting the camera and television: Verify the status of the Video Mode setting on the Setup menu. You have two options: NTSC and PAL. Select the video mode used by your part of the world. (In the United States, Canada, and Mexico, NTSC is the standard.)

After you select the necessary Setup menu options, grab your video cable, turn off the camera, and plug the cable into the camera. The connection port for a standard A/V cable is found under the door on the left side of the camera, as shown on the left in Figure 8-25. Look for the HDMI out port under the cover on the right side of the camera, shown on the right in the figure.

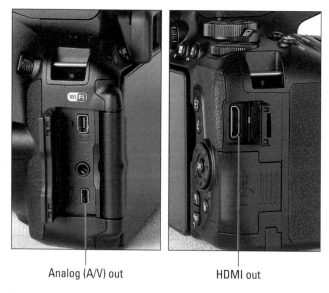

Analog (A/V) out   HDMI out

Figure 8-25: The video-out ports are under the little rubber doors on the sides of the camera.

The smaller plug on the A/V cable attaches to the camera. The yellow plug goes into your TV's video jack; the white one, to the left audio channel jack; and the red one, to the right audio channel jack. For HDMI playback, a single plug goes to the TV.

At this point, I need to point you to your TV manual to find out exactly which jacks to use to connect your camera. You also need to consult the manual to find out which channel to select for playback of signals from auxiliary input devices. Then just turn on your camera to send the signal to the TV set. If you don't have the latest and greatest HDMI CEC capability (or you lost your remote), control playback using the same techniques as you normally do to view pictures on your camera monitor. You can also run a slide show by following the steps outlined in Chapter 11.

9

Working with Picture and Movie Files

*E*very creative pursuit involves its share of cleanup and organizational tasks. Painters have to wash brushes, embroiderers have to separate strands of floss, wood-crafters have to haul out the wet/dry vac to suck up sawdust. Digital photography is no different: At some point, you have to stop shooting so that you can download and process your files.

This chapter explains these after-the-shot tasks. First up is a review of several in-camera file-management operations: rate files, delete unwanted files, and protect your best work from accidental erasure. Following that, you can get help with transferring files to your computer, processing files that you shot in the Raw (NEF) format, preparing images for online sharing, and using the camera's built-in Wi-Fi system to send pictures to a smartphone or tablet. Along the way, I also introduce you to Nikon's free photo software, Nikon ViewNX 2, which offers an easy way to handle many of these jobs.

Rating Photos and Movies

Using your camera's Rating feature, you can assign a rating to a picture or movie file: five stars for your best shots, one star for those you wish you could reshoot, and so on. You can even assign a Discard rating to flag images that you think you want to delete.

Rating pictures has several benefits. First, when you create a slide show, as outlined in Chapter 11, you can tell the camera to display only photos that have a certain rating. (If you want people to think you're an awesome photographer, don't include anything that has less than a five-star rating.) Second, assigning the Delete tag makes it easy to spot the rotten apples amid all your great photos and movies when you take the step of erasing files. Finally, if you use Nikon ViewNX 2 to view your files after downloading, you can sort pictures according to rating, making it easier to cull your photo collection and gather your best work for printing and sharing.

Before showing you how to rate photos, I need to share one rule of the road: If you protect a photo using the feature described in the later section "Protecting Photos," you can't alter the file in any way — and that includes assigning a rating to it. See the aforementioned section to find out how to remove protected status from a file, if necessary.

Assuming that the file isn't protected, you can assign a rating in two ways:

- **Choose Rating from the Playback menu.** Select Rating, as shown on the left in Figure 9-1, to display image thumbnails, as shown on the right. Select the photo or movie you want to rate by tapping it or pressing the Multi Selector right or left to move the yellow highlight box over the image. Rotate the Command dial or swipe your finger up or down to scroll the screen vertically.

  To assign a rating, you can tap the thumbnail according to how many stars you want to assign: tap once for one star, twice for two stars, and so on. You also can tap the Set symbol at the bottom of the screen. Either way, a symbol representing the rating appears with the thumbnail, as labeled in the figure.

  The problem with these touchscreen methods is that there's no way to lower the rating or remove it after you tap. You also can't get to the Discard rating via touchscreen. For full control, assign the rating by pressing the Multi Selector up or down. Select the symbol that looks like a trash can to select the Discard rating. (Refer to the right screen in Figure 9-1.)

Star rating   Discard rating

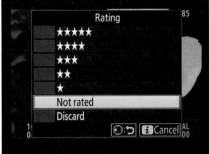

Figure 9-1: You can rate a batch of photos by choosing Rating from the Playback menu.

For a closer view of a selected photo, tap the Zoom symbol at the bottom of the screen or press the Zoom In button. Tap the return arrow (top-right corner of screen) or release the button to return to thumbnails view.

To rate another photo, select it and repeat the process. Tap OK or press the OK button to exit to the Playback menu.

✓ **Set the camera to playback mode, display the photo or movie, and press the *i* button.** The screen shown on the left in Figure 9-2 appears over your photo or first frame of your movie. Select Rating to display the second screen in the figure. Tap the rating you want to assign or use the Multi Selector to highlight it and then press the OK button.

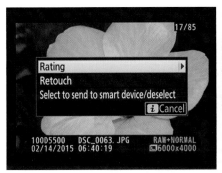

Figure 9-2: During playback, press the *i* button and select Rating to access the rating options.

When you view your pictures or movies in playback mode, the rating appears with the image or on the first frame of the movie. Figure 9-3 shows you where to find the rating in the default display mode (File Information mode). For more about playback display modes, see Chapter 8.

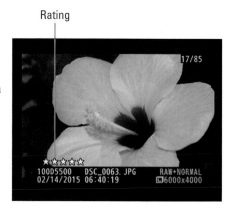

Rating

17/85

★☆☆☆☆
100D5500   DSC_0063. JPG   RAW+NORMAL
02/14/2015 06:40:19   6000x4000

Figure 9-3: The current rating appears here in File Information playback mode.

Deleting Photo and Movie Files

You have three options for erasing files from a memory card when it's in your camera. The next few sections give you the lowdown.

 One note before you begin: None of the Delete features erase pictures or movies that you protect via the option that I outline in the upcoming section "Protecting Photos." To erase protected files, you must first remove the file protection.

Deleting files one at a time

 During picture playback, you can use the Delete button to erase photos and movie files. But the process varies depending on the current playback mode:

- ✔ In single-image view — that is, you're viewing each photo or movie one at a time — press the Delete button.

- ✔ In thumbnails view (displaying 4, 12, or 80 thumbnails), select the photo you want to erase and then press Delete.

 - ✔ In calendar view, select the date that contains the image. Then press the Zoom Out button or tap the Zoom Out symbol to activate the thumbnail list. Select an image and press Delete.

You then see a message asking whether you really want to erase the file. If you do, press Delete again. To cancel the process, press the Playback button.

 By default, still photos appear briefly on the monitor after the shot is recorded. (You enable or disable this feature via the Image Review option on the Playback menu.) During this instant review period, you can press the Delete button to trash the file immediately. But you have to be quick or else the camera returns to shooting mode.

Deleting all files

Open the Playback menu, select Delete, and then select All, as illustrated in Figure 9-4. When the camera asks you to verify that you want to delete all your pictures and movies, select Yes.

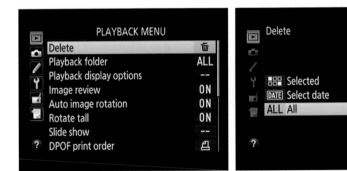

Figure 9-4: To delete all files on the memory card, use this Playback menu option.

 If your memory card contains multiple folders, these steps delete only pictures in the folder that is currently selected via the Playback Folder option on the Playback menu. See the section "Choosing Which Images to View," in Chapter 8, for information.

Deleting a batch of selected files

When you want to get rid of more than a few files — but not erase all pictures and movies on the card — don't waste time erasing each file, one at a time. Instead, you can tag multiple files for deletion and then take them all out to the trash at one time.

To start, select Delete from the Playback menu. You then see the screen shown on the left in Figure 9-5, which offers two options for selecting specific files to erase:

 ✔ **Selected:** Use this option if the files you want to delete weren't all taken on the same day. Choose Selected to display a screen of thumbnails, as shown on the right in the figure. Select the first photo you want to delete by tapping it or by using the Multi Selector or Command dial to move the yellow box over it. Then tap Set or press the Zoom Out button. A trash can appears in the upper-right corner of the thumbnail. In the figure, the two photos in the top-right corner of the screen are tagged for erasure.

If you change your mind, tap Set or press the Zoom Out button again to remove the Delete tag. To undo deletion for all selected photos, press the Playback button or tap the return arrow in the upper-right corner of the screen.

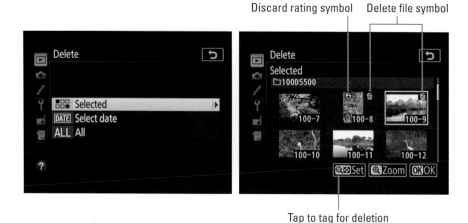

Discard rating symbol   Delete file symbol

Tap to tag for deletion

Figure 9-5: This Delete menu option offers a quick way to delete a batch of photos.

 For a closer look at the selected image, tap the Zoom symbol onscreen or press and hold the Zoom In button. To exit the magnified view, release the button or tap the return arrow.

One important note: Images that you tag with the Discard rating, as explained in the first section of this chapter, are *not* officially marked for the trash heap. When you view your files, you see the Discard rating symbol, labeled on the right in Figure 9-5; when you select the photo via the Delete menu, you see the symbol marked Delete File in the figure. That's the symbol that triggers the camera to dump the file.

✔ **Select Date:** Use this option to quickly delete any record of that day you'd rather not remember. After choosing Select Date, as shown on the left in Figure 9-6, you see a list of dates, as shown on the right. To trash all files from that date, put a check mark in box to the left of the date. You can either tap the box or highlight the date and press the Multi Selector right to toggle the check mark on and off.

Can't remember what photos are associated with the selected date? Try these tricks:

 • To display thumbnails of all files recorded on the selected date, tap the Confirm box at the bottom of the screen or press the Zoom Out button.

 • While thumbnails are displayed, tap Zoom or press the Zoom In button to magnify the selected thumbnail.

• To return from thumbnails view to the date list, tap the Back button (bottom of the screen, marked with the Zoom Out button symbol) or press the Zoom Out button again.

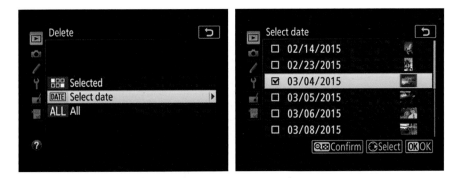

Figure 9-6: With the Select Date option, you can quickly erase all photos taken on a specific date.

After tagging files for deletion or specifying a date to delete, tap OK or press the OK button. Select Yes when the camera asks for confirmation that you want to erase the files.

 You have one alternative way to quickly erase all files shot on a specific date: In the Calendar display mode, highlight the date and then press the Delete button. You see the standard confirmation screen; press Delete again to wrap up. Visit Chapter 8 for the scoop on Calendar display mode.

Protecting Photos

You can protect picture and movie files from accidental erasure by giving them *protected* status. After you take this step, the camera doesn't allow you to delete the file from your memory card, whether you press the Delete button or use the Delete option on the Playback menu.

 I also use the Protect feature when I want to keep a handful of pictures on the card but delete the rest. Rather than use the options I describe in the preceding section to select all the pictures I want to trash, I protect the handful I want to preserve. Then I set the Delete menu option to All and dump the rest. The protected pictures remain intact.

 Formatting your memory card *does* erase even protected pictures. In addition, when you protect a picture, it shows up as a read-only file when you transfer it to your computer. Files that have the read-only status can't be altered until you unlock them in your photo software. (In Nikon ViewNX 2, select the image and then choose File ⇨ Protect Files ⇨ Unprotect.)

Remember, too, that locking the file prevents you from assigning a rating to it — so rate photos before giving them protected status. (Refer to the first section of this chapter for information about the Rating feature.)

To protect a file, take these steps:

1. **Display the picture or movie file you want to protect in single-image view.**

   Or, in Thumbnails view or Calendar view, select the file thumbnail. (Either tap it or use the Multi Selector or Command dial to surround it with a yellow selection box.)

2. **Press the AE-L/AF-L button, highlighted in Figure 9-7.**

   See the key symbol to the lower left of the button? That's your reminder that you use the button to lock a picture. A key symbol also appears with locked photos during playback, as shown in Figure 9-7.

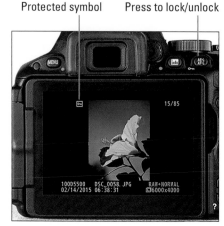

Protected symbol   Press to lock/unlock

Figure 9-7: Press the AE-L/AF-L button to give an image protected status.

To remove protection, display or select the image and then press the AE-L/AF-L button again.

Taking a Look at Nikon's Free Photo Software (ViewNX 2)

When you're ready to move pictures and movies from your camera to your computer, you need some type of photo program to download, view, and manage the files. If you don't already have a favorite photo program, the free software that Nikon provides, Nikon ViewNX 2, may be all you need. Along with features that enable you to download, view, and organize your photos, the program offers basic editing tools as well as a Raw-file converter. Figure 9-8 offers a look at the ViewNX 2 window as it appears when you use Image Viewer display mode, one of three options available from the View menu.

Nikon ViewNX 2 is available for download from the Nikon website (in the United States, www.nikonusa.com). Just head for the Support section of the website, where you'll find a link to camera software. Be sure to download the latest version: At the time I write this chapter, it's Version 2.10.3. Older versions of the software lack support for all D5500 file features.

I don't have room to provide a complete tutorial in using Nikon ViewNX 2, but upcoming sections show you how to use the program to download pictures to your computer, process Raw files, and shrink a high-resolution file to a size that's suitable for online sharing.

Click to hide/display focus point

Focus point

Click to hide/display metadata

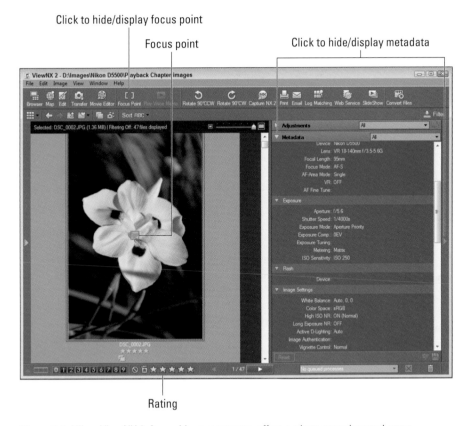

Rating

Figure 9-8: Nikon ViewNX 2, free with your camera, offers a photo organizer and some photo-editing functions.

Before I dig into those file-handling features, I want to spotlight a few Nikon ViewNX 2 features that may make it worth your while to install the program even if you already have another program that you use regularly:

✔ **Viewing image metadata:** *Metadata* is hidden data that includes the camera settings you used to take the picture. If you added a descriptive label through the Image Comment feature that I cover in Chapter 10, it's also stored as metadata.

To display metadata, click an image thumbnail and then display the Metadata panel, located on the right side of the program window (refer to Figure 9-8). If the panel is hidden, choose Window➪Edit or click the triangle on the far right side of the window, and then click the triangle at the top of the panel. (I labeled both controls in the figure.) Many other photo programs also display metadata but sometimes can't reveal data that's very camera-specific.

✔ **Viewing the focus point:** Here's a trick that you can't do in other photo programs: Click the Focus Point button, labeled in Figure 9-8, to display a red rectangle that indicates which focus point (or points, in some cases) the camera used to establish focus, which can be helpful when you're trying to troubleshoot focus problems. You don't see the point if you used manual focusing, and it also may not appear if you used continuous autofocusing.

✔ **Viewing the assigned picture rating:** If you used the Rating feature described earlier in this chapter, the rating appears at the bottom of the screen (refer to Figure 9-8) and in the Tags section of the Metadata panel (not shown in the figure). You can change the rating or assign ratings to unrated photos in Nikon ViewNX 2 as well. To sort photos by rating, choose View⇨Sort Thumbnails By⇨Rating.

For complete details on using these and other program features, select Help⇨ViewNx 2 Help, which opens the built-in user manual.

At press time, Nikon was preparing to release the successor to ViewNX 2, which it calls Nikon ViewNX-i. So check the Nikon website for information about this upcoming program and also check into Nikon's pro-level offerings (which, sadly, are not free).

Downloading Pictures to the Computer

You can move picture and movie files to your computer in two ways:

✔ **Connect the camera to the computer via a USB cable.** The cable you need is supplied in the camera box.

✔ **Use a memory card reader.** With a card reader, you simply pop the memory card out of your camera and into the card reader. Many computers and printers now have card readers, and you also can buy stand-alone readers for less than $30.

I recommend using a card reader because sending pictures directly from the camera requires that the camera be turned on during the download process, wasting battery power. However, I include information about cable transfer in the next section, in case you don't have a card reader. To use a card reader, skip ahead to "Starting the transfer process."

What about wireless transfer, you ask? Well, there is one way to do it: You can buy Eye-Fi memory cards, which have wireless connectivity built in. You can find out more about these cards and how to set them up to connect with your computer at the manufacturer's website, www.eye.fi. Also check the Eye-Fi details provided in the D5500 manual; look for the section related to the Eye-Fi Upload option on the Setup menu. (The menu item appears only when an Eye-Fi card is installed.) I don't cover these cards in this book.

As for the camera's Wi-Fi feature, it enables you only to connect to Android- and iOS-based phones, tablets, and other smart devices. You can't use it to download files to your computer wirelessly. For details about using the Wi-Fi features, see the end of this chapter.

Connecting via USB

To link your camera to your computer via the provided USB cable, take these steps:

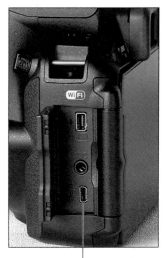

USB port

Figure 9-9: The port for connecting the USB cable is hidden under the rubber door on the left side of the camera.

1. **Check the level of the camera battery.**

   If the battery is low, charge it before continuing. Running out of battery power during downloading can cause problems, including lost picture data. Alternatively, if you purchased the optional AC adapter, use it to power the camera during downloading.

2. **Turn on the computer and give it time to finish its normal start-up routine.**

3. **Turn off the camera.**

4. **Insert the smaller of the two plugs on the USB cable into the USB port on the side of the camera.**

   Look under the rubber door on the left side of the camera for this port, labeled in Figure 9-9.

5. **Plug the other end of the cable into a USB port on the computer.**

6. **Turn on the camera.**

   What happens now depends on the photo software you have installed on your computer. The next section explains the possibilities and how to proceed with the transfer process.

7. **When the download is complete, turn off the camera and then disconnect it from the computer.**

Starting the transfer process

After you connect the camera to the computer or insert a memory card into a card reader, what happens next depends on the software installed on your computer. Here are the most common possibilities and how to move forward:

✔ **An installed photo program automatically displays a photo-download wizard.** For example, the downloader associated with Nikon ViewNX 2, Adobe Lightroom, iPhoto, or another photo program may leap to the forefront. Usually, the downloader that appears is associated with the software that you most recently installed.

On a Windows-based computer, the Windows operating software may present a box of transfer options. Figure 9-10 shows this dialog box as it appears in Windows 7. By default, clicking the Import Pictures and Videos link brings up Windows' own file-transfer program, but you can click Change Program to choose any other photo program.

If you don't want a program's downloader to launch whenever you insert a memory card or connect your camera, you can turn off that feature. Check the software manual to find out how to disable the auto launch.

✔ **Nothing happens.** Don't panic; assuming that your card reader or camera is properly connected, all is probably well. Someone simply may have disabled all the automatic downloaders on your system. Just launch your photo software and then transfer your pictures using whatever command starts that process.

As another option, you can use Windows Explorer or the Mac Finder to drag and drop files from your memory card to your computer. You connect the card through a card reader, and the computer sees the card as just another drive on the system. Windows Explorer also shows the camera as a storage device when you cable the camera directly to the computer. So the process of transferring files is exactly the same as when you move any other file from a CD, DVD, or flash drive onto your computer. (With some versions of the Mac OS, including the most recent ones, the Finder doesn't recognize cameras in this way.)

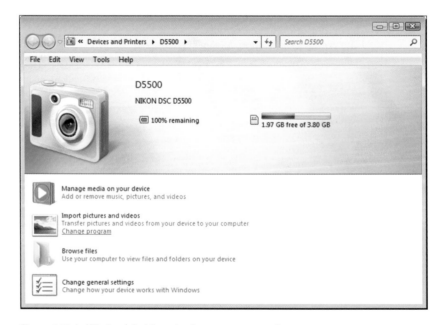

Figure 9-10: In Windows 7, this option box may appear when you connect your camera or memory card to the computer.

In the next section, I provide details on using Nikon ViewNX 2 to download your files. If you use another program, the concepts are the same, but check the program manual to get the details. In most programs, you also can find lots of information by simply clicking open the Help menu.

Downloading using ViewNX 2

Built into ViewNX 2 is a downloading tool called Nikon Transfer 2. Follow these steps to use it to transfer pictures to your computer:

1. **Attach your camera to the computer or insert a memory card into your card reader.**

   Depending on what software you have installed on your system, you may see a dialog box asking you how to download your photos. If the window that appears is the Nikon Transfer 2 window, shown in Figure 9-11, skip to Step 3.

   If nothing happens, travel to Step 2, which shows you how to launch the Nikon Transfer 2 software if it didn't appear automatically.

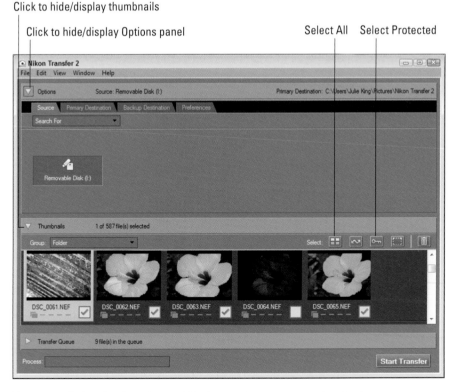

Figure 9-11: Select the check boxes of the images that you want to download.

2. **Launch Nikon Transfer 2 (if it isn't already open).**

   Open Nikon ViewNX 2 and then choose File⇨Launch Transfer or click the Transfer button at the top of the window. The window shown in Figure 9-11 appears. (If you use a Mac, the window decor is slightly different, but the main controls and features are the same.)

3. **Display the Source tab to view thumbnails of your pictures, as shown in the figure.**

   Don't see any tabs? Click the Options triangle (refer to Figure 9-11) to display them. Then click the Source tab. The icon representing your camera or memory card should be selected, as shown in the figure. If not, click the icon.

   Thumbnails of your files appear in the bottom half of the dialog box. If you don't see the thumbnails, click the Thumbnails triangle (refer to Figure 9-11) to open the thumbnails area.

4. **Select the files that you want to download.**

   Click a thumbnail to highlight it and then click the box in the lower-right corner of the thumbnail to select that image or movie for downloading. Here are a few tips to speed up this process:

   - *Select protected files only.* If you used the in-camera function to protect pictures, you can select just those images by clicking the Select Protected icon (refer to Figure 9-11).

   - *Select all files.* Click the Select All icon, also labeled in the figure.

5. **Click the Primary Destination tab to display options for handling the file transfer, as shown in Figure 9-12.**

Select storage folder

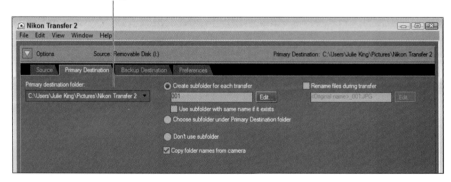

Figure 9-12: Specify the folder where you want to put the downloaded images.

Specify these options:

- *Primary Destination Folder:* Open this drop-down list and choose the folder on your computer's hard drive (or external drive) where you want to put the pictures.

- *Create Subfolder for Each Transfer:* By default, the program creates a new folder inside the storage folder you selected. Then it puts all the pictures from the current download session into that new subfolder. You can either use the numerical subfolder name that the program suggests or click the Edit button to set up your own naming system.

- *Use Subfolder with Same Name If It Exists:* If the folder shown in the Create Subfolder box already exists, select this check box to avoid overwriting existing photo files. The program automatically assigns new filenames to the downloaded photos if the folder contains images that have the same filenames as the downloading ones.

- *Choose Subfolder Under Primary Destination Folder:* Select this option to put files into a subfolder that already exists inside the primary destination folder or to create a new folder there. After you choose the option, look for the Primary Destination text that appears in the upper-right corner of the dialog box. A drop-down list showing current subfolders appears; you can select one of those folders or delete the name of the current subfolder and type a new name.

- *Don't Use Subfolder:* If you choose this option, pictures go into the primary folder.

- *Copy Folder Names from Camera:* Select this option to retain the folder structure of the memory card. That folder is placed inside whatever folder or subfolder you select via the other options.

Yowza. Don't ever say that the program developers didn't want you to have plenty of storage folder flexibility.

6. **Tell the program whether you want to rename the picture files during the download process.**

If you do, select the Rename Files during Transfer check box. Then click the Edit button to display a dialog box where you can set up your new file-naming scheme. Click OK after you do so to close the dialog box.

7. **(Optional) Set a backup destination.**

This feature enables you to download photos to your primary drive and to a backup drive at the same time. To set up the dual transfer, click the Backup Destination tab, select the Backup Files box, and then use the other panel options to specify where you want the files to go.

8. **Click the Preferences tab to set the rest of the transfer options.**

On this tab, you find more options that control how the program operates. Rather than cover all of them, which are explained quite nicely in the program's Help system (access it via the Help menu), I want to highlight just three critical options:

- *Transfer New Files Only:* This option, when selected, ensures that you don't waste time downloading images that you've already transferred but are still on the memory card.

- *Delete Original Files after Transfer:* **Turn off this option**. Otherwise, your pictures are automatically erased from your memory card when the transfer is complete. Always make sure the pictures really made it to the computer before you delete them from your memory card. (See "Deleting Photos and Movie Files" to find out how to use the Delete function on your camera.)

- *Open Destination Folder with the Following Application after Transfer:* You can tell the program to immediately open your photo program after the transfer is complete. Choose ViewNX 2 to view, organize, and edit your photos using that program. To choose another program, open the drop-down list, choose Browse, and select the program from the dialog box that appears. Click OK after doing so.

Your choices remain in force for any subsequent download sessions, so you don't have to revisit this tab unless you want the program to behave differently.

9. **Click the Start Transfer button.**

It's located in the lower-right corner of the program window. After you click the button, the Process bar in the lower-left corner indicates how the transfer is progressing. What happens when the transfer completes depends on the choices you made in Step 8; if you selected Nikon ViewNX 2 as the photo program, it opens and displays the folder that contains your just-downloaded images.

Processing Raw (NEF) Files

Chapter 2 introduces you to the Raw file format. The advantage of capturing Raw files — NEF files on Nikon cameras — is that you make the decisions about how to translate the original picture data into an actual photograph. You take this step by using a software tool known as a *Raw converter.* To process your NEF files, you have the following free options:

⤴ **Use the in-camera processing feature.** From the Retouch menu, you can process Raw images right in the camera. You can specify only limited image attributes, and you can save the processed files only in the JPEG format, but still, having this option is a nice feature.

> ✔ **Process and convert in ViewNX 2.** ViewNX 2 also offers a Raw process-
> ing feature. Again, the controls for setting picture characteristics are a
> little limited, but you can save the adjusted files in either the JPEG or TIFF
> format (TIFF is better at holding onto the original image quality than JPEG).
>
> TIFF stands for Tagged Image File Format and has long been the stan-
> dard format for images destined for professional publication.

The next two sections show you how to convert Raw files using your camera
and ViewNX 2. If you're a dedicated Raw shooter, however, you may want
to invest in a program that offers a bit more control over Raw processing
than these two options. One program to consider is Nikon's own pro-level
software, Nikon Capture NX2 (www.nikon.com); again, watch for news of
the program's new incarnation, Capture NX-D, too. Other popular programs
include three Adobe offerings: Adobe Photoshop, Adobe Lightroom, and
Adobe Photoshop Elements (www.adobe.com). Visit the respective websites
for details about each program; in some cases, you can download a free
30-day trial to find out before you buy whether the program is to your liking.

Processing Raw images in the camera

By using the NEF (RAW) Processing option on the Retouch menu, you can
create a JPEG version of a Raw file right in the camera. Follow these steps:

1. Press the Playback button to switch to playback mode.

2. Display the picture in the full-frame view.

If necessary, you can shift from thumbnails view to single-image view by
pressing OK. Press OK twice if you're in calendar view. (Chapter 8 has
details on these playback modes.)

3. Press the *i* button.

You see the screen shown on the left in Figure 9-13.

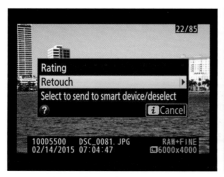
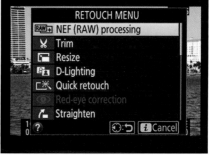

Figure 9-13: Select Retouch (left screen) and then scroll to the NEF (RAW) Processing
option (right screen).

4. **Select Retouch to display the Retouch menu.**

5. **Select NEF (RAW) Processing, as shown on the right side of Figure 9-13.**

   You must scroll to the second page of the Retouch menu to get to the option.

   After you choose NEF (RAW) Processing, you see a screen similar to the one in Figure 9-14, which is where you specify which settings you want the camera to use when creating the JPEG version of the Raw image. Press the Multi Selector down or swipe your finger down the monitor to access the second page of options, shown in Figure 9-15.

6. **Set the conversion options.**

   Along the right side of the screen, you see a column offering the conversion options labeled in Figures 9-14 and 9-15. Select any setting by tapping it or highlighting it and pressing the Multi Selector right. You then uncover the options available for that setting. Make your choice, select a setting, and press OK or tap the return arrow in the upper-right corner of the screen to return to the main Raw conversion screen. Or, if a triangle appears to the right of an option name, press the Multi Selector right or tap the option name again to uncover additional settings.

   If you're not familiar with all the settings, the following list offers a few general recommendations and points you to the chapter where you can get more information:

   - *Image Quality:* Choose Fine to retain maximum picture quality. See the Chapter 2 section related to the JPEG format for details on this option.

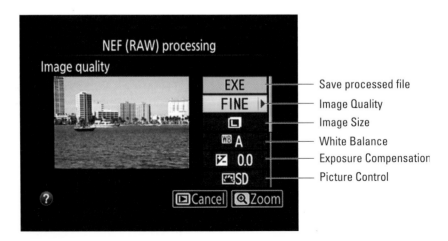

Figure 9-14: These Raw conversion options are on the first page of the menu screen.

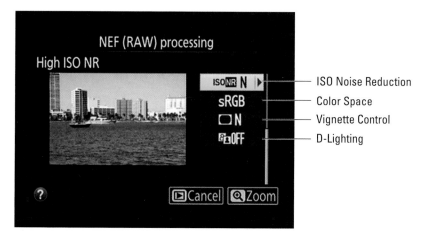

Figure 9-15: Scroll to page two to access these additional conversion settings.

- *Image Size:* Chapter 2 explains this one, too. Choose Large to retain all the original image pixels.

- *White Balance:* Unless image colors appear to be wrong, stick with the default, Auto. Otherwise, experiment with each setting to see which one renders colors most accurately. Check out Chapter 5 for details about White Balance.

- *Exposure Compensation:* With this option, which I cover in Chapter 3, you can adjust image brightness. When using this feature for Raw conversion, you're limited to a range of –2.0 and +2.0; when shooting, you can choose from settings ranging from –5.0 to +5.0. Raise the value for a brighter image; lower it for a darker shot. The camera updates the preview to indicate how your setting will affect the picture.

- *Picture Control:* This option, detailed in Chapter 5, enables you to adjust color saturation, contrast, and image sharpness. As with the White Balance and Exposure Compensation settings, the screen updates to show you the effect of the selected Picture Control. To fine-tune the look applied by the Picture Control, tap the Adjust symbol at the bottom of the screen or press the Multi Selector right.

- *ISO Noise Reduction:* If your picture looks *noisy* — that is, marred by a speckled look — playing with this setting may help eliminate the flaw. See Chapter 3 for an explanation of this feature, which is designed to reduce the amount of noise in pictures shot using a high ISO Sensitivity setting.

- *Color Space:* This setting determines whether the camera sticks with the default color space, sRGB, or the larger Adobe RGB color space when converting your photo. Stick with sRGB until you digest the Chapter 5 section that details this option.

  - *Vignette Control:* If the corners of your image appear unnaturally dark, experiment with this option to see whether it can correct the problem. See Chapter 3 for more about Vignette Control.

  - *D-Lighting:* To brighten the darkest part of your picture without also brightening the lightest areas, try adjusting this setting, which is the post-capture equivalent of the Active D-Lighting option that I cover in Chapter 3.

You can magnify the image by pressing the Zoom In button or tapping the Zoom icon at the bottom of the screen. Release the button or tap the return arrow to return to the normal display.

7. Select EXE on the first conversion screen (refer to Figure 9-14) and press OK.

The camera records a JPEG copy of your Raw file and displays the copy in the monitor. The camera assigns the next available file number to the image, so the number of the original and the number of the processed JPEG don't match. You see the little Retouch menu symbol (the box with a paintbrush) with the JPEG copy during playback.

You also can access the Raw processing tool by displaying the Retouch menu and choosing NEF (RAW) Processing. The camera displays thumbnails of Raw images; select an image and then tap OK or press the OK button to get to the processing options.

Processing Raw files in ViewNX 2

In Nikon ViewNX 2, you can convert your Raw files to the JPEG format or, for top picture quality, to the TIFF format. Follow these steps to try it out:

1. Open ViewNX 2 and click the file that you want to process.

You may want to set the program to Image Viewer mode, as shown in Figure 9-16, so that you can see a larger preview of the image. Just choose View ⇨ Image Viewer to switch to this display mode. To give the photo even more room, also hide the Browser panel, which normally occupies the left third of the window, and the Filmstrip panel that usually runs across the bottom of the window. Choose Window ⇨ Browser and Window ⇨ Filmstrip to toggle those window elements on and off.

2. Display the Adjustments panel (refer to Figure 9-16).

Show and hide this panel and the Metadata panel by choosing Window ⇨ Edit or by clicking the triangle on the far right side of the window. You can then display and collapse the individual panels by

Click to hide/display Adjustments panel

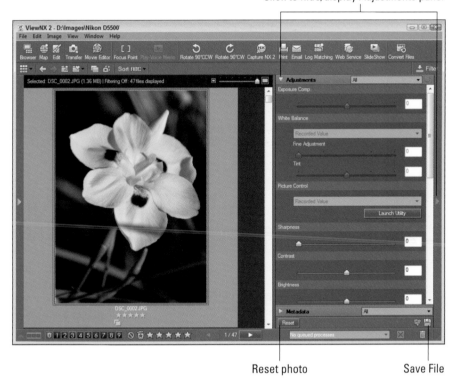

Reset photo   Save File

Figure 9-16: Display the Adjustments panel to tweak Raw images before conversion.

clicking the triangles to the left of their names. (I labeled the triangles in the figure.) To allow the maximum space for the Raw conversion adjustments, collapse the Metadata panel, as shown in the figure.

3. **To display all available settings, choose All from the Adjustments drop-down list (top of the Adjustments panel; refer to Figure 9-16).**

4. **Use the panel controls to adjust the image.**

   The preview in the image window reflects the default conversion settings chosen by Nikon, but you can play with any of the settings. You may need to use the scroll bar on the right side of the panel to scroll the display to see all the options. If you need help understanding any of the options, open the built-in Help system (via the Help menu), where you can find descriptions of how each adjustment affects the image.

   To return to the original image settings, click the Reset button at the bottom of the panel (refer to Figure 9-16).

5. Click the Save button (refer to Figure 9-16).

This step stores your conversion settings as part of the image file but doesn't actually create the processed image file. Don't worry, though. Your original Raw data remains intact; all that's saved with the file is a "recipe" for processing the image, which you can change at any time.

6. To save the processed file, choose File ➪ Convert Files.

You see the Convert Files dialog box, shown in Figure 9-17.

7. Choose TIFF (8 Bit) from the File Format drop-down list.

TIFF is the best format because it retains your processed file at the highest image quality. (This format has long been the preferred format for print publication.) Don't choose JPEG; as explained in Chapter 2, the JPEG format applies *lossy compression,* thereby sacrificing some image quality. If you need a JPEG copy of your processed Raw image for online sharing — TIFF files won't work for that use — you can create one by following the steps laid out in the upcoming section "Prepping online photos using ViewNX 2."

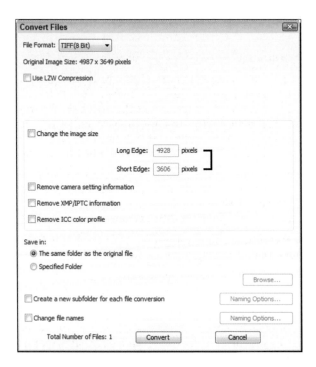

Figure 9-17: To retain the best image quality, save processed Raw files in the TIFF format.

As for the *8 Bit* part of the option name: A *bit* is a unit of computer data; the more bits you have, the more colors your image can contain. Although you can create 16-bit TIFF files in the converter, some photo-editing programs either can't open them or limit you to a few editing tools, so I suggest you stick with the standard, 8-bit image option unless you know your software can handle the larger-bit images.

8. **Deselect the Use LZW Compression option.**

   Although LZW compression reduces the file size somewhat and does not cause any quality loss, some programs can't open files that were saved with this option enabled, so turn it off.

9. **Deselect the Change the Image Size check box.**

   This step ensures that you retain all the original pixels in the processed image.

10. **Deselect each of the three Remove check boxes.**

    If you select the check boxes, you strip image *metadata* — the extra text data that's stored by the camera — from the file. Unless you have some specific reason to do so, clear all three check boxes so that you can continue to access the metadata when you view the processed image in programs that know how to display metadata.

11. **Select a storage location for the processed TIFF file.**

    You do this in the Save In area of the dialog box. Select the top option to save your processed file in the same folder as the original. Or, to put the file in a different folder, select the Specified Folder button. If you do, you see the name of the currently selected alternative folder below the button; change the storage destination by clicking the Browse button and then selecting the drive and folder where you want to put the file.

    By selecting the Create a New Subfolder for Each File Conversion check box, you can put your TIFF file into a separate folder within the destination folder. With this check box enabled, click the Naming Options button and then specify how you want to name the subfolder.

12. **Specify whether you want to give the processed TIFF a different filename from the original Raw image.**

    To do so, select the Change File Names check box, click the Naming Options button, and enter the name you want to use.

    If you don't change the filename, the program gives the file the same name as the original Raw file. However, you don't overwrite that Raw file because you're storing the copy in a different file format (TIFF). In Windows, the filename of the processed TIFF image has the three-letter extension TIF.

13. **Click the Convert button.**

    A window appears in order to show you the progress of the conversion process. When the window disappears, your TIFF image appears in the storage location you selected in Step 11.

One neat thing about working with Raw images is that you can easily create as many variations of the photo as you want. For example, you might choose one set of options when processing your Raw file the first time and then use an entirely different set to create another version of the photo. Just be sure to give each processed file a unique name so that you don't overwrite the first TIFF file you create with your second version.

Preparing Pictures for Online Sharing

Have you ever received an e-mail containing a photo so large that you can't view the whole thing on your monitor without scrolling the e-mail window? This annoyance occurs because monitors can display only a limited number of pixels. The exact number depends on the screen resolution setting, but suffice it to say that today's digital cameras produce photos with pixel counts in excess of what the monitor can handle.

Thankfully, newer e-mail programs incorporate features that automatically shrink the photo display to a viewable size. In Windows Live Mail, for example, photos arrive with a thumbnail link to a slide show viewer that can handle even gargantuan images. That doesn't change the fact that a large photo file means longer downloading times, though — and if recipients choose to hold onto the picture, a big storage hit on their hard drives.

Sending a high-resolution photo *is* the thing to do if you want the recipient to be able to generate a good print. However, it's polite practice to ask people if they *want* to print 11 x 14 glossies of your new puppy before you send them a dozen 24-megapixel (MP) shots.

For simple onscreen viewing, I suggest limiting your photos to fewer than 1,000 pixels on the longest side of the image. This strategy ensures that people who use an e-mail program that doesn't offer the latest photo-viewing tools can see the entire picture without scrolling the viewer window.

This size recommendation means that even if you shoot at your camera's lowest Image Size setting (2992 x 2000), you wind up with more pixels than you need for onscreen viewing. Some new e-mail programs have a photo-upload feature that creates a temporary low-res version for you, but if not, creating your own copy is easy. If you're posting to an online photo-sharing site, you may be able to upload all your original pixels, though many sites have resolution limits.

In addition to resizing high-resolution images, check their file types; if the photos are in the Raw (NEF) or TIFF format, you need to create a JPEG copy for online use. Web browsers and e-mail programs can't display Raw or TIFF files.

You can tackle both bits of photo prep in ViewNX 2 or by using the Resize option in your camera. The next sections explain both methods.

Prepping online photos using ViewNX 2

For pictures already downloaded to the computer, you can create small-sized JPEG copies for online sharing using ViewNX 2. Just click the image thumbnail and then choose File⇨Convert Files. When the Convert Files dialog box appears (see Figure 9-18), set up things as follows:

- ✏ **Select JPEG as the file format.** Make your selection from the File Format drop-down list.

- ✏ **Set the picture-quality level.** Use the Quality slider (refer to Figure 9-18) to set the picture quality, which is controlled by how much JPEG compression is applied when the file is saved. For best quality, drag the slider all the way to the right, but remember the trade-off: As you raise the quality, less compression occurs, which results in a larger file size. (See Chapter 2 for more information about JPEG compression.)

- ✏ **Set the image size (number of pixels).** To resize the photo, select the Change the Image Size check box and then enter a value (in pixels) for the longest dimension of the photo. The program automatically fills in the other value.

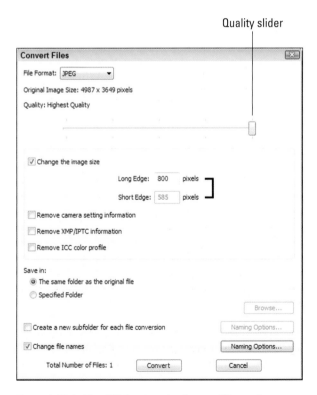

Figure 9-18: In ViewNX 2, select the Convert Files option to create a web-friendly version of a photo.

✔ **Select all three Remove check boxes (refer to Figure 9-18).** Selecting these options removes unnecessary camera metadata, which reduces image file size.

The rest of the options work just as they do during Raw conversion; see "Processing Raw files in ViewNX 2," earlier in this chapter, for details.

If you're resizing a JPEG original, be sure to give the small version a new name to avoid overwriting that original.

Resizing pictures from the Retouch menu

The in-camera resizing tool, found on the Retouch menu, works on both JPEG and Raw images. With both types of files, your resized copy is saved in the JPEG format. You can get the job done in two ways:

✔ **Resize a single photo:** Set the camera to playback mode, display the photo in single image view (or select it in thumbnails or calendar view), and press the *i* button. On the screen that appears, select Retouch and press the Multi Selector right to display the Retouch menu, as shown on the left in Figure 9-19.

Select Resize to display possible image sizes (refer to the right side of Figure 9-19). The first value shows the pixel dimensions of the small copy; the second, the total number of pixels, measured in megapixels. After you select a size, the camera asks permission to create the resized copy; answer in the affirmative to go forward.

✔ **Resize a batch of photos:** Display the Retouch menu and choose Resize to display the left screen in Figure 9-20. Select Choose Size to set the pixel count of the small images. Then choose Select Image, as shown in the figure, to display thumbnails of your photos.

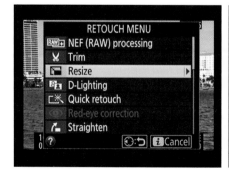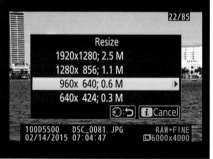

Figure 9-19: Use the Resize option to create a low-resolution version of a picture.

Select the image you want to resize (just tap its thumbnail or use the Multi Selector to move the yellow highlight box over it). Then tap Set (bottom of screen) or press the Zoom Out button to tag it with a resize icon (refer to the right side of Figure 9-20). Select the next photo, rinse, and repeat. After tagging all the photos, tap OK or press the OK button to display the go-ahead screen; select Yes to create your small copies.

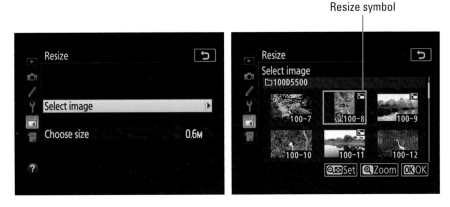

Figure 9-20: To resize a batch of photos, it's quicker to do the job via the Retouch menu.

In both cases, the camera duplicates the selected images and *downsamples* (eliminates pixels from) the copies to achieve the size you specified. The small copies are saved in the JPEG file format, using the same Image Quality setting (Fine, Normal, or Basic) as the original. Raw originals are saved as JPEG Fine images. Either way, your original picture files remain untouched.

Small-size copies appear during playback marked by a Resize symbol next to the file size (lower-right corner), as shown in Figure 9-21. Next to the symbol, you see the resolution (pixel count) of the resized image.

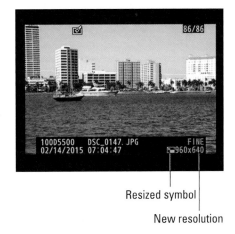

Figure 9-21: The Resize icon indicates a small-size copy.

Taking Advantage of Wi-Fi Transfer

Your camera's Wi-Fi feature enables you to connect your camera wirelessly to certain "smart" devices: specifically, Android and Apple iOS-based phones, tablets, and media players (such as Apple's iPod touch).

 Before you can enjoy this function, you must install the Nikon Mobile Wireless Utility app on your device. For Android-based devices, search for the app at the Google Play Store; for Apple iOS devices, head for the Apple App store. The application is free, but if you've never downloaded any apps, you have to register for an account and give a credit card number (required in case you ever want to download fee-based apps). Be sure to read the details on the download page to make sure that your device is running the required operating software to use the app.

After installing the app, you can perform the following functions:

- **Use the smart device to view photos that are on the camera memory card.** Depending on the size of your device, this enables you to get a little larger view of your photos than the camera's monitor offers.

- **Transfer photos from the memory card to the smart device.** You can then view the photos, upload them to Facebook or other social media sites, or attach them to e-mail or text messages via your device's normal wireless network or cell-based data connection.

- **Use the smart device to trigger the camera's shutter.** You see the live scene on your device screen, just as you see the scene on the camera monitor when you use Live View mode. Then you tap a button on your device to trigger the shutter release.

There are a few critical limitations to this feature:

- **Wi-Fi is for photos only.** You can't view, transfer, or shoot movies using your smart device.

- **You can't connect the camera to a computer via a standard wireless network.** The camera's Wi-Fi only works on a *peer-to-peer* basis: That is, the two devices must be able to talk to each other directly rather than over an intermediate network.

- **Wi-Fi transfer is disabled when your camera is connected to a computer or television.** So unplug the USB or video cable before you attempt a Wi-Fi transfer.

- **You can't adjust camera settings while the camera is connected to your device.** If you want to use your phone or tablet as a remote shutter trigger, you must select all picture settings *before* you connect the camera. If you need to change settings between shots, you have to uncouple the camera and the smart device, select the new settings, and then connect the two devices again. Boo.

✔ **The Wi-Fi feature is a battery hog.** The feature's insatiable appetite for battery juice is why Wi-Fi is disabled by default. The remote-shutter trigger function is also disabled automatically if the battery level on either the camera or the device drops below the level that the camera thinks it needs to perform its job. Long story short: If you routinely use the Wi-Fi functions, consider investing in a spare battery so that you don't run out of power during a shoot.

The next two sections provide a general overview of the Wi-Fi functions. Because the specific steps you take to use the app — and even the available app features — depend on your device, I can't provide full details on each function. However, if you head to the following Nikon web pages, you can download excellent, step-by-step instructions, complete with screen shots of where to tap to access the various app features:

✔ **Android:** `http://nikonimglib.com/ManDL/WMAU/index.html.en`

✔ **iOS:** `http://nikonimglib.com/ManDL/WMAU-ios/index.html.en`

Connecting the camera to your device

To connect your camera to your smart device, take these steps:

1. **Open the camera's Setup menu and select Wi-Fi, as shown on the left in Figure 9-22.**

   You see the Wi-Fi setup screen shown on the right in the figure.

2. **Select Network Connection and then choose Enable.**

   You're returned to the Wi-Fi setup screen. The Wi-Fi symbol shown in the figure blinks to let you know that your camera is now sending out its Wi-Fi signal. The same icon blinks in the Information display and in the default Live View display while Wi-Fi is enabled.

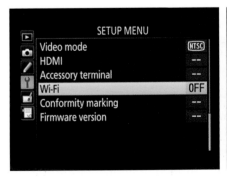
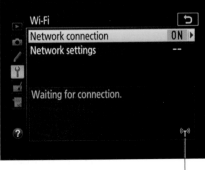

Wi-Fi symbol

Figure 9-22: Enable Wi-Fi via the Setup menu.

3. **Select Network Settings, as shown on the left in Figure 9-23, to display the screen shown on the right.**

4. **Select a connection option.**

Which option you use depends on your device:

- *Push-button WPS (Android only):* Some Android devices offer a WPS (Wi-Fi Protected Setup) feature that enables you to initiate a connection just by pushing a button. If your device has this feature, choose Push-button. The camera displays a screen prompting you to press the WPS button on the device and begins searching for a connection.

- *PIN-entry WPS (Android only):* If your device uses a PIN (personal identification number) for wireless security, select this option from the screen on the right in Figure 9-23. On the next screen, enter the PIN and then choose OK to attempt the connection.

- *View SSID (Android or iOS):* When you choose this option, you see the screen shown on the left in Figure 9-24. Your camera is assigned an SSID number *(Service Set Identifier),* and, after a few moments, the SSID appears as an available network on your smart device. Select the camera's SSID on your device, and then choose the Connect option on the device.

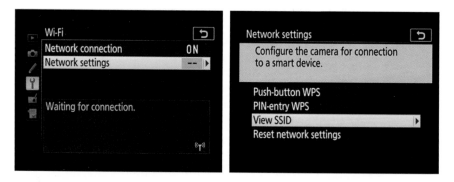

Figure 9-23: Here's the launch screen for configuring the camera to connect with your smart device.

If the stars are in alignment and the devices connect, you see the confirmation screen shown on the right in Figure 9-24 and the Wi-Fi symbol stops blinking. (It may take a few moments for the devices to shake hands.)

5. **Launch the Nikon Wireless Mobile Utility app on your device.**

The initial app screen offers two main options: Take Photos and View Photos, as shown in Figure 9-25. (This figure and others to follow show how the app screens appear on my Android tablet; the design varies

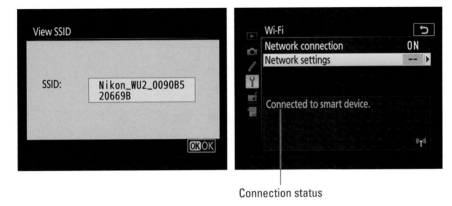

Connection status

Figure 9-24: Choose the camera's SSID (left) from the list of available networks on your smart device; the message shown on the right appears when the connection is made.

depending on your device and its operating system.) Somewhere on the screen, you should also see an icon that lets you access other app settings; usually, the icon looks like a little wheel. Again, for details, download and review the app user guide from the web addresses given in the preceding section.

6. **To sever the connection and turn off Wi-Fi, set the Wi-Fi option on the camera's Setup menu to Off.**

Viewing photos on the smart device

After connecting your camera with the device and firing up the WMU app, tap View Photos on the smart device. You see a screen similar to the one shown on the left in Figure 9-26. Tap the option labeled Pictures on Camera. After a few seconds, thumbnails of your images appear, as shown on the right in the figure, and you can view your pictures using the same techniques you use to view photos that you take with your smart device.

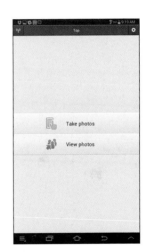

Figure 9-25: The initial app screen gives you the option to view or shoot photos.

Transferring photos to the device

While you're viewing your photos on the device, you can use options built into the WMU app to tag photos for transfer to the device. You can also set the size of the file you want to download. But an easier option is to use a

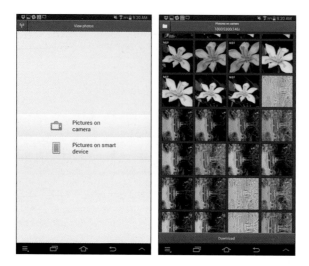

Figure 9-26: You can display thumbnails of photos stored on the camera's memory card.

camera feature that enables you to tag all photos you want to transfer. To try it out, open the camera's Playback menu and choose Select to Send to Smart Device, as shown in Figure 9-27. You see thumbnails of your images, as shown on the right in the figure.

To tag a photo for transfer, tap the Set icon at the bottom of the screen or press the Zoom Out button. You then see a symbol like the one shown on the right in the figure. To remove the transfer tag, tap Set or press the Zoom Out button again. After choosing all your photos, tap OK or press the OK button. Now when you select the option on the smart device that transfers photos, your tagged files are automatically downloaded.

Selected for transfer

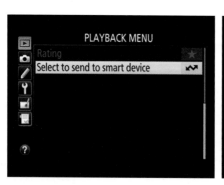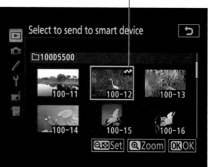

Figure 9-27: Use this menu option to tag a batch of files for transfer to your smart device.

During playback mode, you can tag an individual photo for transfer by pressing the *i* button, which displays the mini-menu shown on the left in Figure 9-28. Choose the Select to Send to Smart Device/Deselect option, as

Selected for Wi-Fi transfer

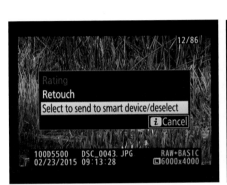 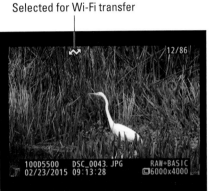

Figure 9-28: During playback, press the *i* button and then choose this option to tag a photo for wireless transfer.

shown in the figure, to add the tag. (Choosing the option once adds the transfer tag; choosing it again removes the tag.) The "marked for transfer" symbol appears on the image during playback, as shown on the right in the figure. (The symbol appears in various places depending on your playback display mode, which you can read about in Chapter 8).

 If you shot the picture in the Raw (NEF) format, it is automatically converted to the JPEG format during the transfer process so that it's ready for online sharing.

Taking pictures via the smart device

To use your smart device as a remote shutter release, connect the devices, launch the WMU app, and then tap the Take Photos button (refer to Figure 9-25). The camera automatically shifts to Live View mode, and the live preview appears on the smart device screen, along with some shooting data, such as the shutter speed and f-stop, as shown in Figure 9-29. A focus box appears on the preview; tap your subject to place the focus box

Set tablet as remote trigger

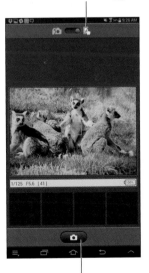

Tab to take picture

Figure 9-29: The Live View preview appears on the device screen; tap the camera icon to trigger the shutter.

over it and set focus. (The exact focusing procedure depends on the current Live View autofocusing settings; Chapter 4 has details.) The focus box turns green when focus is achieved.

Make sure that the option at the top of the screen is set to the icon that shows a finger on the tablet; this tells the app that you want to use the tablet to trigger the shutter. Then tap the camera icon at the bottom of the screen to trigger the shutter release. (Again, the figure shows the screen as it appears on my Android tablet; the specific design may vary if you use a different device or operating system.)

Through the app options, you can specify whether you want the picture to be automatically downloaded after it's captured. You also can delay the shutter release by enabling the app's self-timer option.

Again, you must set all picture options *before* connecting the camera to the device; you can't change settings after the two devices are paired. Neither can you record movies this way; this function is for still photos only.

Exploring two special printing options

The camera offers two features that enable you to print directly from the camera or memory card:

✔ **DPOF (Digital Print Order Format):** With this option, accessed via the DPOF Print Order option on the Playback menu, you select pictures from the memory card to print and then specify how many copies you want of each image. Then, if your photo printer has a memory-card slot that's compatible with your camera's cards and supports DPOF, you simply pop the memory card into that slot. The printer reads the "print order" and outputs only the requested copies of the selected images. You use the printer's own controls to set paper size, print orientation, and other print settings.

✔ **PictBridge:** If you have a PictBridge-enabled photo printer, you can connect the camera to the printer by using a USB cable. The PictBridge interface appears on the camera monitor, and you use the camera controls to select the pictures you want to print. Using PictBridge, you specify additional print options from the camera, such as page size and whether to print a border around the photo.

For more information about both printing options, see the electronic version of the camera manual, available for download from the Support section of the Nikon website.

Part IV
The Part of Tens

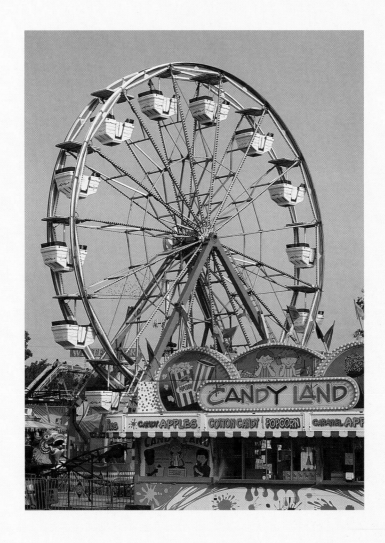

Enjoy an additional Part of Tens article about ten cool digital photography websites at www.dummies.com/extras/nikon.

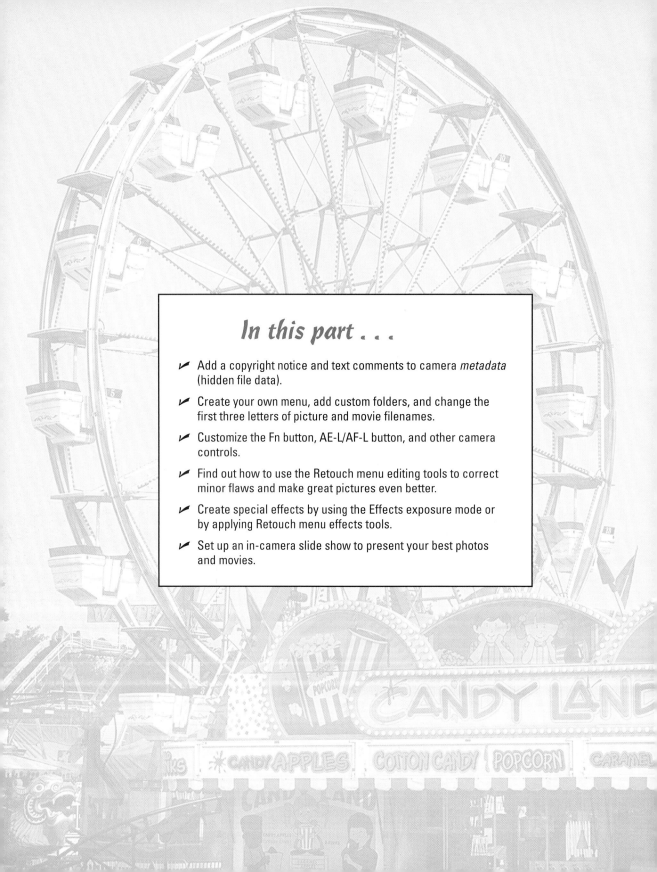

In this part . . .

- Add a copyright notice and text comments to camera *metadata* (hidden file data).

- Create your own menu, add custom folders, and change the first three letters of picture and movie filenames.

- Customize the Fn button, AE-L/AF-L button, and other camera controls.

- Find out how to use the Retouch menu editing tools to correct minor flaws and make great pictures even better.

- Create special effects by using the Effects exposure mode or by applying Retouch menu effects tools.

- Set up an in-camera slide show to present your best photos and movies.

Ten More Ways to Customize Your Camera

*A*s you've no doubt deduced, Nikon is more than eager to let you customize almost every aspect of the camera's operation. This chapter discusses customization options not considered in earlier chapters, including ways to embed a copyright notice in your picture files, create custom folder and file names, and even tweak the function of external controls.

Adding Hidden Image Comments and Copyright Notices

Through the Image Comment feature, you can add hidden text comments to your picture files. Suppose, for example, that you're traveling on vacation and visiting a different destination every day. You can annotate all the pictures you take on a particular outing with the name of the location or attraction. Similarly, the Copyright Information option enables you to tag files with your name, date, and other copyright data.

The text doesn't appear on the photo itself; instead, it's stored with other *metadata* (hidden data, such as shutter speed, date and time, and so on). You can view metadata during playback in the Shooting Data display mode (see Chapter 8) or along with other metadata in Nikon ViewNX 2 (see Chapter 9).

The next two sections explain both features.

Adding an image comment

Select Image Comment from the Setup menu, as shown on the left in Figure 10-1. Select Input Comment as shown on the right in the figure, to display the keyboard screen shown on the left in Figure 10-2.

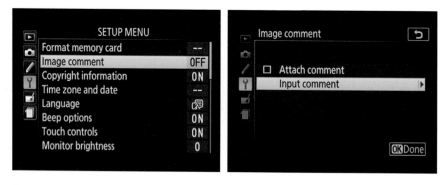

Figure 10-1: You can tag pictures with text comments through this feature.

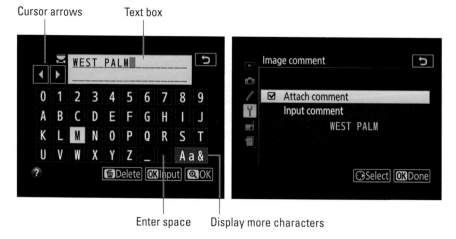

Figure 10-2: After creating your comment text (left), select the Attach Comment box (right) and then press OK or tap Done.

Enter text using these methods:

- ✒ **Enter a character:** If the touch screen is enabled (check the Touch Controls setting on the Setup menu), tap a character in the keyboard. You also can use the Multi Selector to highlight a character and then tap the OK Input symbol at the bottom of the screen or press the OK button. Your comment can be up to 36 characters long.

  To access lowercase characters, numbers, and symbols, select the last "key" in the keyboard. Select the empty box just to the left of that key to enter a space. I labeled these keys in Figure 10-2.

- ✒ **Move the text cursor:** Tap the cursor arrows (see figure) or rotate the Command dial. (The symbol just above the arrows represents the Command dial.) For big cursor moves, rotating the Command dial is the fastest option.

- ✒ **Delete a letter:** Move the cursor under the letter and tap the Delete symbol at the bottom of the screen or press the Delete button.

After entering your comment, tap the rightmost OK symbol (the one marked with a magnifying glass) or press the Zoom In button to display the screen shown on the right in Figure 10-2. You should see your text comment underneath the Input Comment line. Now place a checkmark in the Attach Comment box by tapping the box or pressing the Multi Selector right. Finally, press the OK button or tap the OK Done symbol to exit to the Setup menu. The Image Comment menu item should now read On.

To disable the feature, just revisit the screen shown on the right in Figure 10-2 and remove the checkmark from the Attach Comment box. Press or tap OK to make your decision official.

Adding a copyright notice

To add a copyright notice, choose Copyright Information from the Setup menu, as shown on the left in Figure 10-3. You see the screen shown on the right in the figure. (If you have not yet entered copyright data, the Artist and Copyright boxes will appear empty.)

From there, you take the same steps as when embedding comment text. Select Artist to display the keyboard screen and then use the techniques outlined in the preceding section to enter your name. Then select Copyright data to add that information. The Artist field can hold 36 characters; the Copyright field, 54 characters.

After entering your data, select Attach Copyright Information to turn on the checkmark in the accompanying box, as shown on the right in the figure. Then press the OK button or tap OK Done. To disable the copyright embedding, turn the Attach Copyright Information option off.

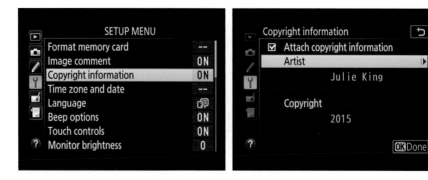

Figure 10-3: You also can tag files with copyright information.

Creating a Custom Storage Folder

By default, your camera stores all images in one folder, which it names 100D5500. Folders have a storage limit of 999 images; when you exceed that number, or the last photo you stored in that folder had the file number 9,999, the camera creates a new folder, assigning a name that indicates the folder number — 101D5500, 102D5500, and so on.

If you choose, you can create your own folder-numbering scheme. For example, perhaps you sometimes use your camera for business and sometimes for personal use. To keep your images separate, you can set up one folder numbered 200D5500 for work images and use the regular 100D5500 folder for personal photos.

To create a new storage folder, follow these steps:

1. **Display the Shooting menu and select Storage Folder.**

   The number you see for the menu option reflects the first three numbers of the folder name. On the menu, you see only those three numbers; during playback, you see the entire folder name (100D5500, for example) in playback modes that show the folder name.

2. **Choose Select Folder by Number.**

   You see the screen shown in Figure 10-4, with the current folder number shown in the middle of the screen.

   A folder icon next to the folder number indicates that the folder already exists. A half-full icon like the one in Figure 10-4 shows that

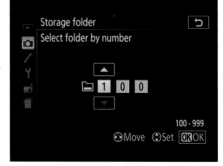

Figure 10-4: Use this screen to create a new folder.

the folder contains images. A full icon means that the folder is stuffed to its capacity (999 images) or contains a picture with the file number 9999. Either way, that full icon means that you can't put any more pictures in the folder.

3. **Assign the new folder a new number.**

   After selecting a number box, tap the up/down arrows or press the Multi Selector up/down to change the number. When you create a new folder, the little folder icon disappears because the folder doesn't yet contain any photos.

4. **Tap the OK symbol or press the OK button.**

   The camera creates your new folder and automatically selects it as the current storage folder.

Each time you shoot, make sure to verify that the folder you want to use is shown for the Storage Folder option. If not, select that option and then choose Select Folder by Number to enter the folder number (if you know it) or choose Select Folder from List to pick from a list of all available folders.

Customizing Filenames

Normally, image filenames begin either with the characters DSC_, for photos captured in the sRGB color space, or _DSC, for images that use the Adobe RGB color space. (Chapter 5 explains color spaces.) But the D5500 enables you to change to any three-letter prefix your prefer. So, for example, you could replace DSC with TIM if you're taking pictures of your brother Tim's family and then change the characters to SUE when you move to cousin Sue's house.

Follow these steps:

1. **Open the Shooting menu and select File Naming, as shown on the left in Figure 10-5.**

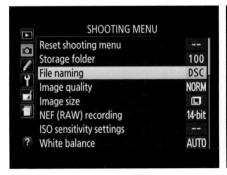
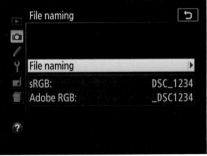

Figure 10-5: This option enables you to change the first three characters of filenames.

You see the screen shown on the right in the figure. The current file naming structure for sRGB and Adobe RGB files appears on the screen.

2. **Select File Naming to display the text entry screen shown in Figure 10-6.**

3. **Enter three custom characters.**

Use the same text-entry techniques as you do when adding image comments, explained at the start of this chapter. Note that your filename is limited to the characters shown in Figure 10-6. You can't use a space or underscore in the filename.

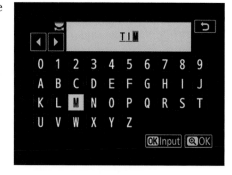

Figure 10-6: This keyboard works similarly to the one used for adding image comments.

4. **Press the Zoom In button or tap the rightmost OK symbol at the bottom of the screen.**

You return to the Shooting menu; the File Naming option should reflect the changes you just made.

Creating Your Own Menu

Keeping track of how to access all the D5500's options can be a challenge, especially when it comes to those that you adjust through menus. To make things a little easier, you can build a custom menu that holds up to 20 of the options you use most frequently. Here's how:

1. **Display the My Menu menu, shown in Figure 10-7.**

This menu shares a slot in the menu list with the Recent Settings menu. The menu icon for the My Menu menu is labeled in the figure. If the Recent Settings menu appears instead, scroll to the end of that menu, select Choose Tab and then select My Menu. The My Menu screen then appears.

2. **Select Add Items.**

You see a list of the other camera menus.

3. **Select the menu that contains an option you want to add to your menu.**

You see a list of all available options on that menu. For example, I chose the Shooting menu to display the options shown on the left in Figure 10-8.

A few items can't be added to a custom menu. A little box with a slash through it appears next to those items (for example, the Reset Shooting Menu option shown in Figure 10-8).

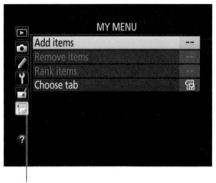

Recent Settings/My Menu icon

Figure 10-7: You can create a custom menu to hold up to 20 of the settings you access most often.

4. **Select the item you want to add.**

Either tap the item or use the Multi Selector to highlight it and then press the OK button. You see the Choose Position screen, as shown on the right in Figure 10-8, where you can change the order of your menu items. For now, just press OK or tap the return arrow at the top of the screen to return to the My Menu screen; the item you just added appears at the top of that screen.

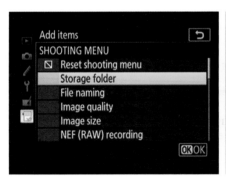
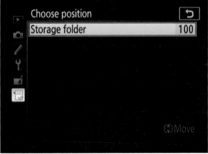

Figure 10-8: Select an item and press OK to add it to your menu.

5. **Repeat Steps 2–4 to add more items to your menu.**

When you get to Step 3, a check mark appears next to any item that's already on your menu.

After creating your custom menu, you can reorder and remove menu items as follows:

✓ **Change the order of menu options.** Display the My Menu screen and highlight Rank Items, as shown in Figure 10-9. You see a screen that lists all your menu items in their current order. You can then use the touch-screen or Multi Selector and OK button to shuffle the list:

- *Touchscreen:* Tap an item, tap the Move icon that appears at the bottom of the screen, and then tap the spot in the list where you want to put the item. Tap OK to lock the item in its new home.

- *Multi Selector:* Highlight the item, press OK, press the Multi Selector up/down to choose the new list position, and then press OK again.

When you're happy with the order of the menu items, tap the return arrow or press the Multi Selector left to return to the My Menu screen.

✔ **Remove menu items.** On the My Menu screen (refer to Figure 10-9), select Remove Items and press OK. You see a list of current menu items, with an empty box next to each item. To remove an item, check its box. (You can tap the box or use the Multi Selector to highlight the item and then press the Multi Selector right.) After tagging all the items you want to remove, press or tap OK. You see a confirmation screen asking permission to remove the item; select OK to go forward.

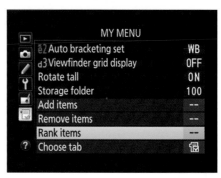

Figure 10-9: Choose Rank Items to change the order of menu items.

Adjusting Automatic Shutdown Timing

When the camera is in shooting mode, its *standby timer* feature saves battery power by shutting off the Information display and viewfinder after a period of inactivity. Similarly, the camera limits the Image Review period (the length of time your picture appears immediately after you press the shutter button), the length of time the Live View display remains active, how long a picture appears in playback mode, and how long menus remain onscreen.

You can control the auto-shutdown timing through the Auto Off Timers option, found in the Timers/AE Lock section of the Custom Setting menu and shown on the left in Figure 10-10.

You get four choices, as shown on the right in the figure, which produce the following shutdown times:

- ✔ **Short:** Standby Timer (affects Information display and viewfinder), 4 seconds; Live View, 5 minutes; Image Review, 4 seconds; playback/menus, 20 seconds.

- ✔ **Normal (default setting):** Standby Timer, 8 seconds; Live View, 10 minutes; Image Review, 4 seconds; playback/menus, 5 minutes.

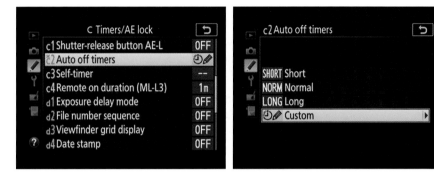

Figure 10-10: Customize auto shutdown timing here.

✐ **Long:** Standby Timer, 1 minute; Live View, 20 minutes; Image Review, 20 seconds; playback/menus, 10 minutes.

✐ **Custom:** Choose this setting to specify delay times for the Standby Timer, Live View display, Image Review period, and Playback/menu display individually.

To disable Image Review altogether, head for the Playback Menu and set the Image Review item to Off.

Changing the Look of the Information Display

By default, the Information display appears as shown on the left in Figure 10-11, with the three large circular graphics representing, from left to right, the shutter speed, f-stop, and ISO settings. As you adjust the f-stop setting, the center of its circle grows or shrinks to represent the opening and closing of the aperture. If you prefer, you can switch to the simpler design shown on the right in the figure. You also can change the background color from black to blue or light gray.

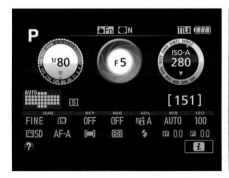
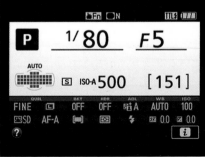

Figure 10-11: You can alter the display style of the Information screen.

Select the design via the Info Display Format option on the Setup menu. You can specify the design used for the P, S, A, and M exposure modes separately from the one used for the other modes. Note that in this book, I use the black background for all Information screens, but the default background color for modes except P, S, A, and M is gray.

Keeping the Information Display Hidden

Also found on the Setup menu, the Auto Info Display option offers another way to customize the Information display. When this option is On, as it is by default, the Information display appears whenever you press the shutter button halfway and release it. If you disable the Image Review feature (via the Playback menu), the Information display also appears after you take a picture.

Turn off the Auto Info Display option, and the Information screen appears briefly when you first turn on the camera, but after that, you must press the Info button to display it. Instructions in this book assume that you stick with the default setting (On). But because the monitor is one of the biggest drains of battery power, you may want to set the option to Off if you have a lot of shooting left to do and the battery is running low.

 Directly below this menu option is the similarly named Info Display Auto Off setting. This setting, when enabled, tells the camera to shut off the monitor display as soon as the eye sensor atop the viewfinder detects that you put your eye to the viewfinder. I see no reason to turn this option off. You can only look at one display at a time, and having the monitor turned on while you're looking through the viewfinder is just wasting battery power.

Customizing a Few Buttons

A few camera buttons can be modified to perform functions different from their default purposes. Again, instructions in this book assume that you haven't modified the buttons, but after you master your camera, you may want to take advantage of these options. You can customize the following buttons:

 ✔ **Function (FN) button:** Establish this button's behavior via the Assign Fn Button option, found on the Controls submenu of the Custom Setting menu and shown in Figure 10-12.

By default, pressing the button accesses the ISO setting; press the button while rotating the Command dial to change the ISO value. But you can choose from a list of other options, as shown on the right in Figure 10-12. (Be sure to scroll to the second page of the list to access all the options.)

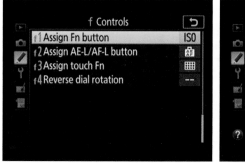 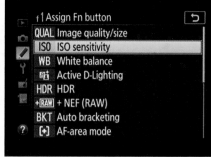

Figure 10-12: You can assign any number of jobs to the Function button.

To see an information screen that tells you what each Fn button setting does, tap the question mark icon at the bottom of the screen or press the Zoom Out button. To exit the information screen, tap the return arrow or press the Zoom Out button again.

✔ **AE-L/AF-L button:** This button is related to the autoexposure and auto-focusing systems. You can set the button to perform the following functions via the Assign AE-L/AF-L Button option, also found in the Controls section of the Custom Setting menu:

- *AE/AF Lock:* This is the default setting. Focus and exposure remain locked as long as you press the button.

- *AE Lock Only:* Autoexposure is locked as long as you press the button; autofocus isn't affected. (You can still lock focus by pressing the shutter button halfway.)

- *AE Lock (Hold):* This one locks exposure only with a single press of the button. The exposure lock remains in force until you press the button again or the exposure meters turn off.

- *AF Lock Only:* Focus remains locked as long as you press the button. Exposure isn't affected.

- *AF-On:* Pressing the button activates the camera's autofocus mechanism. If you choose this option, you can't focus by pressing the shutter button halfway.

✔ **Shutter button:** The Timers/AE Lock section of the Custom Setting menu offers an option called Shutter-Release Button AE-Lock. This option determines whether pressing the shutter button halfway locks focus only or locks focus and exposure.

At the default setting, Off, only focus is locked; exposure is adjusted up to the time you take the shot. If you change the setting to On, your half-press of the shutter button locks both focus and exposure. (Remember that you also have the option of using the AE-L/AF-L button to lock exposure and focus together, as outlined in Chapters 3 and 4.)

Assigning a Touch Function Role

You may be wondering about the purpose of the little Fn symbol that appears by default at the top of the Information display, labeled in Figure 10-13. Tapping the symbol does nothing, so what gives?

Touch Function assigned

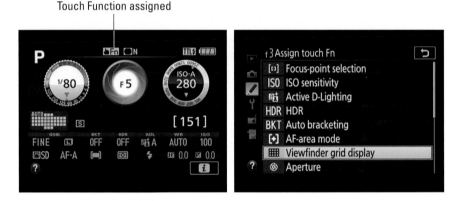

Figure 10-13: The Fn symbol (left) indicates that you assigned any of several roles to the Touch Function feature (right).

The symbol indicates that a feature Nikon refers to as Touch Function is enabled. That means that you can tap a specific region of the Information dispay to quickly adjust a setting. By default, your tap toggles the viewfinder grid display on and off.

Where you can tap to activate the assigned function depends on the position of the monitor. When the monitor is flat on the camera back, you can tap any empty area within the right half of the screen. If you swing the monitor out and away from the camera, you can tap any empty area throughout the whole screen.

To determine what functions you can assign, open the Controls submenu of the Custom Settings menu. Then choose Assign Touch Fn to display the list of settings, shown on the right in Figure 10-13. Again, you can tap the question mark symbol or press the Zoom Out button to find out the result of each option.

Scroll to the second page of the options list to reveal the None setting. If you select this setting, the Fn symbol disappears from the top of the Information display, indicating that tapping the Touch Function area of the screen has no result. This setting is perfect for those of us whose noses sometimes touch the screen, resulting in an unintended Touch Function action.

The Touch Function setting *does not* enable or disable the rest of the touch-screen functions. To control those functions, use the Touch Controls option on the Setup Menu. Choose Enable to enable all touch operations; Playback Only to turn on touch control only during playback; and Disable to turn off the touchscreen altogether.

Reversing the Command Dial Orientation

When you shoot in certain exposure modes, you rotate the Command dial when adjusting shutter speed, aperture, and Exposure Compensation. By default, rotating the dial to the right raises the value that's being adjusted. If that setup seems backward to you, you can tell the camera that you prefer to rotate the dial to the right to lower the values.

To do so, cruise to the Controls section of the Custom Setting menu and select Reverse Dial Rotation, as shown on the left in Figure 10-14. You see the second screen in the figure, where you can modify the dial orientation separately for Exposure Compensation and shutter speed/aperture adjustment. (Note that the Exposure Compensation setting also affects the dial's performance when you adjust Flash Compensation.)

Placing a check mark in the box next to the option reverses the dial orientation. You can toggle the box on and off by tapping it or by highlighting it and then pressing the Multi Selector right. Tap OK or press the OK button to finalize things.

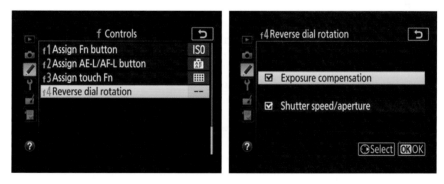

Figure 10-14: For people who like to go left when everyone else goes right, this option reverses the orientation of the Command dial.

Ten Fun (And Practical) Features to Explore on a Rainy Day

In This Chapter

▷ Applying Retouch menu filters

▷ Removing red-eye

▷ Correcting crooked horizon lines, lens distortion, and perspective

▷ Tweaking exposure, contrast, and color

▷ Cropping away excess background

▷ Having fun with special effects

▷ Creating a slide show

*E*very photographer produces a clunker now and then. When it happens to you, don't be too quick to press the Delete button, because many common problems are surprisingly easy to fix. In fact, you often can repair your photos right in the camera, thanks to tools found on the Retouch menu.

This chapter starts with the basics of navigating the Retouch menu and then provides specific instructions for using its most useful photo-repair tools. Following that, I clue you in on a few special-effects tricks, including shooting in Effects mode, and walk you through the process of creating a slide show so that you can show off your photos at the next family gathering.

Applying the Retouch Menu Filters

You can get to most Retouch menu features in two ways:

✔ **Display the menu, shown on the left in Figure 11-1, select a retouching tool, and then select the photo you want to edit.** After you select a retouching tool, you see thumbnails of your photos, as shown on the right in the figure. The yellow highlight box indicates the selected photo. Tap the photo you want to adjust to display settings related to the selected tool. (You also can use the Multi Selector to move the yellow box over the photo and then press the OK button.)

If a photo can't be altered, an X appears over the thumbnail; I labeled the symbol in the figure. Normally, you get the no-go signal because you already applied a certain Retouch menu option to a picture. For example, you can't edit a photo after you crop it using the Trim tool. (A Retouch symbol like the one labeled in the figure indicates a previous edit to the photo.)

Retouch menu icon

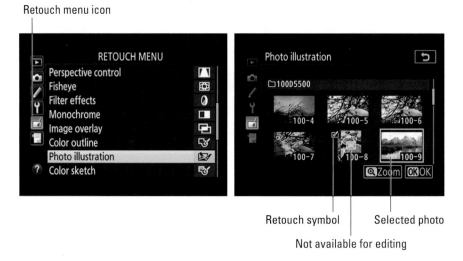

Figure 11-1: After selecting a Retouch menu option (left), select the photo you want to edit (right).

✔ **Switch the camera to playback mode, display your photo in single-frame view, and press the i button.** (For this step, you can't use the touchscreen.) The screen shown on the left in Figure 11-2 appears. (Now the touchscreen controls are available.) Select Retouch to display the Retouch menu superimposed over your photo, as shown on the right. Select a tool to display options related to that tool.

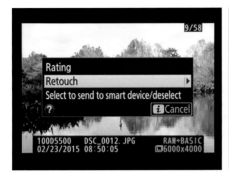 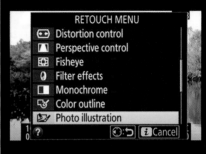

Figure 11-2: In single-frame playback view, press the *i* button to access the Retouch menu.

 By default, you see other picture data, such as filename, on the playback screen. To declutter your view, enable the None option via the Playback Display options on the Playback menu. Then press the Multi Selector up or down until you get to the None display mode, which shows just your image and any relevant Retouch menu tool data.

I prefer the second method, so that's how I approach things in this chapter, but it's entirely a personal choice. However, you can't use the *i* button method to access the Image Overlay menu item. That feature, which combines two Raw (NEF) photos to create a third, blended image, is available only when you display the Retouch menu by pressing the Menu button. (The section "Combining Two Photos with Image Overlay," near the end of this chapter, explains the Image Overlay feature.)

A few other facts to note:

- ✓ **Your originals remain intact.** When you apply a Retouch menu tool, the camera creates a copy of your original photo and makes the changes to the copy.

- ✓ **All Retouch menu tools work with either JPEG or Raw (NEF) originals except Image Overlay and NEF (Raw) Processing.** Those two tools work only with Raw files. See the Chapter 2 discussion about the Image Quality setting for an explanation of JPEG and Raw (NEF). Chapter 9 explains the NEF (Raw) Processing tool.

- ✓ **Retouched copies for all alterations except Image Overlay are saved in the JPEG file format.** The retouched copy uses the same JPEG quality setting as the original (Fine, Normal, or Basic). Retouched copies of Raw originals are saved in the JPEG Fine format. For Image Overlay, the retouched image is stored using the current Image Quality and Image Size settings. (Chapter 2 discusses the Image Size setting also.)

- ✓ **You can apply each correction to a picture only once.** The exception, again, is Image Overlay. If you save the composite in the Raw format, you can combine the composite with a third Raw image. In fact, you can keep combining photos until your memory card is full, if the urge hits you.

✓ **The camera automatically assigns the next available file number to the retouched image.** Make note of the filename of the retouched version so that you can easily track it down later.

✓ **Certain filters enable you to temporarily display a magnified preview of the "after" image.** If so, you see the word *Zoom* along with a symbol that looks like the Zoom In button at the bottom of the screen. (You can get a glimpse of this symbol in Figure 11-3.) To magnify the preview, either hold down the Zoom In button or tap the Zoom symbol. To return to the display that shows thumbnails for the original plus the edited version, release the button or tap the return arrow in the top-right corner of the magnified display.

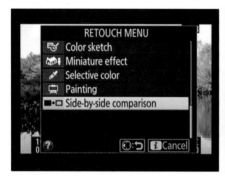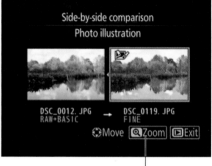

Tap to magnify preview

Figure 11-3: Use Side-by-Side Comparison to see whether you prefer the retouched version to the original.

✓ **You can compare the original and the retouched version by using the Side-by-Side Comparison menu option.** Here's an option you can't access by pressing the Menu button to bring up the Playback menu. Instead, display either the original or the retouched version in full-frame playback. Then press the *i* button, choose Retouch, and select Side-by-Side Comparison. You see the original image on one side and the retouched version on the other (refer to Figure 11-3). At the top of the screen, a label indicates the Retouch tool that you applied to the photo.

These tricks work in Side-by-Side Comparison display:

• If you applied more than one Retouch tool to the picture, press the Multi Selector right and left to display thumbnails that show how each tool affected the picture.

- If you create multiple retouched versions of the same original — for example, you create a monochrome version, save it, and then crop the original image and save that — use a different technique to compare the versions. First, press the Multi Selector right or left to surround the After image with the yellow highlight box. Now press the Multi Selector up and down to scroll through the retouched versions.

- To temporarily view the original or retouched image at full-frame size, use the Multi Selector to highlight its thumbnail and then press the Zoom In button or tap the Zoom symbol onscreen. Release the button or tap the return arrow to return to Side-by-Side Comparison view.

To exit the Side-by-Side Comparison display and return to normal playback, first move the highlight box over the image you want to display (the original or the altered version). Then press the Playback button or tap the Exit symbol in the lower-right corner of the screen.

Removing Red-Eye

For portraits marred by red-eye, give the Red-Eye Correction filter a whirl, as shown in Figure 11-4. If the camera detects red-eye, it applies the filter and displays the results on the screen.

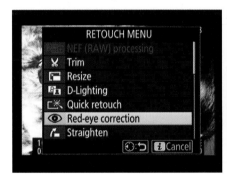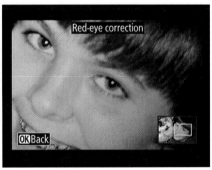

Figure 11-4: The Retouch menu offers an automated red-eye remover.

Tap the Zoom icon at the bottom of the preview window or press the Zoom In button to magnify the display, so that you can closely inspect the repair, as shown on the right in the figure. If you're cool with the job the camera performed, tap or press OK twice: The first press returns the display to normal magnification; the second makes the change official. To instead cancel the repair, press the Playback button.

Note that the filter can correct only red-eye; it can't fix animal eyes that a flash has turned white, yellow, or green.

Straightening Tilting Horizon Lines

I have a knack for shooting with the camera misaligned with respect to the horizon, which means that photos like the one on the left in Figure 11-5 often wind up crooked. Luckily for me, the Retouch menu offers a Straighten tool that can rotate tilting horizons back to the proper angle, as shown on the right.

Original   Straightened

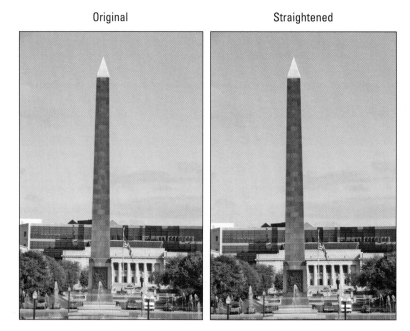

Figure 11-5: You can level crooked photos with the Straighten tool.

After you choose the filter from the Retouch menu, you see a screen similar to the one in Figure 11-6, with a grid superimposed on your photo to serve as an alignment aid. Press the Multi Selector right to rotate the picture clockwise; press left to rotate counterclockwise. Each press spins the picture by about 0.25 degrees. You can achieve a maximum rotation of 5 degrees. Press OK to create the straightened copy.

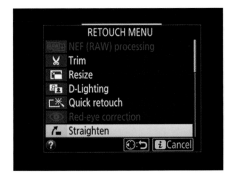
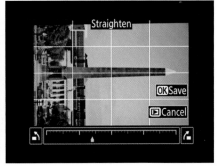

Figure 11-6: Press the Multi Selector right or left or tap or drag on the scale to set the rotation direction and amount.

To achieve this rotation magic, the camera must crop your image and enlarge the remaining area — that's why the After photo in Figure 11-5 contains slightly less subject matter than the original. (The same cropping occurs if you make this kind of change in a photo editor.) The camera updates the display as you rotate the photo so that you can get an idea of how much of the original scene may be lost.

Removing (Or Creating) Lens Distortion

Certain lenses can produce a type of distortion that causes straight lines to appear curved. Wide-angle lenses, for example, often create *barrel distortion,* in which objects at the center of a picture appear to be magnified and pushed forward — as if you wrapped the photo around the outside of a barrel. The effect is easy to spot in a rectangular subject like the oil painting in Figure 11-7. Notice that in the original image, on the left, the edges of the painting bow slightly outward. *Pincushion distortion* affects the photo in the opposite way, making center objects appear smaller and farther away.

If you notice either type of distortion, try enabling the Auto Distortion Control option on the Shooting menu. This feature attempts to correct distortion as you take the picture. Or you may prefer to wait until after reviewing your photos and then use the Distortion Control tool on the Retouch menu to try to fix things, as I did for the second image in Figure 11-7. Less helpful, in my opinion, is a related Retouch menu filter, Fisheye, that creates distortion to replicate the look of a photo taken with a fisheye lens.

With either filter, you lose part of the original image area as a result of the distortion correction, just as you do with the Straighten tool. So if you're shooting a photo that you think may benefit from these filters, frame your subject a little loosely.

Slight barrel distortion

After Distortion Correction filter

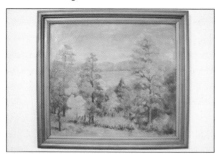
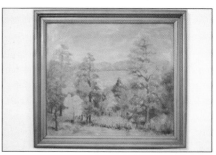

Figure 11-7: Barrel distortion makes straight lines appear to bow outward.

Here's how the Retouch menu filters work:

- **Distortion Control:** After selecting the filter from the Retouch menu, you see the screen shown on the left in Figure 11-8. An Auto option is available for some lenses, as long as you didn't apply the Auto Distortion Control feature when taking the picture. As its name implies, the Auto option attempts to automatically apply the correct degree of correction. If the Auto option is dimmed or you prefer to do the correction on your own, select Manual to display the screen shown on the right in the figure. Move the yellow marker under the scale (by tapping, dragging, or pressing the Multi Selector left/right) to adjust the image. Move the marker right to reduce barrel distortion; move it left to reduce pincushioning. Tap OK or press the OK button to save a copy of your original with the correction applied.

- **Fisheye:** Selecting this filter presents a screen similar to the one shown on the right in Figure 11-8. Again, move the marker under the scale to set the distortion amount.

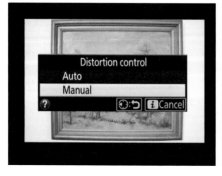
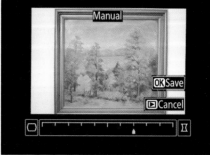

Figure 11-8: The Distortion Control filter can reduce barrel distortion.

Correcting Perspective

When you photograph a tall building and tilt the camera upward to fit it all into the frame, an effect that's referred to as *convergence* or *keystoning* occurs. This effect causes vertical structures to tilt toward the center of the frame. Buildings sometimes even appear to be falling away from you, as shown in the left image in Figure 11-9. (If the lens is tilting down, vertical structures instead lean outward, and the building appears to be falling toward you.) Using the Retouch menu's Perspective Control feature, you can right those tilting vertical elements, as I did to produce the right image in Figure 11-9.

Original

After perspective correction

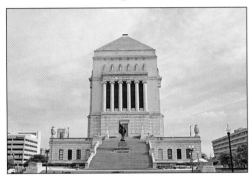 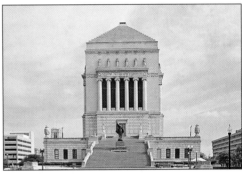

Figure 11-9: The original photo exhibited convergence (left); applying the Perspective Control filter corrected the problem (right).

Note, though, that as with the Straighten, Distortion Correction, and Fisheye tools, the Perspective tool results in some loss of area around the perimeter of your photo. So again, when shooting this type of subject, frame loosely — that way, you ensure that you don't sacrifice an important part of the scene due to the correction.

After you select the filter, as shown on the left in Figure 11-10, you see a grid and horizontal and vertical scale, as shown on the right. Use the touchscreen controls or press the Multi Selector left and right to move the out-of-whack object horizontally; shift the marker up and down the vertical scale to rotate the object toward or away from you. When you're happy with the results, tap OK or press the OK button.

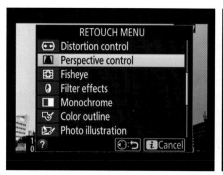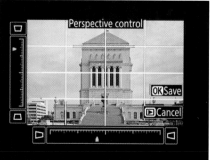

Figure 11-10: Move the marker along the vertical scale to rotate the subject toward or away from you; use the horizontal scale to rotate the object to the right or left.

Manipulating Exposure and Color

You also have access to these Retouch filters that adjust exposure and color:

✔ **D-Lighting:** Chapter 3 explains Active D-Lighting, which brightens too-dark shadows in a way that leaves highlight details intact. You can apply a similar adjustment to an existing photo by choosing the D-Lighting filter from the Retouch menu. I used the filter on the photo in Figure 11-11, where strong backlighting left the balloon underexposed in the original image.

Original image

D-Lighting, High

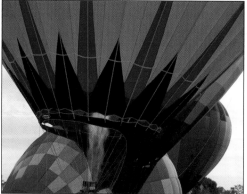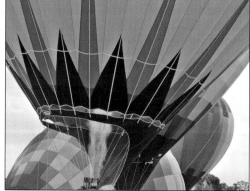

Figure 11-11: An underexposed photo (left) gets help from the D-Lighting filter (right).

When you choose this filter, you see before-and-after views of the image, as shown in Figure 11-12. Set the strength of the adjustment via the

Effect option. (You can use the touchscreen or press the Multi Selector left or right.)

Also note the Portrait Subjects option, which is underneath the Effect option and dimmed in the figure. If the camera recognizes faces in the photo, you can select this option to limit the exposure adjustment to areas around the face (or faces). However, only three faces (maximum) are considered for this special exposure change. Also, you must have captured the photo with the Auto Image Rotation option on the Setup menu enabled. A checkmark in the Portrait Subjects box means that the feature is turned on; tap the box or select it and press OK to turn the feature off.

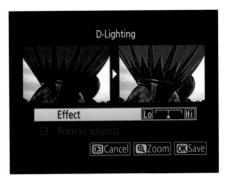

Figure 11-12: Set the strength of the D-Lighting adjustment via the Effect option.

You can't apply D-Lighting to a picture taken using the Monochrome Picture Control, introduced in Chapter 5. Nor does D-Lighting work on pictures to which you've applied the Quick Retouch filter, covered next, or the Monochrome filter, detailed a little later in this list.

✔ **Quick Retouch:** This filter increases contrast and color saturation and, if your subject is backlit, also applies a D-Lighting adjustment to restore some shadow detail that otherwise might be lost. As with D-Lighting, you can choose from three levels of Quick Retouch correction. And the same restrictions apply: You can't apply the filter to monochrome images or on pictures that you adjusted via D-Lighting.

✔ **Filter Effects:** The Filter Effects option offers filters that are designed to mimic the results produced by traditional lens filters. The first two are color-manipulation filters. The other two, Cross Screen and Soft, are special-effects filters; you can read about both later in this chapter.

The color filters work like so:

  • *Skylight filter:* Reduces the amount of blue to create a subtle warming effect.

  • *Warm filter:* Produces a warming effect that's just a bit stronger than the Skylight filter.

✔ **Monochrome:** With the Monochrome Picture Control feature, covered in Chapter 5, you can shoot black-and-white photos. As an alternative, you can create a black-and-white copy of an existing color photo by applying the Monochrome option on the Retouch menu. You can also create sepia and *cyanotype* (blue and white) images via the Monochrome option. Figure 11-13 shows you examples.

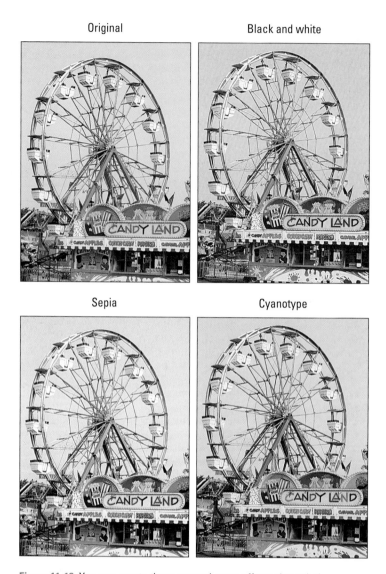

Figure 11-13: You can create three monochrome effects through the Monochrome tool on the Retouch menu.

You can't apply certain Retouch menu options to your photo after you do the conversion; the D-Lighting, Quick Retouch, and Soft filters are among those that don't work on a monochrome copy. (Obviously, filters related to color adjustment also are no longer available.) So use those filters before heading to the Monochrome option.

After selecting Monochrome from the Retouch menu, select the type of image you want to create (black-and-white, sepia, or cyanotype) and tap OK or press the OK button. You then see a preview of the result; for the Sepia and Cyanotype filters, you can set the intensity of the tint by tapping the Darker and Lighter symbols at the bottom of the preview (or pressing the Multi Selector up and down). To make the monochrome copy, tap OK or press the OK button again.

Cropping Your Photo

To *crop* a photo means to trim away some of its perimeter. Cropping can often improve an image, as illustrated by Figure 11-14. When shooting this scene, I couldn't get close enough to fill the frame with the ducks, as shown on the left. So I cropped the image after the fact to achieve the composition on the right.

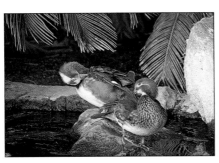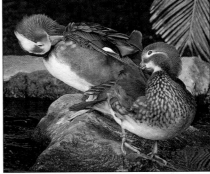

Figure 11-14: Cropping creates a better composition and eliminates background clutter.

The Retouch menu's Trim tool enables you to create a cropped copy of a photo right in the camera. However, always make this your *last* editing step because after you crop, you can't apply any other fixes from the Retouch menu.

After you select Trim from the menu, you see the screen shown in Figure 11-15. The yellow box represents the cropping frame; anything outside the box won't appear in your cropped image.

Adjust the size, position, and proportions of the crop frame as follows:

✔ **Set the crop aspect ratio:** You can crop to one of five aspect ratios: 3:2, 4:3, 5:4, 1:1, and 16:9. The current aspect ratio appears in the upper-right corner of the screen. (Refer to Figure 11-15.) To cycle through the other settings, tap that aspect ratio readout or rotate the Command dial.

✔ **Adjust the cropping frame size**: For each aspect ratio, you can choose from a variety of crop sizes, which depend on the size of the original. The sizes are stated in pixels, such as 3600 x 2880. The current crop size appears in the upper-left corner of the screen.

If you're cropping in advance of printing the image, remember to aim for at least 200 pixels per linear inch of the print — 800 x 1200 pixels for a 4 x 6 print, for example.

Use these techniques to change the crop-frame size:

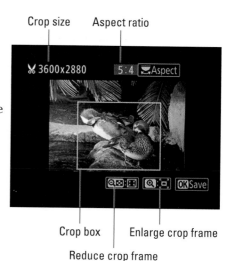

Crop size   Aspect ratio

Crop box | Enlarge crop frame
Reduce crop frame

Figure 11-15: The yellow box indicates the cropping frame.

- *Reduce the size of the cropping frame.* Press and release the Zoom Out button or tap the Zoom Out icon. Each tap or press of the button further reduces the crop size.

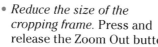

- *Enlarge the cropping frame.* Press the Zoom In button or tap the Zoom In icon. Again, press or tap as many times as needed to generate the crop size you want.

✔ **Reposition the cropping frame.** Drag your finger inside the crop frame or press the Multi Selector up, down, right, or left.

To create the cropped copy of your photo, press the OK button or tap OK on the touchscreen.

When you view the cropped image in Playback mode, a scissors symbol appears next to the Image Size readout (lower-right corner of the frame) to tell you that you're looking at a trimmed photo.

For help reducing the size (resolution) of your photo without cropping the image, flip to Chapter 9 and investigate the section related to the Resize option of the Retouch menu.

Playing with Special Effects

For photographers who want to alter reality beyond what you can achieve with the tools mentioned so far, the Retouch menu offers a number of special-effects filters. And through the Effects exposure mode, you can add certain effects at the moment you capture the image — you don't have to shoot the picture and then tweak it through the Retouch menu. The Effects exposure mode also enables you to record movies using special effects.

The next section describes the remaining Retouch menu effects; following that, I show you how to take advantage of the Effects exposure mode.

Applying special effects via the Retouch menu

For after-the-shot special effects, check out these Retouch menu options:

✔ **Cross Screen:** This filter, one of the Filter Effects options, adds a starburst effect to the brightest part of the image, as shown in Figure 11-16.

Original | Cross Screen Filter Applied

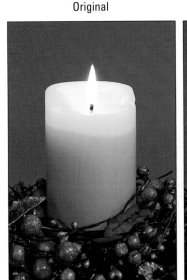
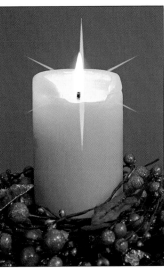

Figure 11-16: The Cross Screen filter adds a starburst effect to the brightest parts of the photo.

After you select the filter, you see a preview along with options that enable you to adjust the number of points on the star, the intensity of the effect, the length of the star's rays, and the angle of the effect. To update the preview after changing a setting, select Confirm; when you're happy with the effect, select Save.

✔ **Soft:** Also on the Filter Effects menu, the Soft filter blurs your photo to give it a dreamy, watercolor-like look. You can choose from three levels of blur: Low, Normal, and High.

✔ **Color Outline:** Select this option from the Retouch menu to turn your photo into a black-and-white line drawing. (And please don't ask me why this filter isn't called Black-and-White Outline.)

✔ **Photo Illustration:** This effect produces a cross between a photo and a bold, color drawing; you can see an example in Figure 11-2, at the start of this chapter. Use the filter's Thickness option to adjust the look of the effect.

✔ **Color Sketch:** This filter creates an image similar to a drawing done in colored pencils; Figure 11-17 shows you an original (left) and its altered cousin (right). You can modify the effect through two options: Vividness, which affects the boldness of the colors; and Outlines, which determines the thickness of outlines.

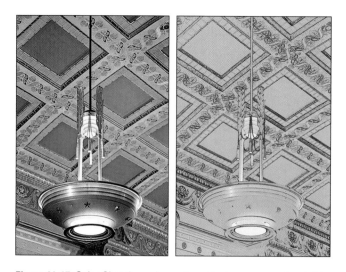

Figure 11-17: Color Sketch produces the effect you see on the right.

✔ **Miniature Effect:** Have you ever seen an architect's small-scale models of planned developments? The Miniature Effect filter attempts to create a photographic equivalent by applying a strong blur to all but one portion of an image, as shown in Figure 11-18. The left photo is the original; the right shows the result of applying the filter. For this example, I set the focus point on the part of the street occupied by the cars.

The Miniature Effect filter works best if you shoot your subject from a high angle — otherwise, you don't get the miniaturization result.

After choosing the filter from the Retouch menu, you see a yellow box over the photo, as shown in Figure 11-19. The box represents the area that will remain in focus. Adjust its size and position as follows:

Original   Miniature Effect filter

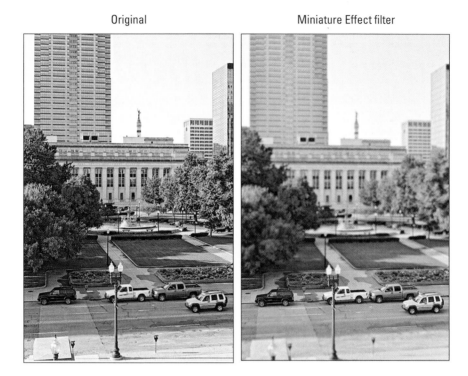

Figure 11-18: The Miniature Effect filter throws all but a small portion of a scene into very soft focus.

- *Rotate the box 90 degrees:* Tap the icon in the upper-right corner of the screen (refer to Figure 11-19) or press the Zoom Out button.

- *Position and resize the box:* Touchscreen control is easiest: To adjust the box size, tap the left icon in the top-right corner of the screen; to reposition the frame, just drag inside the box. If the touchscreen is disabled, turn to the Multi Selector. When the focus box is oriented as shown in Figure 11-19, press up/down to resize the box; press

Resize frame

Focus frame   Rotate frame

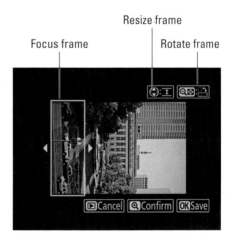

Figure 11-19: Position the yellow box over the area that you want to remain sharply focused.

right/left to move it. If the box is oriented horizontally, use the opposite maneuvers.

- *Preview the effect:* Tap Confirm or press the Zoom In button.

When you get a result you like, tap OK or press the OK button.

✔ **Selective Color:** This effect *desaturates* (removes color from) parts of a photo while leaving specific colors intact. For example, in Figure 11-20, I desaturated everything but the yellows and peaches in the rose.

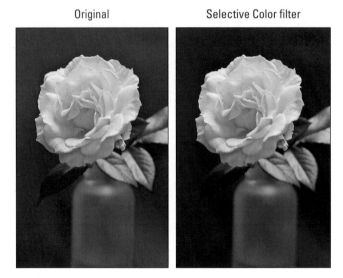

Figure 11-20: I used the Selective Color filter to desaturate everything but the rose petals.

After choosing the effect from the Retouch menu, you can select up to three colors to retain and specify how much a color can vary from the selected one and still be retained. Make your wishes known as follows:

- *Select the first color to be retained.* Use the Multi Selector to move the yellow box, labeled *Color selection box* in Figure 11-21, over the color. (You can also tap the screen to position the box, but tapping the precise pixel that picks up the color you want to retain is tricky.) Next tap the AE-L/AF-L icon in the upper right corner of the screen (refer to the left screen in Figure 11-21) or press the AE-L/AF-L button. The chosen color appears in the first color swatch at the top of the screen.

- *Set the range of the selected color.* Rotate the Command dial or tap the Change symbol (bottom of the screen) to display a preview of the desaturated image and highlight the number box to the right of the color swatch, as shown on the right in Figure 11-21. Then use the touchscreen arrows or Multi Selector to choose a value from 1 to 7. The higher the number, the more a pixel can vary in color from the selected hue and still be retained. The display updates to show you the impact of the setting.

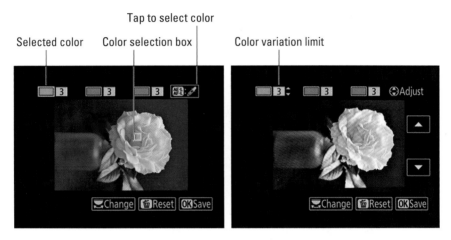

Figure 11-21: To select a color you want to keep, move the yellow box over it and tap the AE-L/AF-L symbol or press the AE-L/AF-L button.

- *Choose one or two additional colors.* Rotate the Command dial or tap Change to highlight the second color swatch and then repeat the selection process. To choose a third color, lather, rinse, and repeat.

- *Fine-tune your settings.* You can keep rotating the Command dial or tapping Change to cycle through the color swatch and range boxes, adjusting each as necessary.

- *Reset a color swatch box.* To empty a selected swatch box, tap Reset or press the Delete button. To reset all the swatch boxes, hold down the Delete button until a message asks whether you want to get rid of all selected colors. Select yes to go forward.

- Save a copy of the image with the effect applied. Tap OK or press the OK button.

✔ **Painting:** The last special effect on the Retouch menu, this one produces a vividly colored, loosely rendered version of your photo.

Shooting in Effects mode

When you set the Mode dial to Effects, as shown in Figure 11-22, you can apply special effects on the fly: That is, the effect is added as the camera writes the picture to the memory card.

Live View switch

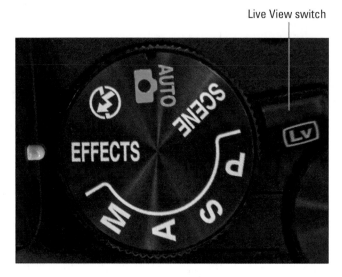

Figure 11-22: Effects mode lets you apply special effects to movies and still photos.

For still photos, I prefer to capture my originals sans effect and then work from the Retouch menu to alter them. That way, I wind up with one normal image and one with the effect applied, just in case I decide that I prefer the unaltered photo to the effects version. Shooting in Effects mode also brings up another problem: To create the effects, the camera puts most picture-taking controls, such as White Balance and Metering mode, off limits.

However, Effects mode does offer some artistic filters not available on the Retouch menu. In addition, it enables you to add effects to movies, which isn't possible on the Retouch menu. So even though I suspect that you won't find a use for the Effects mode very often, I'd be remiss if I didn't spend a little time discussing it.

As soon as you set the Mode dial to Effects, an icon representing the selected effect appears in the upper-left corner of the Information display, as shown on the left in Figure 11-23. Tap that icon or rotate the Command dial to shift to the screen shown on the right, where you can select a different effect. Browse through the effects by tapping the left/right touchscreen arrows or rotating the Command dial. Press the shutter button halfway and release it to return to shooting mode.

Effect symbol

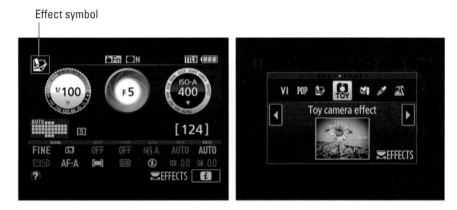

Figure 11-23: Rotate the Command dial or tap the scroll arrows to access the various effects.

Several effects offer settings you can tweak to alter the result. But you can't get to these settings unless you switch to Live View mode. (Rotate the Live View switch, labeled in Figure 11-22.) Live View also enables you to see a live preview of the selected effect, as shown on the left in Figure 11-24. Use the process just described to select a different effect. The OK Set symbol, highlighted on the left in Figure 11-24, indicates that you can fine-tune the effect. Tap that symbol or press OK to access the settings, as shown on the right. After making your adjustments, tap OK Done or press OK to return to the live preview. (If you see the OK Set sign on the preview, you can tap it at any time to readjust the effect settings.)

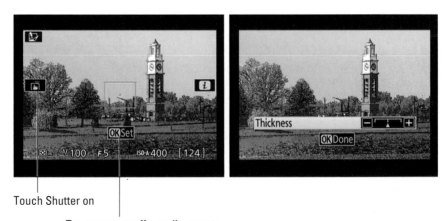

Touch Shutter on

Tap to access effect adjustments

Figure 11-24: In Live View mode, you can preview and adjust Effects mode settings.

Effects mode offers the following choices:

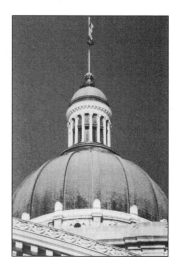

Figure 11-25: The Night Vision effect creates an exceptionally noisy black-and-white image.

- **Night Vision:** Use this setting in low-light situations to produce a grainy, black-and-white image that resembles what you see with night-vision goggles. Figure 11-25 has an example. To achieve the grainy effect, the camera uses a high ISO Sensitivity setting — that high ISO produces noise, which results in the grainy look. How high the ISO climbs and, thus, how much noise becomes visible, depends on the ambient light.

  A few critical points about Night Vision mode:

  - *Autofocusing is available only in Live View mode.* For viewfinder photography, you must focus manually.

  - *Flash is disabled, as is the AF-assist lamp.* The whole idea is to create a picture taken in little light, after all.

  - *Use a tripod to avoid blur.* A slow shutter speed is needed to capture the image in dark conditions, and you must be careful to avoid camera movement during the exposure. If your subject is moving, it can appear blurry even if the camera is on a tripod.

  - *You can capture the photo only in the JPEG format.* You select this setting via the Image Quality option on the Shooting menu. Raw (NEF) files aren't compatible with the Night Vision effect.

- **Super Vivid:** Choose this setting for hypersaturated, super-contrasty images.

- **Pop:** One step less intense than Super Vivid, this mode amps up saturation only.

- **Photo Illustration:** This setting produces the result shown in Figure 11-24: a bright, poster-like effect. Two warnings: You must focus manually to shoot a movie in this mode, and your finished "movie" looks more like a slide show made up of still images.

- **Toy Camera Effect:** This mode, also compatible only with the JPEG file format, is designed to create a photo or movie that looks like it was shot by a toy camera — specifically, the type of toy camera that produces images that have a vignette effect (corners of the scene appear darker than the rest of the image).

In Live View mode, you can adjust two options: Vividness, which affects color intensity; and Vignetting, which controls the amount of vignetting.

✔ **Miniature Effect:** This one is also a duplicate of the one on the Retouch menu; Figure 11-18 shows an example of the result. Again, the filter works by blurring all but a small portion of the scene, which you specify by positioning the red focus frame that appears in Live View mode.

To set up this effect, press OK or tap the OK icon to display horizontal markings that indicate the width of the sharp-focus region. Use the Multi Selector or touchscreen controls to adjust the width and position of the in-focus region. When you achieve the look you want, press or tap OK again.

A few other limitations also apply: Flash is disabled, as is the AF-assist lamp. If you use the Continuous Release mode, the frames per second rate is reduced. You must set the Image Quality option (Shooting menu) to JPEG for still photography, and, when autofocusing, you can't use any AF-area mode except Single Point. (Chapter 4 discusses this autofocus option.)

For movies, sound recording is disabled, autofocus is disabled during recording, and movies play back at high speed. (The high-speed playback means that a movie that contains about 45 minutes of footage is compressed into a 3-minute clip, for example.)

✔ **Selective Color:** Use this effect to create an image in which all but one to three colors are desaturated, just as when you use the Selective Color option on the Retouch menu. Figure 11-20 has an example.

To choose the colors you want to retain and specify the range of similar colors that are included, switch to Live View and then press OK. At the top of the screen, you see three color-swatch boxes and a value next to each box. In the middle of the screen, you see a small white box, which is the color selector box. Set up the effect as follows:

- *Choose a color to retain:* Frame the image so that the white selection box is over the color you want to preserve. Then tap the eyedropper icon in the upper-right corner of the screen or press the Multi Selector up.

- *Set the color range:* After you select a color, the color range value to the right of the color box becomes active. Press the Multi Selector up or down to adjust the color range value. A higher value retains a broader spectrum of similar shades than the one you chose.

- *Choose additional color to retain:* Rotate the Command dial to select the second color swatch box and repeat the process of choosing a color and setting its range value. (You also can simply tap the color box to select it.)

- *Deselect a color:* Change your mind about retaining one of your chosen colors? Select its color swatch and then press the Delete button. Or hold down the button for a few seconds to delete all your selected colors.

After setting your color preferences, tap the OK icon or press the OK button to lock in your decisions and hide the options.

Note that just as with the preceding Effects settings, you're limited to using JPEG as the file type when you use the Selective Color mode. Flash is disabled.

✔ **Silhouette:** Choosing this setting ensures that backlit subjects will be captured as dark silhouettes against a bright background, as illustrated in Figure 11-26. To help ensure that the subject is dark, flash is disabled.

✔ **High Key:** A *high key* photo is dominated by white or very light areas, such as a white china cup resting on a white doily in front of a sunny window. This setting is designed to produce a good exposure for this type of scene, which the camera otherwise tends to underexpose in response to all the high brightness values. Flash is disabled.

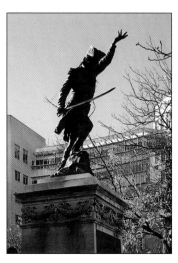

Figure 11-26: The Silhouette effect can produce an interesting result when you photograph dark subjects set against a bright background.

How does the name relate to the characteristics of the picture? Well, photographers refer to the dominant tones — or brightness values — as the *key tones.* In most photos, the *midtones,* or areas of medium brightness, are the key tones. In a high key image, the majority of tones are at the high end of the brightness scale.

✔ **Low Key:** The opposite of a high key photo, a low key photo is dominated by shadows. Use this mode to prevent the camera from brightening the scene too much and thereby losing the dark and dramatic nature of the image. Flash is disabled.

After selecting an effect, you can exit Live View to take the picture using the viewfinder if you prefer. Or, to record a movie, remain in Live View mode and just press the red movie-record button to stop and start recording.

One final note: In Live View mode, be sure to check the status of the Touch Shutter, represented by the symbol shown in Figure 11-24. When the symbol appears as in the figure, tapping the screen sets focus and releases the shutter. To turn off the shutter-release function, tap the Touch Shutter icon (the word Off then appears with the icon). If the Effects mode permits autofocusing, you can still tap the screen to set focus.

Combining Two Photos with Image Overlay

The Image Overlay feature on the Retouch menu enables you to merge two existing Raw images. I used this option to combine a photo of a werewolf friend, shown on the left in Figure 11-27, with a nighttime garden scene, shown in the center. The result is the ghostly image shown on the right. Oooh, scary!

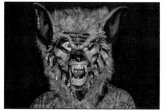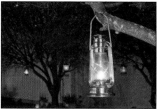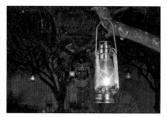

Figure 11-27: Image Overlay merges two Raw (NEF) photos into one.

On the surface, this option sounds kind of cool. The problem is that you can't control the opacity or positioning of the individual images in the combined photo. For example, my overlay picture would have been more successful if I could move the werewolf to the left in the combined image so that he and the lantern aren't blended. And I'd also prefer to keep the background of image 2 at full opacity in the overlay image rather than getting a 50/50 mix of that background and the one in image 1, which only creates a fuzzy-looking background in this particular example.

However, there is one effect that you can create successfully with Image Overlay: a "two views" composite like the one in Figure 11-28. For this image, I used Image Overlay to combine the front and rear views of the antique match striker into the composite scene.

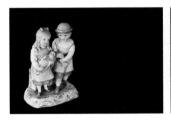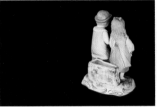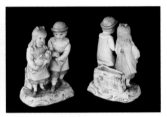

Figure 11-28: If you want each subject to appear solid, use a black background and position the subjects so that they don't overlap.

 For this trick to work, the background in both images must be the same solid color (black seems to be best), and you must compose your photos so that the subjects don't overlap in the combined photo, as shown here. Otherwise, you get the ghostly portrait effect like what you see in Figure 11-27.

To be honest, I don't recommend using Image Overlay for serious photo compositing. Instead, do this kind of work in your photo-editing software, where you have more control over the blend. So in the interest of reserving space in this book for features that I think you will find much more useful, I leave you to explore this feature on your own. The electronic version of the camera manual (available for download from the Support section of the Nikon website) explains the steps involved in using each of them.

Creating a Digital Slide Show

Many photo-editing and cataloging programs offer a tool for creating digital slide shows that can be viewed on a computer or, if copied to a DVD, on a DVD player. You can even add music, captions, graphics, special effects, and the like to jazz up your presentations.

But if you want to create a simple slide show — that is, one that simply displays the photos on the camera memory card one by one — you can create and run the show right on your camera by using the Slide Show function on the Playback menu. And by connecting your camera to a television, as outlined at the end of Chapter 8, you can present your show to a whole roomful of people.

 One important point to note about the Slide Show feature: The pictures displayed in the show depend on the current setting of the Playback Folder option on the Playback menu. If you haven't created any custom folders — a trick you can explore in Chapter 10 — you likely have only one folder on your card, so all pictures will be included in the show. If your memory card does contain multiple folders, choose from these three Playback Folder option: Display photos in the current folder; display all photos shot with the D5500, regardless of folder; or display all photos on the memory card (even if taken by another camera). Note that you may not be able to display photos taken with some cameras.

With that detail out of the way, follow these steps to present a slide show:

1. **Display the Playback menu and select Slide Show, as shown on the left in Figure 11-29.**

   You see the screen shown on the right in the figure.

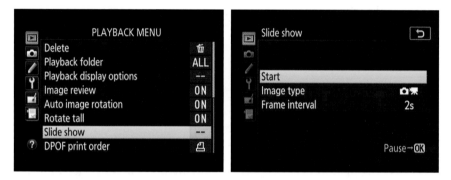

Figure 11-29: Choose Slide Show to set up automatic playback of all pictures on your memory card.

2. **Set the Image Type and Frame Interval options.**

   Select Image Type to specify whether you want the show to include photographs and movies, photos only, or movies only. If you rated pictures, a topic I cover in Chapter 9, you can specify how many stars a photo or movie must have to be worthy of display.

   The Frame Interval option you choose determines how each image will be displayed. You can set the interval to 2, 3, 5, or 10 seconds.

   To exit the selection screens, tap the return arrow in the upper right corner of the monitor or press the OK button.

3. **To start the show, select Start.**

   When the show ends, you can select one of three options: You can choose to restart the show, adjust the frame interval, or exit to the Playback menu.

During the show, control playback as follows:

- ✓ **Pause/restart:** Press OK to pause; to resume playback, select Restart. While the show is paused, you can adjust the frame interval if needed.

- ✓ **Skip to the next/previous image manually.** Press the Multi Selector right or left.

- ✓ **Change the information displayed with the image.** Press the Multi Selector up or down to cycle through the display modes. See Chapter 8 for help understanding the various modes.

- ✓ **Adjust movie sound volume.** Press the Zoom In button to increase the volume; press the Zoom Out button to decrease it.

- ✓ **Exit the show before the last slide:** You have three options:
    - *To return to regular playback,* press the Playback button.
    - *To return to the Playback menu,* press the Menu button.
    - *To return to picture-taking mode,* press the shutter button halfway.

Index

• E •

• *N* •

About the Author

Julie Adair King is the author of many books about digital photography and imaging, including the best-selling *Digital Photography For Dummies.* Her most recent titles include a series of *For Dummies* guides to popular digital SLR cameras, including the *Nikon D5300, D3300, D7100, and D600.* Other works include *Digital Photography Before & After Makeovers, Digital Photo Projects For Dummies, Julie King's Everyday Photoshop For Photographers, Julie King's Everyday Photoshop Elements,* and *Shoot Like a Pro!: Digital Photography Techniques.* When not writing, King teaches digital photography at such locations as the Palm Beach Photographic Centre. A native of Ohio and graduate of Purdue University, she resides in West Palm Beach, Florida.

Author's Acknowledgments

I am deeply grateful for the chance to work once again with the wonderful publishing team at Wiley. Rebecca Senninger, Carmen Krikorian, Michelle Hacker, Steve Hayes, and Mary Corder are just some of the talented editors and designers who helped make this book possible. And finally, I am also indebted to technical editor Dave Hall, without whose insights and expertise this book would not have been the same.

Publisher's Acknowledgments

Executive Editor: Steven Hayes

Development Editor: Rebecca Senninger

Technical Editor: David Hall

Editorial Assistant: Claire Brock

Sr. Editorial Assistant: Cherie Case

Project Manager: Michelle Hacker

Project Coordinator: Kumar Chellapa

Cover Image: Main image Ron Wise; Camera and Back Cover images courtesy of Julie Adair King